HELLO TOWNS!

Other Books by
SHERWOOD ANDERSON

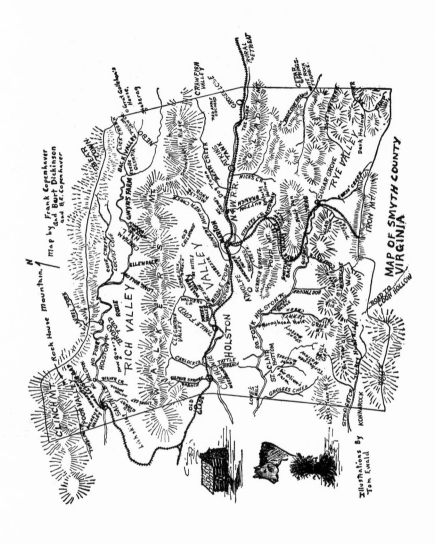

MAP OF SMYTH COUNTY VIRGINIA

Map by Frank Copenhaver and Burt Dickinson and B.F. Copenhaver

Illustrations By Tom Ewald

HELLO TOWNS!

by
SHERWOOD ANDERSON

PAUL P. APPEL, *Publisher*

MAMARONECK, N.Y.

1970

To my friends,

MR. and MRS. BURTON EMMETT

A number of the articles and tales of life in the town and other things built up out of the imagination because of living here have been printed in *Vanity Fair* and in other newspapers and magazines.

LET ME EXPLAIN

Writing is not an occupation. When it becomes an occupation a certain amateur spirit is gone out of it. Who wants to lose that?

And there is no place for the artist in American life. Even if I were a rich man, and I am not, I would not know what to do with myself if I had no occupation but writing. I like to write as the impulse comes to me, like love-making for example. I began writing some fifteen or twenty years ago. At that time I was employed in an advertising agency in Chicago.

I was not interested in advertising. I wrote advertisements of plows, soap, perfumes, etc. I did not care particularly whether or not the men who made these articles got rich selling them.

I was interested in the men. I made friends among them. Many of these friendships I have kept.

But I hated my occupation. When my books began to sell a bit and my name became known I quit.

So there I was. I was a man without an occupation. For a time I drifted from place to place.

I could not afford to live much in cities. "All right. I will be a countryman," I said to myself.

When this impulse came to me I was with the lady "E,"

7

riding on a country road, in the Southwestern Virginia hills. We had just come up out of a charming little upland valley. In the valley there was just room for one farm.

"Let's buy that farm," I had said laughingly. The idea made me feel magnificent. To own a farm. How marvelous. "Let us try living here, being farmers. A fellow ought to try that once in a life."

It happened that at the moment I had a little money. We had knocked at the door of the house. Two children came out. They had told us their mother, a widow, had gone afoot to a nearby town. "But would she sell this farm?"

"Yes, she would. We want to move to West Virginia."

Well there was an impulse I had never had. Never had I wanted to move to West Virginia.

We drove on presently and met the woman in the road. She had a copper kettle on her head. It was time for the making of applebutter. As you will know, this was in the early fall.

And what a country this is in the fall, how gorgeous it is. A man lives here in a sea of color, swims in it. Color has always excited me. I am excited by women, by color, by good prose.

And so I stopped this woman in the road. "Do you want to sell your farm?" She did. "And how much?" The price was surprisingly low. Can a farm with a house on it be bought at such a price? Why I had that much money myself.

I took the farm.

Afterward "E" and I went drifting off to Europe and I sat during a winter in Paris cafés wondering why I was there. We came back. We began to live on our farm. A little more money came in. We built a house. Building a house was an experience too but I will not write of it.

We had now a farm and a house but I had still no occupation. I tried farming a bit. And strolled about.

"Well, here I am," I said to myself, "I have plenty of time to write. Why do I not write?" When I was employed in a large advertising agency in the city I was always crying out for quiet.

It was quiet enough on my farm, in the hill valley in Virginia. Sometimes it was ghastly quiet.

I was alone hour after hour. I had built me a little cabin, away from the house, where I could be alone, I went and sat in it.

There were paper and pencils and books along the wall. At last I had got myself what is called "a study." My God!

I could write nothing. I sat laughing at myself.

Birds have nests, it seems, for raising their young but they do not make love in the nest. They make love among the branches of the trees or on roofs of houses in the city. They make love when they meet one they can love.

But you are not a bird.

Some twenty miles away from my farm there is a town. The name of the town is Marion. I began going down there, standing about before the stores, walking about the streets. It was a good town, not too large, not too small.

Another fall came and there was a fair held. I went day after day.

Well, horses were being raced, cattle shown. In the grandstand at the fair men and women were greeting each other. I sat alone. I have never felt more lonely in my life.

And then a man came to me. He had heard there was a writer,

*living back in the hills. He was himself interested in writing.
"How ideal it is," he said.*

"To live like that?"

"Yes."

*"It is terrible," I said. "I cannot live like that. The silence is
terrible. There is too much of it." I began talking to the man
eagerly. "Is there anything I could do here, in this town? Could
I work here?"*

*He suggested that I might buy the local weekly newspapers.
There were two of them, one Democratic and the other Republican.*

"But how is that arranged? How is that done?"

*He explained. How simple it was. The man who owned both
papers had no politics at all. He turned over so much space to
the Republicans each week and an equal amount of space in the
other paper to the Democrats.*

"He lets them say what they please?"

"Yes."

*"And he does not have to be either a Democrat or a Repub-
lican?"*

"No."

*My heart was beating now. "Would he sell the papers? Could
I buy them?"*

He thought I could.

*Well, I had left the man. I was so excited I could not talk
any more. Here was something I had always wanted to do. I
drove madly back to the farm.*

*"E," I called. "Yes." "I am going to buy two newspapers. I am
going to run them."*

"But where will you get the money?"

"I don't know. I will get it all right."

I have always had this supreme faith about getting money. I cannot tell where it comes from. And I always get it.

"Will you lend me some money?"

"No."

"Will you lend me some money?"

"No.

"No. No. No. No. No. No. No. No."

"Yes."

That's how it is done.

CONTENTS

13

JANUARY

CONTENTS

CONTENTS 17

A BEGINNING

Every week the pages of the paper are to be filled. The new editor, who is also an author, knows but few people of the town. He has moments of dread. At times he says to himself—"Why have I arranged to do this? Why have I let myself in for this?"

The town nestles among the hills. "There are all these people walking up and down the street. Will they come to like me? Will I like them?"

It is going to be a peculiarly intimate relation. The small town weekly is not a daily. It is not a question of gathering news.

He drives his car down to the town and parks it on Main Street. Since Sinclair Lewis wrote his book he has been hating the words, "Main Street." "I will call it something else," he says to himself. He hates all expressions that become, as is said, "a part of the language." He is to hate later the name "Elmer Gantry," as representing preachers and "Babbitt," as representing the business men of the American small town.

"The names are lies in themselves," he is saying to himself. "They are too easy. There is too much malice in them."

And now he is walking along the street. Perhaps people are pointing him out. "That is our new editor. He also writes books. What do you suppose he is like?"

Alas, some of them may have read some of the editor's books. The thought sends a little shiver down his back. "They may have taken them literally," he is saying to himself.

But are books not to be taken so? Certainly not. Books are books. They are to be taken as books.

But who will understand that?

Now be quiet. Quit being frightened.

The Rialto, Marion, Va.

FIRST WEEK OF
NOVEMBER

∾∾∾

FROM THE PAPER

"Your new editor came into town Monday. Children prancing in the streets at night, dancing, song, laughter, cheers. Girls and boys in fancy costumes.

"Fool that I am I thought it was because all Marion was so glad the new editor had arrived.

"It was only Halloween."

Shooting at Groseclose
NEWS

A dramatic shooting occurred last Friday at Groseclose. Oscar K. Harris, a well-known man in this county, drove to Groseclose late on Friday afternoon. He was accompanied by his wife. W. A. Sult, the victim of the shooting, is an employee in the post office at Groseclose. Calling him to one side, Mr. Harris is said by eyewitnesses to have talked with him for some time, presumably about some letters Mr. Harris held in his hand.

The shooting occurred at 4:15 Friday.

Suddenly drawing a pistol Mr. Harris began to shoot. As the victim ran he followed, still firing. What was perhaps the fatal shot caught Mr. Sult in the back of the neck. He fell forward dead.

Owing to the prominence of the Harris family the shooting has stirred the whole community. Many rumors are passing from mouth to mouth through the streets. Mr. Harris was brought to Marion immediately after the shooting but as yet his attorneys have given out no statement and Mr. Harris himself would not give an interview.

There have been many rumors connecting the shooting with Joseph Deboe, now serving a term in the federal penitentiary at Atlanta, but as we go to press none of the rumors as to the cause of the shooting can be confirmed.

Around this whole affair there is at present an air of mystery. When Mr. Harris is brought up for his preliminary hearing no doubt much of the mystery will be cleared up. The shooting was dramatic and sudden and has been followed by complete silence. The elopement of one of Mr. Harris' daughters, a student of the Radford State Teachers College, with J. W. Deboe last year has added a touch of significance to this shooting. It is generally thought Mr. Sult had something to do with the Deboe matter.

W. A. Sult was formerly a merchant at Groseclose and Oscar K. Harris is the ticket agent for the Norfolk and Western at Cooper, W. Virginia. Mr. Harris was to have had his preliminary hearing on Monday but because of the illness of his attorney, the Hon. B. F. Buchanan of Buchanan & Buchanan, the hearing has been set forward to Thursday, November 3rd.

LATER

The preliminary hearing of O. K. Harris was held Thursday morning at 9:30 before Justice Dickinson. Jones Ambers, Mrs. Simmerman, a young man named Medley and E. F. Sult, brother of the dead man, were examined. It was established that Sult was shot four times in the body, once in the arm and once in the back of the neck. O. K. Harris was bound over to the Circuit Court.

Chilhowie, Va., Nov. 2nd, 1927.

Editor Smyth County News,
Marion, Va.
Dear Sir:

I would like to drop a few lines in one of your columns if you have room.

I understand that some one in Marion reported that I, R. L. Brown, candidate for Justice of the Peace of Marion District, was a bootlegger. I am not writing this letter merely for the sake of my election, but I do want to let the good people of Marion know where I stand on the Liquor question. I would refer you to the people of Marion and elsewhere if they believe that report. I would like for him to ask the good business people of Chilhowie whether or not there has ever been any talk of that kind about me, also the good people of Saltville and not only this but to recognize that I was Justice of the Peace for eight years in Washington County. They can ask their Judge John Stewart in regard to my reputation of being a bootlegger. If the man that reported such a false report as this would oppose liquor, as I oppose it, don't think we would have near as much drinking as we do.

Respectfully,

R. L. BROWN

adv.

The New Frankness

EDITORIAL

There has been a distinct change come over the modern world. Some years ago Mr. Theodore Dreiser published a book called, "Sister Carrie." It was suppressed as immoral but after some years was republished. It is a fine book but I doubt if it would strike any one as immoral now.

Mr. Mark Twain wrote a book before he died. It was a frank discussion of his beliefs about life. When he had written it it seemed to him so terrible that he was afraid to have it published. When he died the manuscript of the book was put away in a safe. It was to be published only after a hundred years had passed.

As a matter of fact it was published ten years after his death and shocked no one. In the ten years the world has moved up with a great rush and in particular the American world.

I myself have lived through much change. Several of my own books that have, when published, been condemned as too frank are accepted everywhere now. There is a great mistake commonly made by older people about the younger generation.

What has happened is that there is an increased curiosity about life. The younger generation has got onto much of the bunk older people talk. What is the use my trying to make my son or daughter think I have led a pure life if I haven't? Few of us have. I know I haven't.

The young man or woman does not expect the impossible from the father or mother. They do expect a little indulgence, an attempt at understanding. To try and give them that, to be as frank as we can about our own experiences with life, is about all we can do for them.

SECOND WEEK OF
NOVEMBER

An editor's thoughts—not published. Terror. These people. Suppose they find me out.

Can I do this thing? What do I know of all these lives?

I have been out of a small town too long. How close it is here. I cannot breathe.

These people have known each other always. They must know everything about each other. I could not bear to have everything known about me.

I do not want to be intimate with people. Why did I come here to a small town?

I have lived too long in cities. In the city I could go around the first corner and be lost. I was one more figure moving through the city streets with many thousands of other figures.

I am known in a small literary and intellectual circle. How easy to avoid all such circles.

Here I can avoid no one. All will be found out about me.

The men in my shop—how nice they are. They are watching me. I am boss here. They are wondering what I will be like.

I have eminence of a sort in some places but there is no eminence here. Here I must stand on my own feet. Will the men here in the shop like me? Already I like them.

They come to work in the morning. They laugh. They quarrel a little. I feel awkward with them.

Group Feeling

EDITORIAL

When I was little more than a boy I went into the army. I was a private soldier. I remained in the army for a year. It was an odd experience. In our family we had all been intense individualists. Of a sudden I found myself living intimately with a great many other men. How I longed for privacy. At night I slept in a tent with six other men. Later, when I looked back upon that time, I thought they had all been on the whole rather considerate, but there was one night, I recall, when I crawled out of the tent and went walking in a moonlit road. I walked a long way and went into a wood and slept.

The loneliness, the quiet of the woods cured me. I had begun to hate the men with whom I was compelled to associate so closely.

On another day I got another angle on my own feelings. The company to which I belonged joined its regiment and we all went away together to fight the Cuban War. One day, with a great many other regiments, we were marching in a road. There might have been twenty thousand men in line. The regiment to which I belonged happened to be near the head of the line. We swung out of a long valley and up the side of a hill. There was the steady rhythmic tread of many feet. A peculiar mass feeling came into me. In feeling myself a part of a great powerful body, I myself felt powerful.

I dare say all of society is organized on this basis. However, whenever I am in a place where there are many men, in a club, or at a meeting of any sort, I feel myself not the same man I am when alone or with one or two other men. Another man I know well, sits near me. In an odd way I do not feel him as the same man with whom I talked yesterday. The mass feeling has got into him too. I dare say that what are called, "Leaders of Men," understand this feeling. They know how to direct other men in groups, in the mass. I have never had for myself any desire to be such a leader. The very notion frightens me.

A few times in my life I have been called upon to make a public address. Well, I have done it. When I got through I felt silly.

Children in particular frighten me. People of my own age are not so bad. Their lives are more like my own. Perhaps I feel that they like myself have no longer the rich possibilities of children.

And the truth is that all of this feeling in me may come largely from the fact that I have for so long a time been a writer. The writer is a solitary beast. He sits for hours working alone in his room. He writes and then tears up and writes again. There he is alone. What he is writing, if it is read at all, will be read by individuals. For example, every writer knows that the writing of, say, a public address, is quite a different matter from writing for the individual. We all, in our public lives, become something we cannot be in our private lives.

There may be people who can remain the same in their public capacity as they are as individuals. Such men are natural public leaders. How happy I would be if I could become such a one, unself-conscious, more direct, if I could ever learn to feel as easy and as natural with many people gathered together as I can with almost any man when I have him alone.

Sleepless Nights

EDITORIAL

A dog keeps barking. You get up and read a book. At night everything is distorted. There is some one else asleep in the next room. You want something in there. Really you do not want anything but sleep. There is a book in the room on a table by your friend's head. Why do you want just that book?

You do not want it at all. You want to make a noise and awaken your friend. You succeed.

He wakes up and stares at you with sleepy eyes. You begin to complain. "I can't sleep," you say. He pretends to be concerned. You begin talking hopefully but now he has rolled over in his bed and is asleep again.

All the world is asleep. Your nerves are jumping. You try to lie quiet but do not succeed. If you are a smoker you smoke many cigarettes. Your throat becomes hot and dry.

O Lord help you. Now you have begun thinking about yourself. You begin thinking up impossibly shrewd things to say to people next day. Suppose you are a writer. You write in fancy with a new and striking eloquence. What marvelous sentences.

You get up and put some of them down. You forget the anguish that prompted them the next morning and hate them.

I dare say you are not a writer. You are a banker, a manufacturer, a merchant, a workingman. You become so clever you amaze yourself. It may be you pile up money, you make a new invention.

There is a man with whom you have had a quarrel. In fancy you meet him on the street. He is a bit impertinent and you knock him down. How many men I have whipped in fancy on sleepless nights. What beautiful women have been in love with me.

After such a night you get up the next morning feeling seedy of course. You go out into the street. All about are people who have just arisen from refreshing sleep. How old you feel. What a dead cold place the world is.

Court News

Nearly the entire time of the court during the last week was taken up with the case of the commonwealth against Andy and Abe Caldwell, Andy, as we understand it, being Abe's son. The jury in this case was as follows: D. J. Tucker, H. B. Cregger, C. B. Scott, M. B. Pafford, W. G. Cornett, S. F. Armstrong, D. W. Corner, W. R. Farris, Roy E. Hubble, E. C. Haislip, A. A. Couthard and C. C. Cornett. The Attorney for the defense was Mr. Robt. Summers of Abingdon.

As nearly as your correspondent could figure this case out it was one grand family row. Rocks were thrown, clipping people here and there about the head, shot guns were fired and a general good time was had by all. There were enough Andys, Buds, Bills, Joes, etc., etc., firing rocks and profanity up and down one mountain road to make us lonesome for Grayson county. Old man Simmons, I think it was, got a couple of good hard rocks on top of his head and nearly died. We had some sturdy feminine testimony in this case. It was very enlightening. The jury decided Andy and Abe would have to pay fifty dollars and break stones for three months. I hope they don't break them on my road.

Court has adjourned until January 14, 1928.

Nebo School Notes

BY A CORRESPONDENT

Our first forest fire for this fall broke out on the south side of Walker's mountain. When it spread to the top of the mountain it could be seen from our school building. You could see it best at night. There were long lines of fire along the side of the mountain. Our foresters kept busy; but when they had put out one fire, they found that another had sprung up, or perhaps several. At one time there were seven different fires blazing fiercely. On Mr. Geo. Harmon's farm you could see them well. At times when the trees were afire there were great blazes. Great clouds of smoke came over from a fire on Brushey mountain which could not be seen from here. Our valley was full of smoke from these fires. They have done a lot of damage. Our mountain road was blocked in places with fallen, burning timber; fences were burned, young trees destroyed, many of our wild animals were run out of the mountains and will probably starve this winter, and some of them perished in the fire.

Great care has been taken to keep the forest from catching fire but some careless somebody let it get out. We are beginning to appreciate our forests and are anxious to protect them for the home and food they provide our game. We look to them to conserve our rainfall and to keep the flow of springs and streams normal; to prevent the washing of soil from the mountain sides and to provide us with beautiful places for camping and picnic grounds. Just before the fire our county forest warden came by and left posters and fire warning notices for us to put up.

Owen Hubble caught an eagle, which weighed ten pounds and

measured seven feet from one tip of its wing to the other. It has a long bill and sharp claws, and is very strong. It can carry a rail or a large turkey gobbler, or a large lamb.

We had a Halloween party Monday evening. The school gave three little plays: "Grandpa and Grandma U. S. Bye," "A Day's Work," and "Which Witch." Dorothy Buchanan and Claudine Robinette dressed in Indian suits, and sang "an Indian lullaby." The fourth and fifth grades gave a "Go to School Song," and "The Landing of the Pilgrims on Plymouth Rock," and last we had some athletic stunts. We charged 10 and 15 cents, and shall get us a basketball with the proceeds.

Some of the farmers are getting through shucking corn and are sowing wheat.

EDITOR'S THOUGHTS

But I cannot write just for the people who read my paper. I shall have to write about them too. I venture to write of them in Vanity Fair. *Afterwards I shall get courage to publish these notes in my paper as well.*

Notes for Newspaper Readers

There is a little alleyway back of the shop. From the window where I sit writing I can, by turning my head slightly, see into the courthouse yard and to the post office door.

The post office is the town gathering place. The morning mail from the east comes in just after eight o'clock. Men begin to gather at about that hour. Back of the glass front of the post office the clerks are at work distributing the mail.

I see the prominent men of the town gathered. There is the judge, three or four lawyers, the merchants, the bankers. This is a

Virginia town. These people have not moved about much. Not many new people have come in. As yet, I feel a little strange here.

There is a poor, bedraggled woman in the alleyway. She has two small children with her. The children look half starved. They are picking up bits of coal and wood and putting them in a basket. Presently she and her children will go home and build a fire. They will huddle about it. The morning is cold.

Thoughts drifting in a man's mind. Mountains rise up out of this valley in all directions. The valley is broad and rich. Ever since I have been in this valley, I have been reading every book I could find about the life here. Every one knows that Virginia is one of our oldest states. In the early days, when all eastern and central Virginia had already been settled for a long time, this country remained untouched.

There was the country east of the mountains. The whites had that. Then came the Blue Ridge Range. Beyond that another range, the tail end of the Appalachians, trailing down across Virginia and into North Carolina.

A rich country of little upland valleys. There was a great salt lick at Roanoke and another near us, at Saltville. Game was abundant. In all of this country, blue grass grows naturally. It is wonderful for fattening stock. During the spring, summer and fall months, thousands of fat cattle and sheep are driven down through our main street to the railroad yards.

Before the white men got over the mountains and into these valleys, all of this country was the happy hunting ground of the Indians. None of the tribes lived here, but the Shawnees, the Chickasaws, the Mingos, even the Indians from Ohio and New York state came here to hunt.

Then the white hunters came, Daniel Boone and the others. They went back over the mountains telling great tales. Settlers came. Each settler picked out his own little valley and built his cabin.

Great land companies were formed to exploit the country. George Washington got in on that. The English governor owed him something for his services during the French and Indian War. George knew how to take care of himself in a financial way. The early settlers in the little valleys had to fight the Indians for their lives on the one hand, and fight it out with the great speculative land company for the very soil under their feet.

An independent people, full of personality. The town has not yet had the problem of assimilating foreign born citizens.

Every one knows every one else. Their fathers were known and their grandfathers. A newcomer like myself—I have been in this country only three years—sees the change going on here that has gone on all over America.

Presently there will be more factories. Labor is plentiful and can yet be bought at a low price. That, in the end, will bring the factories.

The drama of a small town always unrolling before the eyes. Now a crier comes out and calls from the courthouse steps. Court is about to go into session.

It is a case involving mountain people. I go over there. Courts have always frightened me a little. Formerly, when I lived in Chicago, I knew a good many newspaper men. They went freely into the courts, even into the judge's chamber. They spoke freely to the judge, "Hello, Jim," they said.

And there was the sheriff. I have always been afraid of sheriffs. It may be that every writer is instinctively afraid of being arrested. I was arrested once. That was up in Ohio. A sheriff picked me up as a diamond thief. He took me off to a police court. Two or three men in uniform gathered about and began hurling questions at me. I stood trembling. What a queer feeling of guilt.

Now, I go into our courtroom freely. The sheriff and the judge smile at me. Behold, I am a power in the land. I own a newspaper. I even go into the sheriff's office. He and I have a cigarette together.

In the courtroom outside country people are gathered. They are afraid in the presence of the law, as I was once afraid. A court official is telling me about his daughter, who has got a prize in school. I know what he wants. He is proud of his daughter. He wants that put in the paper. It will go in.

In the courtroom I can go into the sacred precincts inside the bar. How brave I am. These days I feel as I did when I was a boy and got a job tending race horses. What did I care about wages? I could consort shoulder to shoulder with the great, with horse-men.

I walked beside drivers of race horses, touched their elbows.

The witness on the stand is lying. He is a small boy. His father and his uncle have had a fight. One has haled the other into court. The fight took place on a country road, just as evening was coming on. The men threw rocks at each other.

The boy has been told a story he must repeat in court. What a ridiculous story. He is swearing that his father stood just so, beside the road. The uncle came along the road, swearing. He threw rocks at the boy's father. The father stood like a statue beside the road. He did not throw any rocks until he had been hit twice. What an amazingly gentle, patient mountain man. Now the lawyers are asking the boy searching questions. He is confused. The color leaves his face. His hands grip the chair in which he sits. I know how the boy feels. He feels as I used to feel when I went into court—before I became an editor and, therefore, brave.

Frightened country people gathered in the courtroom. Presently their turn will come. What a terrible thing is the law.

I am glad I am not a lawyer. I am a newspaper man.

A brother newspaper man has come in. He runs another weekly newspaper in a neighboring town. I have become part of a vast brotherhood. We talk of the cost of getting out a newspaper; how to make the merchants advertise more than they do. Advertising is the breath of our nostrils.

The newspaper man has gone out. After all, running a country weekly is not running a newspaper. In our hearts, we country editors know that. We are not after news. If any one wants news, let them take a daily. We are after the small events of small town people's lives.

The country newspaper is the drug store: it is the space back of the stove in the hardware store: it is the farmhouse kitchen.

There was a man on a gray horse went along a mountain road one day last week. Farmer Cooper was in a distant field and could not make out the rider of the gray horse. He has been bothered ever since. "Ma, who do you suppose it was?" Now he has his weekly copy of our paper. He is sitting in the kitchen, reading.

Aha, there it is. "Ed Barrow, from up Sugar Grove way, rode his gray horse into town on Wednesday of last week. He reports a fine bunch of steers to sell."

An old colonel with a gray beard comes into the office and takes a chair near my own. His hands tremble. In the Civil War he was a Reb. Once there was a raid of Union troops down into this country. There was a battle over near Saltville, just across Walker's Mountain from where we are sitting now.

The old man describes the battle, in which he took part as a young soldier. It was getting toward the end of the war. The Colonel was but a boy then. All of the men of this section had gone off to join Lee before Richmond. Grant was pounding away at Lee during those days. It was near the end of things.

And a battle here—in this quiet place. Old men and boys rushing to the Stars and Bars. Who knows, my own father may have been along on that raiding party. They were trying to get up to the Norfolk and Western Railroad, to tear it up. Stealing chickens on the way, too.

Old men and boys rushing through the hills, the Colonel among them. He describes the battle in the hills; the driving off of the Yanks. It takes an hour to tell. It is a good story. Well, no hurry. We country editors have no dead line. If we do not get to press to-day, we will go to press to-morrow. After the Colonel leaves, leaning heavily on his cane, a heavy-faced woman with a determined jaw comes in.

She wants a piece put in the paper. She had two sons. One of them was killed last year in a railroad accident. With several other boys he was in a Ford. There was moon whisky in the Ford. The driver was reckless. He drove before an on-coming train at a grade crossing and two boys were killed.

The boy's mother has written a piece about the boy. She says he was a good boy and feared God. "I hope," she says in the piece, "that what has happened to Harry will be a warning to his brother, Zeb." Evidently Zeb is a bit out of hand, too.

"Will you print it?" she asks. Surely, we will.

She is followed by a shy, fair maiden in a blue dress.

The maiden also has something to put in the paper. She hands it to me and goes out. I look at the paper. "Miss Ruby Small of Carrollville was in town Tuesday to get her teeth fixed."

Well, well, Ruby, are you having trouble with your teeth, and you so young, too.

There is no question, the dentists of this town should do more advertising in our paper.

Night. Your country editor walks about his town. He belongs to the great brotherhood of the ink pots. He does not have to rush like the city newspaper man, nor does he need to be high toned and literary, like your magazine editor.

Your country editor is thinking up schemes. He is trying to think how to make the merchants of his town advertise more. He thinks of that for a time, and then thinks of his town.

More and more he is growing familiar with it. The threads of its life run through his fingers. He knows, O, what does he not know?

And the people of the town, knowing what he knows, a little afraid, keep passing and looking at him. He is just a little outside their lives. He is something special. He writes. That alone sets him apart.

THIRD WEEK OF
NOVEMBER

Already your editor has a sense of something. On a daily paper life must resolve itself into days. What happened yesterday is past. There are two days here, Tuesdays and Thursdays, our printing days.

Can enough things happen in a town to make up a paper every week. What is news and what is not news?

There are questions to be settled too. We will not handle scandal in our paper. Domestic relations will be let alone. If some man or woman here in our courts get a divorce we will say nothing.

Life is difficult enough without the terror of such publicity.

On the other hand there are people getting into trouble of another sort. A good deal of bootleg whisky is sold about here.

Young men, when they buy the stuff and get drunk, take a sporting chance. If they grow rowdy, get arrested, are put into jail, we will publish the news of it.

There are people here who will not like that. In Virginia family is everything. Young men of good family will get into such trouble. They, or their parents, will come to see us. "Leave it out of the paper, please." "We cannot leave it out." "But have you no sympathy?" "Did you never do anything of the sort?"

"I did it yesterday and may do it to-morrow. If I get into jail I will write the story of it for the paper and send it out of the jail."

FROM THE PAPER

Fine Hunting Weather

The opening of the hunting season on Tuesday the 15th saw Marion with a lot of its best citizens missing. Lovers of the dog, the gun, the woods and the whir of the pheasant or the quail, cutting out for cover, were up and out early. The sportsmen had fine weather and there were some full game bags before night.

Reports from all over the county and from surrounding counties say that the birds are plentiful this year and that the sportsmen will have a happy season.

BUCK FEVER

The Marion Band

EDITORIAL

What does a band mean to a town? Better to ask what is a town without a band? Life in a town goes on, just so. You know how it is. Merchants selling goods, lawyers fighting their cases, farmers coming into town to buy goods. Spring, summer, fall and winter. People in their houses, women cooking, making beds. Life is dull enough.

Days come. See, the men of the band have put on their uniforms and are coming up along the street. The big drum is booming, the horns going.

Just suppose now, in our town, we are visited by some great man. Hurrah now, let's give him a big day. It may be the governor of the state or some other dignitary. Our principal men are going to meet him down at the station. They have their best cars there, the biggest and best cars we have in town, all our leading citizens. And no band. Pshaw. What a frost.

And what about Armistice Day and the Fourth of July?

Or when the fair is on.

Older men, staid citizens of a town may be able to get along without a band, but what about the boys?

When I was a boy my one great yearning was to play the biggest horn in the town band. I never made it. There never was much music in me.

Still and all, I'm not a jealous man. What I can't have I don't want to take away from the other fellow.

I still like a band better than almost anything else in a town. Band music just suits me. There they come up the street. Lately I have only seen the Marion band in action a few times and then they didn't have any drum major. I hope they get one again soon. I like to see the fellow in the big bearskin hat with his staff, stepping high and wide. I'd like to do it myself but I haven't got the figure for it.

And how faithful and devoted the band members are. The men of our Marion band, for example, go off to practice twice a week. Far from getting paid for their work, they do it without pay. The members even pay dues to keep the band going.

Recently, until these last few weeks our Marion band has had a band leader who was paid a good salary because he was a good man. He was there to keep the boys up to snuff and would be there now but that he is sick.

But the boys are at it just the same. They are keeping the band going.

There are men in the Marion band who make a sacrifice every time they go out to play. Bear this in mind. When we want our band most other towns, that haven't any band, would like one, too. Our band gets offers to go all over Southwest Virginia. Such offers almost always come when we need them here and they stay at home. Instead of going out and raking in money they stay here and give their services.

And there are individual members of the band who make a sacrifice every time they go out to play. Do they kick? Not they.

The boys of the band like their band, and so do we. Hurrah, here they come. Music floating on the breeze. Every heart jumping. Life. Music. Zipp.

We like that.

The people of Marion owe it to their band to give it the heartiest kind of support. Get back of them. When they need a little money to keep going, shell out.

A good band is the best investment a town can make. We, in Marion, have a corking good one. Let's stand by it.

N E W S

"Mr. O. K. Harris, who was recently placed in jail in Marion, charged with murder, was led before the bar in custody of the jailer and upon motion by the defendant, by counsel, was ordered confined in the Criminal Department Southwestern State Hospital for the Insane for observation."

People

E D I T O R I A L

I suppose I am by nature a neutral man. Often so-called "bad men" interest me as much or more than good men. In all my life I have never opposed any so-called reform nor have I ever gone in for one.

What interests me is human life. I like people just as they are. I do not want to change any one. Nature seems to have so arranged my mind that I see both sides of every question. I dare say there are few enough sins I have not committed at some time.

Well, I could never be a reformer and that's that.

Life as it is, the meannesses, joys, sorrows, life in cities and towns, the changes always going on in the tone of life.

I began life as a workingman. What strange old fellows I met in some of the shops. I have known profane crusty old fellows who were filled with tenderness inside. Afterward another kind of life, among college professors, big business men, etc.

I found there the same inevitable variations.

In the end what has interested me is the insides of people. You may study people all your life. In the end you know little enough.

FOURTH WEEK OF
NOVEMBER

I shall begin at once putting all sorts of things that come into my own mind into the papers. I cannot be a slave to the papers. I shall let my fancy loose. If the papers fail what does it matter? I have failed many times before.

There are stories here. I shall sell them to magazines when I can. Later I shall publish them in my own papers. There will be this life of the town and my own life outside. There is the life of the fancy too. Perhaps newspapers have become too much newspapers.

A Mountain Dance

A man named Poly Grubb told me the story. His real name is Napoleon. It was fall, a cold day in late November. The wind was icy cold.

I had gone out to hunt rabbits.

I knew Poly. He was a mountain man living with his old father and mother in a cabin up along the road on which I have been living. That day when I saw him my dog was with me. He went to sniff about Poly's legs. Poly was a little nervous. "Will he bite?" he asked in alarm. The question was absurd. My dog is of the sort that can never be persuaded even to growl. When you lose your temper he only wags his tail and looks at you with sorrowful eyes.

Poly and I had met at a place where a bridge crossed the road. It had been snowing all night. He seemed excited. The day before had been quite warm.

Almost at once he began to talk. His eyes were heavy. I could smell moon whisky on his breath.

He began to tell me about a dance he had attended during the night. He grew talkative.

'You must understand that, in our hills every one is quite poor.

The mountain people are poor without being really poor. They do not feel poor.

At first when you go into our mountain country you say to yourself, "What miserable lives these people live." You have come up into the hills, let us say, out of a rich valley.

In the valley there are prosperous towns. People live in comfortable houses. There are automobiles, radios, movies to go to at night.

You travel up into the hills over miserable roads. If during the winter or spring, you are trying to get into the hills in an automobile you have to give it up.

There are small towns, miserable looking places.

Cabins back in the hills. Many of them are without floors. There is just one large room. The whole family lives in it. There is no privacy. Everything concerned with the family life, love making, birth, illness, death, takes place in the one room.

The people cling to their hills. Not far away, a half day's journey in a Ford along the valley road, is an industrial town.

The men could make good wages down there. They do not go.
In the hills there is no work. They raise a little corn, make moon
whisky.

They raise a hog or two, raise beans. Their diet is amazingly
simple.

Among them you will see tall, graceful men, beautiful women.
You look with amazement. There before you in the road walks an
aristocrat. People of the outside world think of these mountain
people as underfed, illiterate and dangerous. They have been fed
up with romances. John Fox, Jr., and others have done what they
could to spread misunderstanding. They were compelled to do
it to manufacture their romances. The romancers are always taking some such toll of peoples.

Newspapers talking about feuds. Songs and stories about sudden
deaths, fierce hatreds.

The people I knew in the hills had, for the most part, soft voices
and gentle eyes.

Poly Grubb was an example. He was tall and slender and spoke
a peculiar dialect. I shall not try to reproduce it.

That November morning on the bridge, as we stood together,
my dog having gone off to hunt rabbits, he began to tell me a story
of the dance of the night before.

He said that in the early evening he was sitting at home. As I
have said, he lives in a mountain cabin with his father and mother,
now both very old. I have seen the house. It looks as if a slight
wind might blow it away.

Moreover, it stands far up in the hills in an exposed place. In
the winter blustering winds tear over the hills. In some way the
cabin, rudely built, with but one room and no floor, survives.

Poly has lived there all his life. Both his father and mother are
almost blind. He had four sisters and several brothers, but they
have married and gone away to other cabins. Poly was the young-
est child. He may be twenty-five.

He would like to marry but will not until his father and mother die.

On the November evening before the morning I saw and talked with him and when he told me this story he said he was sitting alone in the cabin with the old people.

He began to grow restless. Winter was coming on. The winters are long and cold in the mountains. He was wishing for a wife. His father and mother, now that they have grown old, seldom speak. Sometimes Poly has to do the cooking. His mother is too ill to get out of her bed. He has to keep the house in order.

He told me that, as he was sitting by the fireside, the old people having crawled into bed, he grew suddenly restless.

He sprang up and went out of doors. There was a new moon but it did not shed much light. A cold wind blew and in the air there was the promise of snow, the first snow of the winter. Ragged clouds were drifting across the sky.

Later when the snow is deep these mountain cabins are sometimes isolated for weeks at a time.

It was a bad time of the year for a young strong man to be unmarried.

Poly felt that. He was nervous. As he stood by the cabin door the wind whistled through the dry leaves of the oak trees. The oak leaves cling to the trees all winter in our hills.

The wind blowing, the mournful sound of the wind in the trees, the promise of snow in the air, had in some way suggested to Poly's mind the idea that it would be a fine night for a dance. I got from him, when he was talking to me, the notion that the wind had suggested the thought to him. It may just have been the dry leaves dancing on the limbs of the trees.

Evidently the dancing leaves had also suggested the idea to others. The leaves in the trees beside his cabin door were dancing madly, then becoming quiet, then dancing again.

He told me that the noise made by the wind, playing in the dead dry leaves, was like the sound of a fiddle.

Anyway Poly was standing there, like that, and suddenly he began to run up hill through the woods.

As a matter of fact, for some time, Poly had been paying attention to one of the Franklin girls. I knew that from others. There are six girls and several grown boys in the Franklin house. How they all manage to live in the one small cabin I do not know. I presume it is none of my business.

The oldest of the Franklin girls, the one to whom Poly is particularly attentive, is famous as a cook all through the hills. She is a year or two older than Poly.

And so, that night when Poly wanted to dance and when snow was promised and the wind was roaring in the trees, he ran through the woods to her father's house.

The six Franklin girls were all there and some of the boys.

They had all come out of the warm, stuffy cabin and stood by the door, as though waiting for Poly.

There had been nothing arranged, but when he got there others from other isolated cabins in the hills began to arrive.

He suggested to me, without saying the words, that he thought the night had been a little crazy and that all the people of the hills were a little crazy.

Young people kept running up the hill. They filled the Franklin house. Suddenly they all went out of doors. It had begun to snow. The mountain seemed full of voices.

The Franklin house, although it is far up in the hills, is just at the foot of the highest single hill in all this part of the state.

All of the young mountain people, gathered at the Franklin house, began suddenly to climb.

They climbed silently, hurriedly. No one laughed. No one had suggested a dance. How were they going to dance? They had no music.

Half way up there is a winding road. Well, it isn't a road. It is a trail.

When they had got almost up to the road they heard a sound. They all stopped and listened. Then a shout went up.

There was a man in the road, an old man. His name is Wiley Small. He is the best fiddler in all this section. What had brought him outdoors that night and into that lonely hill road Poly said no one knew. He might have had a still in some gully up there.

And anyway, as Poly kept insisting, it was a crazy night. Anything can happen on such a night.

There the old man was, in the road, and he was playing on his fiddle, perhaps to cheer himself on the road. People in the hills are always playing the fiddle or singing on lonely nights. He was playing "Turkey in the Straw."

Up to the old man they all rushed and, grabbing him by the arms, pushed him on up the hill through the brush. He kept demanding a drink and bottles were produced.

All the young men began to drink. Drink loosened their tongues. They sang and shouted. They came to a cleared place and one of the young men began to wrestle with one of the Franklin girls.

The Franklin girls are all big and strong. It was a hard tussle. All the others gathered about.

When the young man had thrown her to the ground she sprang quickly up and they all climbed on up to the top of the hill.

The top of the high hill is almost bare. In the winter the wind howls up there. It had begun to snow.

Quickly a roaring fire was built of dry brush, the sparks flying in all directions, and the dance began.

Poly said the mountain people danced all night. He said it was a crazy, a good dance. He said the couples kept dancing in and out of the fire. The wind was roaring and the sparks flying. More than once, he said, the girls' clothes caught on fire.

No one cared. They all kept dancing and dancing, shouting and

singing. Old Wiley Small kept drinking moon whisky and playing his fiddle.

The young men were all drinking whisky. Poly said that he got
so hot from dancing and from the whisky that the snow on his
cheeks and the cold wind felt like a kiss.

Perhaps he had begun thinking of kisses. When he told me the
story of the dance he may still have been a little drunk. Once or
twice I thought he might fall off the icy bridge on which we stood.

On the mountain, on the night before, the girls and women,
although they had not been drinking, were as excited as the men.

He himself had been, as every one in that section knew, paying
attention to the oldest of the Franklin girls. Her name is Stella.
They have not married, I fancy because of Poly's father and
mother.

They may be waiting for his old mother to die. The old woman
has, no doubt, a prejudice against any other woman coming to live
in her house.

At any rate he is in love with Stella. He intends to marry her.
She is a respectable girl and the most famous cook in the hills.

He said that during the dance he became suddenly enamored of
a little mountain girl that every one knew was a little loose.

He was dancing with her and suddenly he took her away.

He said that Stella Franklin knew and that her brothers knew.
He laughed when he told about it and said he supposed every one
knew. He said he wasn't the only one who went with that particular girl, although he did insist he was the first one.

When I asked him he told me that he did not think that Stella
Franklin cared, at least not much. As I have suggested, when he
talked to me he was still a little drunk. His tongue was loose.

He went away with the mountain girl, whose reputation is not
of the best, and then came back to the dance.

He began dancing then with Stella Franklin. He danced with
her the rest of the night. When the dance broke up, almost at day-

light, he took her home. When I saw him he had just come from her house.

He and Stella, I gathered, had not got home until almost daylight and had sat up together the rest of the night.

They had been making plans. When his old people die it is understood Poly will get the mountain farm.

He told me that, as soon as his mother died, he would marry Stella. He would, he said, if she would have him. And he thought she would.

He seemed proud of the fact that Stella was a good woman. He was proud of the fact that she was a woman who never lost her head. He was proud of the fact that she was a famous cook.

He said he would have to be getting on home to his old people, that he would have to be getting a little sleep.

From what he had said and from a certain swing of his shoulders as he walked off up the road I gathered that the night's adventure had not hurt his chances for the marriage with Stella.

BACK TO THE NEWS
Election Day Shooting
NEWS

Election day saw a bad case of shooting over in Grayson county. Paul Halsey, living on the Fairwood Road, shot a man named Young. As we got the story there had been bad blood between the two men for some time. Their farms joined each other.

As the story is told in Grayson County, Young recently shot a horse belonging to Halsey. It seemed this man Young has been in such trouble before. On election day he went to Halsey's house. As Halsey tells the story, Young invited him out to the barn saying he was sorry he had shot the horse and wanted to settle.

A son accompanied Young on the visit to Halsey. They got Halsey into the barn and then closed the door. The elder Young pulled at a gun and told Halsey to make his peace with God as he was about to die.

The son was in the meantime standing outside the barn and firing shots into Halsey's house.

In the barn a very dramatic scene must have been taking place. Young put his pistol close to Halsey's face and was about to fire when, with a quick upward movement of his arm, Halsey knocked the gun up. The shot went through the roof of the barn.

Halsey then jumped to his feet and getting a pistol out of his pocket began to shoot. One of the shots lodged in the hip of the elder Young, another in his arm. All of this was on election day. Young with his son drove to Troutdale where, in spite of his wounds, he stopped to vote. Then he drove to a doctor at Grant. The doctor being unable to get the bullet lodged in his hip, he was taken to the hospital where, after the bullet had been removed, he escaped by crawling through a window. At the time of this writing his whereabouts is unknown.

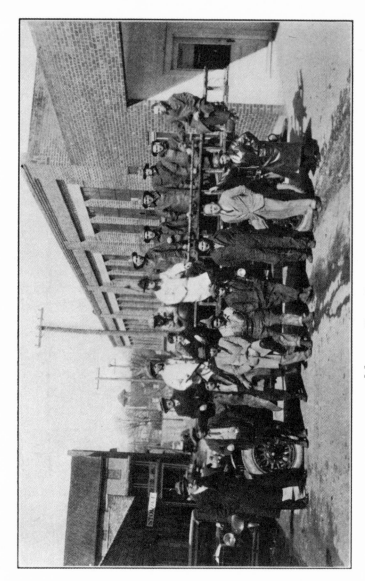

MARION FIRE DEPARTMENT

FIRST WEEK OF
DECEMBER

~~~

*In this climate the days are still fair. The hunters are still
going out into the fields. From the print-shop windows I see them
in their cars. The dogs are riding with them. What intelligent
fellows these bird dogs are. Now and then a man takes me out.
I have even acquired a bird dog of my own. He sleeps at night at
the foot of my bed.*

*I cannot convince these men I am a bad shot. They go forward,
the dogs on the point, the men talking to them—"easy, boy. Hold
it now. Hold it, boy." I am too excited to shoot straight.*

*I am as excited as the dogs. Now the birds go out of cover.
The men shoot, one after another. The birds fall. The men turn
and look at me. "Why did you not shoot?" They think I am
staying back to give them the shots, wishing to be courteous.*

*It is not that. I do not like to be shown up as a bad shot. And
besides I like it better so. By standing back I see it all, the dogs,
the flying birds and the men, when they draw down so steadily
and surely. It is much more fascinating for me to see it all than
to shoot birds.*

49

Our buying the newspapers at Marion has brought down upon us the comments of our brother editors from all over America. Most of the comments take the form of warnings. We are supposed to be in some kind of danger. There hasn't been any one in the shop with a gun yet.

In the Shadows of the Mountains

NEWS

There are three brothers named Jackson, living on Clinch Mountain under the shadow of Red Rock, near Saltville.

About three months ago one of the Jacksons disappeared. No one knows where he went. Probably he just walked off. He may have got a little tired of our country. Before now your faithful correspondent has done little things like that himself.

But that is neither here nor there. The point is that one of the Jacksons disappeared.

All quiet on Clinch Mountain. Then a rumor started. It grew and grew. The rumor ran down the mountain into the valleys. The rumor said that the aforesaid Jackson was not vamoosed but dead.

He was dead and buried secretly under the barn at the Jackson place.

You know how rumors grow. This one grew fine. People got excited. Last Sunday morning they disturbed the sleep of Sheriff Dillard. "Come over here," a tense voice called to him over the long-distance telephone from Saltville.

Always alert to his duty, Sheriff Dillard went. He drove to Saltville and was told the mysterious and horrid tale. Taking under his wing a goodly company of Saltville citizens, including the following, he lit out for Clinch Mountain.

List of illustrious diggers:

Well there was C. H. Holmes, B. G. Thompson, Sam Dillard, Si Feis, Mont Cardwell and several others.

And away they all went. The Jackson place was reached. Picks and shovels were provided. Beside the good diggers from Saltville others came afoot, on horseback and in cars. A great concourse gathered. We are told there were so many present that they lifted up the barn and set it over a fence into a nearby field.

Then they began to dig. They dug for hours in the hot sun. They made a great and magnificent hole.

But alas! no corpse.

They didn't even uncover a mine or a hidden pot of treasure. Nothing came out of the hole but just dirt, and a few rocks.

Sheriff Dillard says it is all right with him. He says he needed a little exercise anyway.

                                                    BUCK FEVER

If we can get on our mailing list every aspiring writer in America we will have a bigger circulation than the *Saturday Evening Post.*

When Knighthood Was in Flower
NEWS

That was a long time ago. It is said, however, that Walter Pierce, out on Walker's Creek, in the Hungry's Mother section, has a lot of the old flare in him.

A few days ago he was driving along the road with his uncle, J. A. Pierce. They came across the Evans boys beside the road. Some other fellows, among them Ed Smith, were with the Evans boys. For a long time there has been bad feeling between the Pierce and Evans factions out that way.

By the story brought out in Justice Dickinson's court, in the trial on Monday, words started between the two factions. Walter Pierce and his uncle got out of the car. It is said that Walter Pierce offered to let himself and any one of the Evans factions be searched for concealed weapons.

Then, when they were found all clean, they were to go into a field and fight it out.

That's the way they used to do things in the old days of Knights and Kings.

No one seemed to want to do it. The Pierces started to get back into the car.

The claim is that a young man named Ed Smith picked up a rock and tried to see if he was good enough to get into the big league. He probably is. Any way, he clipped J. A. Pierce on the forehead with the rock and his doing so cost him $25 in Justice Dickinson's court.

To-day all is quiet on Hungry's Mother.

BUCK FEVER

At Chilhowie, William McVey 15 Kills His Cousin Paul McVey 17

NEWS

The quiet and peace of an unusually beautiful Sunday was broken by a shocking killing at Chilhowie. William McVey, son of Andy McVey, a farmer living near Chilhowie, stabbed and killed his cousin, Paul McVey, son of Harrison McVey, another farmer and the brother of Andy McVey.

The cutting was done with a pocket knife and the boy who did the cutting is but fifteen. His dead cousin was seventeen.

Our correspondent says that the two boys had been playmates for a long time. The two farms were near each other. The boys had been trapping and got into a quarrel over the ownership of a steel trap. They became inflamed by passion and a fight started. In the fight the younger boy drew his pocket knife and stabbed his cousin in the neck. The jugular vein was cut and the boy died within the hour. William McVey was brought to Marion and lodged in the jail here.

Our young Buck Fever, we have taken in here to work with us, is real. He is imagined. He exists. He does not exist. He is a tall young mountain man. He is the fragment of a dream. But who is not that? Who is not the fragment of a dream?

SECOND WEEK OF
DECEMBER

ZEB

Zeb, the print-shop devil, is real enough. In the shop we grow impatient with him, we scold, we threaten. He grins. His mouth is big and he has a big head. The grin spreads over his face. He is as awkward as a bird dog pup. When he begins to grin you cannot scold any more.

People here are very conscious of being Southern. Some months ago I wrote something about the South and published it in a Northern magazine. Now I shall put it in my paper.

The South

The white race is one great family, the black another. In the far east, the yellow men. Families of brown men, scattered over the Pacific—living on islands.

The American Pacific Coast grew alarmed at the way yellow men pushed in and managed to squeeze them out.

Suppose you have, living in the family, in the house with you, a man or woman who wins your affection. There is a reason why you cannot sit with such a one at table, marry, make love with such a one.

Something strange—a strange kind of relationship between men and women—men and men—women and women.

Something tender—often brutal, often fine—making white men something they would not otherwise be—making black, brown, high-brown, velvet-brown men and women something they would not otherwise be.

I have had in mind, for some time now, trying to write several articles about sections of the country in which I have lived. No one will take what I say too seriously. It does not matter. Writing may clarify some of my own thoughts and feelings.

I am living in a valley between mountains cutting the north off from the south and can roll down either way. One roll into West Virginia, another into North Carolina. Of these particular places I shall say nothing. There has been in me always something calling from the north, a voice calling from the south. In regard to the negro I am Southern. I have no illusions about making him my brother.

I have just come from the far south, have been living there for two or three years. The heat and mosquitoes drove me out. Some of these days I shall drift back down there.

Southern nights, soft voices, New Orleans, Mobile, the Mississippi, live oaks, ships, forests—negroes—always the negroes—setting the tempo of life.

Here I find myself sitting at my desk, trying to write of the south—wanting to do it.

Liking negroes—wanting them about—not wanting them too close. In me the southern contradiction so puzzling to the north.

To a man like myself—that is to say to the artist type of man living in America—there is something tremendously provocative in the American south, in all the life of the south. The south is to me not just a place—it is an idea—a background.

Laughter perhaps—leisure—a kind of warm joy in living.

Born in the middle west—a youth spent as a wanderer and factory hand—after years of struggle, trying to be a successful man of affairs in industrial northern cities—I went south for the first time when I was well into middle life.

Something had drawn me south—something I had felt since boyhood. It may have been the reading of Huckleberry Finn—or the talk of my father.

He was a man southern bred and proud of it.

All southern men, men whose people came from the south, tell you about it at once. The notion of a southern aristocracy persists. Whether or not it is justified is another matter. I have always had difficulty deciding just what an aristocrat is.

Innumerable Americans have had the experience of a first southern trip—by train. . . .

The little miserable towns, the badly kept plantations, lean hogs in the streets of towns, lean white men, shabbiness.

Niggers.

Shiftlessness.

I got it all that first time south and landed at last in the old city
of Mobile. This was in the month of February. I went to a hotel.

I did not intend to stay there. I had saved a little money and
wanted to live cheaply, while I wrote a novel. We high-brow
writers have to live low.

It rained—a soft patter of rain in the streets. I put my bags in
my room, ate hastily and went out into the night—my first southern night.

For how many hours did I wander, sometimes in lighted streets
where white men lived, sometimes in little dark negro streets?
At once I felt—how shall I explain? There was something friendly
—in dark figures passing in dark streets, in buildings. Something
friendly seemed to come up out of the warm earth under my feet.

In northern industrial towns at night, as you wander thus
through streets of small houses, there is always something tense
and harsh in voices coming out of houses. Something nervous—
irritable—in people.

Life is too difficult. Everything moves too fast.

The tenseness was in my own voice, that first night in the south.
I had gone south hoping to get it out.

Softness in voices, laughter, an easy careless swing to bodies of
men and women. I walked in a soft cloud of words, not clearly
caught, feeling warmth in sounds, in people.

There was a negro ballad I had once heard Carl Sandburg sing,
a ballad about the boll weevil.

> *"I like this place,*
> *This'll be my home."*

I went murmuring the song—not being a bold singer—have
been murmuring it to myself these last four or five years—while
I lingered in the south.

Being northern, I yet never went south without a feeling of gladness, never have turned back northward without some feeling of inner fear—of sadness.

I got the nigger craze. All northern men of the artist type who go south get it.

Well, for those of us who tell tales, sing songs, work in colors, in stone, the negroes have something—something physical—rhythm —something we want to get into ourselves—our work.

I had not gone the length of wanting the negro to replace the white. I hadn't even gone with Abe Lincoln who said "Just because I want to see justice done the black is no sign I want to sleep with him." I wasn't thinking of justice.

Being in the south, what I most wanted was a decent sort of relationship with white southern men. In Mobile, New Orleans, Baton Rouge—other towns of the south—there is always a difficulty for the northern man to overcome.

It concerns the blacks.

You are in the south and would like to know—because you are a writer, interested in the life about you—something about the relationships of black, brown, yellow and white.

The negro race in the south is so apparently getting lighter. How does that happen? What's going on? White blood constantly creeping in from somewhere.

Northern travelers can't do it all.

Many of the negro women seen in the streets, in cities, on country roads, on river boats, about houses where you go to dine— splendid creatures.

People always whispering things. "Such and such a white man has a touch of the tar pot." It doesn't come in through white southern women. You know that.

I went walking with southern men, eating, drinking, talking with southern men.

Men are what the civilization in which they live makes them.

Be careful now.

A good deal of fear, everywhere in the south, of cheap, snap northern judgments. One of these fellows hot on justice goes south. He sees the negroes doing all the work with their hands—sees them wearing ragged clothes, eating in fence corners like dogs, gets indignant.

He can tell you all about everything in ten days.

I did not want to do it like that. The negro problem is the vast overshadowing problem of the south. No man questions that.

Try down there to associate with the negro; sit with him, eat with him, talk with him.

You would learn nothing. A white man of the right sort will tell you everything better—more clearly. You would get nothing but the contempt of both whites and blacks. Chances are you would deserve it, too.

Some days I sat for hours on the docks—watching negroes work. That wasn't for the negroes' sake. It was for my own sake. The negro had something I wanted. All sensible white men want it. There is a kind of closeness to nature, trees, rivers, the earth, more primitive men have, that men less primitive are all seeking. We want to have the cake and eat it. I know I do.

I remember a morning. I went before daylight to conceal myself in a lumber pile, lay hidden all day, negroes at work all about me.

Later many talks with southern white men. They began to open up a little—saw I hadn't come down there to tell them anything. Some grew immediately angry, flared up. Others got my point of view—seemed to like it.

Suppose strangers always coming into your house to tell you where to hang your pictures, how to place your chairs, how to treat others in your house.

In what bed to sleep. The south has had to stand a lot from the north—God knows.

Yes, it happens—boys in the country—in the cities—brown girls. How are you going to help that?

To say it does not happen—constantly—is foolish. If it did not happen there would be no problem, and there is a problem. If the negro were just an animal. He isn't. Often he is a tremendously attractive man—or alas, woman.

If you think you, being northern, a Puritan perhaps, would run your house better, be more truly what you call "moral," you're a fool.

I remember a brown man laughing. He was sweeping out my room in a house in the country. "White man and brown woman get the fun in this country. White woman and brown man get left."

Well, I have stressed the problem. I like to accept life as it comes up to me. Nothing in the life of the south shocks me. I would take my chances with southern white men and women. Given the same problem I could not handle it better.

It seems to me that what the south needs most now is the artist —not visiting artists—its own—but there is a difficulty.

The south needs southern expression of all phases of southern life in song, prose, painting, music. To get that it needs acceptance of itself, more frankness.

It needs to begin to escape the nonsense about spotless white womanhood, insisting too much upon a kind of purity that is humanly impossible. It needs most of all to wipe out fear of ugly puritanical northern judgments.

The south has got to cleanse itself of the fear of facing itself.

Not an easy job.

The southern problem—that of a race living so intimately with the white race—not living with it at all—fear of race mixture—is the hardest problem any section of the country has to face.

Having lived in the south I believe southern white men handle it as well as northern men ever could—perhaps better.

Chicago, talking of southern violence.

If you go on the theory that exact justice is a human possibility everything is wrong. I do not subscribe to any such theory.

I have a notion that injustice has a place of its own in the scheme of life.

As for the negro, I am sure he is better off in the south than in the north. There, at least, injustice is often tempered by real affection.

The land belongs to the blacks. White men own legally the railroads, the land, the boats on the rivers, the rivers, forests, swamps, but they are nigger boats, nigger rivers, nigger swamps, forests, railroads.

It can't be otherwise.

Any intelligent southern white would agree—laughing—"what of it?"

The negro does the work, the dust of the fields and the water of the rivers and swamps runs through his fingers. No white man anywhere has ever done what the negro has done with the railroad.

Songs of railroads, dreams of railroads—voyages from town to town—a chicken for frying tucked under the arm.

> *"Have you got your ticket bought*
> *O, Lord!*
> *Have you got your ticket bought?"*

Railroading into a nigger heaven.

The land is really the negro's land because he works it, sings of it, loves it.

What of it?

The white man isn't going to let him take it away.

The white man of the south getting at his problem the best he can, perhaps. Having to put up with violent fools in his own race, having to be father to innumerable black children.

The blacks remain children.

In the country—in the south—in many households in cities, the conditions of slavery days not much changed.

A relationship between the races not frankly faced, but faced more than the north suspects.

All sorts of subtle angles—loyalty, tenderness, attempts at justice that do not show on the surface.

The negro unbelievably cunning—"cute" is the word.

Getting for himself in the south—so much the whites do not get and that does not appear on the surface.

The south—the white south getting bolder. Southern white life will yet express itself—really—in song, prose, painting, music.

The negro contributing—doing too much of the contributing now. A second-rate negro poet or artist always getting twice the credit of an equally able white man. That's northern sentimentality.

It is a difficult, delicate job to see the southern white man's angle and see it whole, but the northern man will have to do it if he wants to draw nearer the south.

To go black—think all the hope of future cultural development in the south is in the southern black, because he sings, dances, produces jazz—is hopelessness.

The puzzle remains—two races that when they meet to produce blood mixture must meet in secret, in shame.

The southern problem is the most difficult problem in America. The attitude of the north has never helped much.

I spent a few days at a southern plantation. There were several thousand acres—a village of blacks.

The seasons were long, land cheap.

Two white women owned and ran the place.

We came in the late afternoon and dined in a great room of the old house.

The management of such a house would drive a northern white woman crazy in a week.

The two southern women were handling it easily—naturally.

Delicious food—in vast abundance—dogs, cats, niggers—men, women and children.

Life squirming and writhing everywhere underfoot—nigger life, insect life, animal life.

The niggers worked the land on shares. The arrangement would be called "peonage" by a northern reformer.

Sure, all the niggers in debt to the two women, always in debt.

What grows on the place belongs to every one on the place. The niggers eat, sleep, sing, make love, work some.

As we dined one of the women told me of hogs, chickens, eggs, turkeys always being carried off secretly to be consumed in some cabin.

She had to know her blacks.

If a man stole a hog, needing it—having children to feed, having been ill—having been a good nigger when times were better —she said nothing, laughed and let it go.

She had to know what nigger stole the hog and why.

She managed to let him know she knew without too many words.

There's a way.

Cunning, creeping life all about the two women. They did not dare be afraid.

I stayed four days and went back on "settlement" day.

That is the great day when the negro squares up for his year's work.

Not much chance for the whites to cheat. If they do they lose their niggers.

The negro won't go away physically.

Cheat him and he'll live on you all through the next year, doing no work.

He knows how.

Negroes aren't fools either. Trick niggers among them—but a trick negro is like the trick white workman of the north.

The two women had to know their people.

Niggers on such southern plantations are taken out sometimes and whipped.

I saw a southern white woman whip a negro man for trying to hit another negro man with an axe.

It was about a negro girl they both wanted.

The white woman knew what was coming. She was watching. She stepped in just in time to prevent a murder. Such things are not uncommon in the south.

The two women I visited knew every negro man, every negro woman and child on their place as a northern woman might know the children of her own body.

Plenty of southern white men of the same sort—on other plantations about.

The two white women were doing the job because their white men were all dead. Southern white families—the old ones are dying out. That may be one reason why so many negroes come north.

Just why the old white families are passing is another story. It may be simply the old south's passing, a new south being born. In southern cities the negro labor doesn't sing any more. The south may have to industrialize, like the east, mid-America, the far west, southern city newspapers all say so.

And the dying out of the old families may be due to something else.

The thing not talked about except among intimates—never publicly—in the south.

A gradual loss of personal dignity in white men, due to a condition—thrust into relationships too complex and difficult for the generality of men to handle.

At the plantation I visited, the plantation run by two childless women, the last of their particular family, the problem was touched upon during our visit.

After dining one evening we sat on a wide gallery. There was talk of the old days. Always talk of old days in the south.

Then later a troop of black and brown women came up to the house to sing.

The old work songs, ballads about the life of the negroes on the plantation, were taboo.

An idea had got abroad among the blacks that it was wicked to sing of work, of play. Only songs of a Baptist or Methodist God permitted.

A few wicked niggers, however. They stepped forward and sang of a wreck on the railroad that crossed the edge of the plantation some three miles from the house, of the year when the flu came and so many negroes died.

I have seldom heard the miseries of flu so aptly described.

The wicked negroes having a grand time—singing the ungodly songs—the good ones standing aside and enjoying the wickedness of the wicked.

Puritanism taking hold of the negroes, too.

The two southern white women half heroic figures in my imagination.

I got a slant on them the next day.

We drove to a small town, a southern market town and the half white negroes were all about.

A girl with straight hair and blue eyes—the hair golden brown.

A young negro man with Jewish features, plainly marked.

Traces of white blood everywhere—in blacks—making the blacks not blacks but browns.

I dared to suggest to the women—tentatively of course—well, I asked the question. . . .

Very few of the negroes of that section had ever been twenty miles from home. Few enough northern visitors came that way.

Young white men growing up—getting married—making a new white man's south as a new east, far west and mid-America is always being made.

The woman looked at me with a hard light in her eyes.

"It is true," she said. "It happens. I don't like it."

"One thing I know. You are a northern man and can't judge in such matter, but I am southern through and through." She smiled at me, deciding not to be angry.

"What you suggest happens but southern white men never have anything to do with the matter."

It was the south—all I know of the south. If you of the north lived there do you think you would do the job better?

Southern civilization began with a problem—a war was fought —the problem remains.

It cannot be solved now—in any way I know.

It can be faced.

Facing it may be the one thing needed for the flowering of a truly southern art, a truly southern contribution to an American civilization.

THIRD WEEK OF

DECEMBER

FROM THE PAPER
Nebo School Notes

Owen, Herbert, Mason and Hugh went hunting and bagged mostly rabbits; Connie went visiting "Uncle Charley Edmonds" and "Aunt Alice." The rest of us stayed at home, but we all had a good time.

The hunting season began November 15th and will last until December 31. There seems to be lots of game in the valley and mountains. Our city friends come out to help us hunt, and birds and rabbits live hard. Mr. Bailey and Mr. Robinette of Roanoke were here visiting and hunting. Mr. Bailey killed two pheasants. They were the color of partridges and larger than frying-sized chickens. Mr. Otis Hubble found several pheasants and killed one.

The farmers have been very busy for a week or two killing hogs; now that it has turned warm again some are afraid their meat will spoil; but there is no danger of the back-bones and ribs, for we are working on them three times a day. Hog killing time is great for the little children. They are always up bright and early that morning, but the older we get the less fun we see in it. However, when the meat is cooked and put on the table we can't say we don't like it.

Town Business

N E W S

Mr. T. E. King of the Marion National Bank appeared before the Town Council at its last meeting and urged the settlement of a bill for paying the town's share of the cost of the sidewalk before the new bank building. There was some question as to the amount the town was to pay, but after Mr. King had presented the bank's side of the matter, the council voted to meet the bank at least half way in the matter.

Mr. Wheeler appeared before the council and complained of the waste of water caused by the leakage of the Norfolk and Western water tank.

A committee was appointed to see about the installation of two water plugs on Pearl Avenue.

The matter of housing the machinery of the town was taken up and a committee was appointed with power to act. At present the machinery is housed facing our most fashionable street, that is to say this print shop. Mr. Robert Goolsby, who has the honor of owning the roof over our heads, is kicking at the mess made. We rather sympathize with Mr. Goolsby. There is a hint on the part of the council that both Mr. Goolsby and ourselves may be made happier by moving the whole shebang to some other place. We will not be sad.

The laws of the town, not having been copied or codified since 1893, have been put into definite form by Mayor Dickinson. We look for a printing job from that.

It was decided that, for the month of December, the two town sergeants would be put on duty as follows: Mr. Hays from twelve at night until one the next afternoon, Mr. Snavely from noon until twelve at night. It is almost as soft a job as ours.

Mr. Hays was complimented by the council for his care of the children at the street crossing.

There was some talk of putting up a tin building down our way—this in the machinery matter, but Mr. Dickinson made the good point that a pile of pipe was handsomer than a tin building.

The matter of the crossing at the Presbyterian Church was put over until the next meeting.

The GREAT WHITE WAY came up for discussion again but it is going to cost too much. We would almost be willing to be a street lamp ourselves for what the power companies are threatening to charge. Some hope was held out that the power company might go Democratic and cut prices a little later.

WINTER DAYS IN A SMALL TOWN

Mysterious Checker King Shows Marion His Curves

He came into town about the middle of last week, a rather quiet man with a little black mustache and a nervous step. Perhaps you know that Bill Johnson's shop, down facing the Marion Rye Valley Railroad, is the checker center in Marion. There is a little room back in there, behind the shop, with a stove and a little table with its checker board.

For years now the checker tournaments of Marion have been

fought out in that room. Perhaps Mr. Johnson himself is the champion among our players.

Others who are devotees of the game are Mr. James W. Sheffey, H. A. Stephenson, T. K. Sawyers, Ed Scott, Jess Hankla and Bill Waterson. These men are all good players. No one of them can be dead sure of beating another.

And then this man named Ward came along—at least he said that was his name. He said he had once been a famous surgeon in a big New York hospital. It might have been true. Something had happened to the man all right. What it was no one knew.

He just wandered into the shop one day last week and asked if they played checkers there. They did. Some one asked him to sit into a game. He did.

A few moves and his opponent was whipped. It was hard to see how he did it. He seemed to have no special system. For all the jokes made about the game checkers is about as complex a game as chess. There are a thousand combinations possible.

This man Ward seemingly knew them all. Sometimes he played a tight game and at other times opened wide up. He had our checker players woozy. No one could beat him. He could play and win while reading a newspaper or talking to a bystander. No one in Marion ever saw such checkers. Word ran all over town and all of the latter part of last week the checker headquarters of Marion was crowded. Then the mysterious checker king disappeared as mysteriously as he had come, but for years the men who love checkers will be talking of his game and wishing he had stayed long enough to give them a real chance to get on to his curves.

A Touch of Highlife

NEWS

Those of our subscribers who do not lead as virtuous a life as this editor were a little alarmed on the evening of Tuesday the 24th.

First the lights went out and then there came a howling wind and rain from over Chilhowie way, that threatened for a moment to blow the town away. We saw several real sinners with pale drawn faces, but as they got through that time we will not print their names.

Anyway we are told that the roof of the grandstand at the fair ground blew away.

Also Mr. Arthur L. Cox, whose wife is ill in a Philadelphia hospital and who is doing most of his own work at home and taking care of four children, had a scare. A stray ball of lightning got into his house and burned out all the lights. Must be he is not living as pure a life as most editors live. Not a thing happened to us.

Should Not Have Tied His Shoe Laces

NEWS

We understand Tom Doyle is in trouble again. A year or two ago he was in hot water for walking off with a coat belonging to some one else. Jailer Hopkins got after him and gave him such a hot foot race that he ran right out of the coat.

This time he is accused of taking a pair of shoes belonging to one of the workmen on the Marion Hotel. Well, well, he should not have laced the shoes. It was bad technique. He could not run out of them and was caught and taken before Justice Francis at Chilhowie. He got 30 days and $50.

ADVERTISEMENT

Don't fail to try for the prize at the corn-eating contest at the Marion Hardware on Saturday afternoon of this week. How many kernels of corn will a rooster eat after having been kept from corn since the day before? The winning guesser gets a fine prize.

Wanted His Wife

NEWS

If we were a woman and had to have a husband, William Lambert of Lee County is the man we would want.

When Mr. Lambert wants his wife he wants her. Unfortunately, Mrs. Lambert is a patient in the State Insane Hospital at Marion.

Mr. Lambert came from Lee County to see his wife on the morning of Thursday the 26th. He was allowed to go and visit his wife in her room at the hospital.

Screams from the room. Mrs. Lambert says her husband wanted to take her out of the institution at the point of a big gun.

We will say this—if any one wanted most of the women we know they could get them without a gun.

The attendants at the hospital phoned to Sheriff Dillard. The Sheriff went up and got Mr. Lambert. He was taken before Mayor Dickinson and fined $20 for carrying a loaded revolver. He denies that he threatened the attendants at the hospital or his wife or any one else.

"I only thought it would be a good thing to take a gun along with me when I was going into a strange county," he said. He must have thought he was going into Carroll County or some place like that.

Anyway, Sheriff Dillard has got him a swell new revolver, the county is $20 richer, and poor Mr. Lambert of Lee County is in jail.

BUCK FEVER

Tough Luck in Turkeypen Hollow

NEWS

Sheriff Dillard has a notion that Ellis Cornett, who lives up Kentucky Hollow way, above Atkins, ought to see a doctor about his eyesight and smelling organs. The sheriff was up that way one day last week. They dug up two barrels of perfectly good mash in a barn just 147 steps from Ellis Cornett's door.

The barrels, it seemed, were set down in the ground under some boards and straw and the mash in it was about ready to be run off. It got run off on the ground.

And such a smell, the sheriff said. Mr. Cornett swore he did not know it was there. He was up before Justice Dickinson and as he has several small children at home the justice let him go on $500 bond agreed to between Mr. Cornett and his wife.

He is to appear before the grand jury at its next meeting late in February.

FOURTH WEEK OF
DECEMBER

Old Plow Horse

No doubt he will not see the grain in shock;
    Fifteen years—a long span for a horse:
A dozen seed-times has he pulled my plow
    As years went trooping in their lazy course.

I was young: the young have buoyant hearts;
    He was mettlesome—his bay neck curved:
I could pull a line with steady hand
    Oh, it was seldom that my mold-board swerved!

Glad am I my seed is in the loam;
    I am weary, full of muscle-sting;

I have put the clanking trace-chains by
Alien hoofs will tramp my fields next spring.

Stranger hands may even hold these reins;
I have hope that I will thresh the sheaves;
But there is much of peril for the old,
Between brown harvest and the first green leaves.

JAY G. SIGMUND

Letters keep coming in—many people in many places who
would like to work on this paper. Tired out city people we knew
somewhere in our wandering wanting to live closer to the hills
and the grass roots. We wish we could give them all a chance
but if we took any one else on, we would have to fire Buck Fever.
Buck says there isn't any ex-city man going to get his job if he has
to work for his stall room.

Human Misery

NEWS

When it sinks low enough and gets caught in the trap of life,
human life can be both dangerous and terrible.

Thomas Patterson, who says he is from Martinville, West
Virginia, drifted into town on Monday. The man is a dope. You
know what that means. When he got to Marion he was desperate.
He went first to the office of Mayor Dickinson and then to Dr.
Weindell. The M. D. could not supply him with the drug he
craved. He got desperate and ugly and attacked Doctor Weindell,
striking him in the face and cutting his lip. Then he fled. It was a
brutal and uncalled for attack.

It would not do of course to let such a man run loose. Men and
boys took up the chase. Highway policeman Jack Williams, Rush
Hayes, Sheriff Dillard, all got busy.

Patterson was cornered at the East End Filling station and

showed fight. He was however surrounded and without further injury to any one was lodged in jail. Every one breathed a bit easier.

It happens that this writer never sees a thing of this sort without an inward shudder. It was a gray dismal day. I cannot escape this trick of identifying myself with such a poor human. As he runs through the street I imagine myself running. I imagine myself also the victim of some terrible habit, driven to desperation, brutalized.

Buck Fever, our star reporter, was missing for a half day last week and has been very mysterious about it. He may have been home, for a visit to Coon Hollow, or he may have been out courting. If you have the lowdown on Buck let us know. We are trying to check up on him.

Here Comes the Band
EDITORIAL

One of the first signs of the decay of a town is when it cannot get up enthusiasm to support a band. The Marion band needs support. Most people don't know it. Marion is so used to having a good band that it takes the institution for granted.

Do you realize that our Marion Band has over two thousand dollars invested in instruments, to say nothing of uniforms?

It has always been a straight band. During the eighteen years of its life it has gone to a good many other towns. No one ever saw one of the boys drunk or misbehaving.

In order to keep themselves up to snuff the boys practice twice a week. They pay a dollar a month out of their own pockets. This isn't fair. They should not be asked to do that. The money goes to pay rent for a hall in which to practice and other incidental expenses. Who will pay the yearly dues for one band boy? This paper will receive it for them. Some of the boys are behind in their dues. A good many of them work hard for their money. When they get behind they do not feel like coming around to practice and the band suffers.

Only last Armistice Day our band had an offer to go to another town. They could have gotten $250 for the day. They stuck to Marion. They have always stuck. We ought to stick to them.

There is soon to be a show put on in town a part of the proceeds of which go to the band. Support that when it comes along. If you feel like chipping in to pay some fellow's dues for a year we will be glad to hear from you.

Every town that is a town needs a good band, Marion has one. Let's stand by them.

Cattle Rustler Picked Up Near Marion

NEWS

You don't have to go to the movies to get wild west life in our little town. Writers of wild west tales come on down here to live. Bring your money with you. We're a little short ourselves. We have got excitement here now.

One day last week, Jack Williams, the Lee Highway cop, got word that there was a famous cattle rustler somewhere in this country. Jack got busy, went out and got him, took his guns off him and brought him in. He picked him up over near Wytheville but what sort of a place is that to keep a desperate man in? He brought him right on over here to Marion to our own favorite little old county jail. Buck Fever helped him.

Buck says the cattle rustler's name is Sam Russell and that he hails originally from over in Grayson County. He was out west though when he got into this mess. Buck's story is that he rustled a bunch of cattle out in western Missouri, drove them to a strange town, insured them there, getting the insurance money, then drove them to another town and sold them. Buck wanted us to try and do the same thing with this paper and we did approach Mr.

Gills, the well known insurance agent, but he frowned on us.

ITEMS

Nellie the print-shop cat was missing one morning last week and Zeb our printer's devil was heart-broken. Nellie came in later. She is getting as elusive as Buck Fever. She and Buck may be up to the same game. They are both under suspicion.

Bill Wright, the banker, and Brown Wells came over from Troutdale to see our plant. Joe put their names on a lino-type. They were already subscribers. They report shooting good in the hills, but did not say what kind of shooting.

Join the Glory List

EDITORIAL

The Marion Publishing Company doesn't intend to become a crusader. You know how city papers are. Well, we make no pretensions to being a big city paper. We are just a little old country weekly, that's what we are.

City papers are always getting up a crusade for some good cause. They uplift this one or that one. Sometimes whole sections of society get uplifted like that. It's wonderful.

We aren't, however, quite so ambitious. Up to date we have taken up but one cause and that is the Marion Band. It may be the only one we ever will take up. And we are not doing that out of any altruistic purpose. It's just because we like to hear the band play. We like to see them parade. When a big day comes we like to see them put on their uniforms and come blowing their heads off up Main Street.

Flags flying, every one feeling fine. Life is drab enough on ordinary days. We have never found any way to be a canary bird ourself.

What we want is to see the band boys have a little money in the treasury. We want band concerts on summer nights. O hearts of gold, who will put up $5 a year over a period of five years to get and keep our band in bang-up financial condition? We are making this appeal not only to Marionites but to all people in the surrounding country who read this paper and who like to come to our town when there is something stirring, or on summer nights to hear the band play.

You know this paper is getting quite a circulation in the outside world too. Men at a distance, who remember their own town band, can chip in. They don't need to stop at five. They don't need to sign up for five years. Anything addressed to box K, Marion, and marked "F OR THE BAND" will get to the boys.

I will sign up for .... years, for the sum of ....
dollars a year to put and keep the Marion Band on a sound financial basis.

Names will not be printed if you do not wish it.

The King of England, President of France, President of the United States, Senators, Politicians, Millionaires, Rich Authors, Poor Ones, Farmers, Merchants, any one welcome.

If you do not want to sign up for more than one year or cannot give $5 do not let that stop you.

Cut this out, sign your name, put in a bill and mail.
JOIN THE GLORY LIST.

Fatal Shooting at Konnarock

NEWS

At seven o'clock on Tuesday evening, the 21st, word was phoned into the sheriff's office that there had been a fatal shooting at Konnarock. The man shot was well known in Konnarock. Here is the story as we have been able to gather it.

Two deputy sheriffs, McDaniels of Smyth County and Garland Patton of Washington County, had gone into the mountain near Konnarock bearing felony warrants against General Trivett and his nephew, also named Trivett. On a former visit to the same section the same officers had found a still. The two Trivetts were nearby, cutting wood, apparently for the still. The Trivetts had left their guns leaning against the still house and the officers grabbed the guns and when the men ran shot at them. The Trivetts escaped.

On the same day officers went back into the same section bearing the felony warrants. They found another still but no men. Later as they were walking along a mountain road they met the Trivetts and at once a battle of guns began.

After an exchange of several shots the Trivetts ran off. The younger man escaped and has not been found.

General Trivett, after running some distance turned into the brush. The officers followed and found him lying on the ground. He got up and there were some words. "I'm shot." "You fellows shot me," he said. As the officers had the drop on him he walked along with them for some distance and then fell to the ground. The officers carried him to their car and took him into Konnarock from where they phoned over to the sheriff's office in Marion. Sheriff Dillard, Prosecutor Funk, Jailer Hopkins and Justice Dickinson went over at once. By the time they got to Konnarock General Trivett was dead.

Why Joe

We ask our readers to remember that we are but a small shop, with but a few employees. Often you will find in our papers grammatical errors and misspelled words. We have in our office here a lino-type machine that got a bad start in life. Joe, the lino-type operator, watches it constantly, but it will not behave. Perhaps when it was younger it would not go to school. Lord knows what gets wrong with it sometimes.

For example, only the other day, one of our most respected advertisers advertised cotton underwear. The machine made it coffin underwar. You see the machine had just been working on death notices. Such things happen.

The Day
EDITORIAL

Five or six o'clock in the morning. The sun not yet up. Every-thing inside is at loose ends. Presently you will gather yourself together for the day. Every day is a something special. It is like a house. The foundations for the day have to be laid, the walls have to be put up.

Men are fortunate who have definite tasks. I have always envied bricklayers. There the bricks are. They are all of one size. You must lay every brick just so. A definite task like that takes your mind off yourself and others. You get up in the morning and begin to lay bricks. As you work your mind clears. You speak to your fellow workman. The day gets going all right.

Such people as lawyers, doctors, school teachers, bankers, manu-facturers, preachers, editors, writers, people whose work is at least partly mental, the tone such people set for their day is all im-portant.

The task the school teacher has to face daily would frighten me. There is a whole room full of children. Children are usually quick and responsive. The day starts. What is the teacher's mood? It will effect every one of the pupils.

Formerly I knew personally a good many actors. I used to go around to see them after the show, in their dressing rooms. There was the actor reading the same part every evening. No two per-formances were just alike. There were the same words, the same gestures. Something that should have existed between the actor and his audience would not come to life. Many a time have I seen an actor come off the stage utterly discouraged. He dropped into a chair. "What a rotten performance I gave to-night," he said shaking his head.

He was the same man he had been on other nights, was well and strong. What was the matter with him?

It must be that with preachers the same thing happens. The challenge given them is something terrific. We go to hear them expecting them to give us something we have not got in ourselves, that is to say the strength and inclination toward gentleness, love, all of the finer attributes.

And they, poor men, have daily to go through the same little annoyances the rest of us do.

The business man, the head of some large enterprise. What a pack of worries for him. He has not only to think of production but of finance, of holding his men in line, of selling what he manufactures. Some manufacturers get rich. I do not envy them what they have to go through to get there.

The day exists as a day. The sun comes up or it rains or snows. I get up early on some days and walk about in the streets. People look outwardly alike, but inside themselves what is going on? There is in me a great curiosity about people. On the whole, I think it is sympathetic. Often in the early morning I lose courage. I run and grab a book and begin to read or I hurry to my typewriter and begin putting down words as I am doing now.

Any little definite thing I can do helps me in laying the foundation for my own day.

REPRINTED FOR MY OWN PAPERS FROM
VANITY FAIR

A Criminal's Christmas

A STORY

Every man's hand against me. There I was in the darkness of the empty house. It was cold outside and snow was falling. I crept to a window and raising a curtain peered out. A man walked in the street. Now he had stopped at a corner and was looking about. He was looking toward the house I was in. I drew back into the darkness.

Two o'clock, four o'clock. The night before Christmas.

Yesterday I had walked freely in the streets. Then temptation came. I committed a crime. The man hunt was on.

Always men creeping in darkness in cities, in towns, in alleyways in cities, on dark country roads.

Man wanted. The man hunt. Who was my friend? Who could I trust? Where should I go?

It was my own fault. I had brought it on myself. We were hard up that year and I had got a job in Willmott's grocery and general store. I was twelve years old and was to have fifty cents a day.

During the afternoon of the day before Christmas there was a runaway on Main Street. Every one rushed out. I was tying a package and there—right at my hand—was an open cash drawer.

I did not think. I grabbed. There was so much silver. Would any one know? Afterward I found I had got six dollars, all in quarters, nickels and dimes. It made a handful. How heavy it felt. When I put it in my pocket what a noise it made.

No one knew. Yes they did. Now wait. Don't be nervous.

You know what such a boy—twelve years of age—would tell himself. I wanted presents for the other kids of our family,—wanted something for mother. Mother had been ill. She was just able to sit up.

When I got out of the store that evening it was for a time all right. I spent a dollar seventy-five. Fifty cents of it was for mother —a lacy-looking kind of thing to put around her neck. There were five other children. I spent a quarter on each.

Then I spent a quarter on myself. That left four dollars. I bought a kite. That was silly. You don't fly kites in the winter. When I got home and before I went into the house I hid it in a shed. There were some old boxes in a corner. I put it in behind the boxes.

It was grand going in with the presents in my arms. Toys, candy, the lace for mother.

Mother never said a word. She never asked me where I got the money to buy so many things.

I got away as soon as I could. There was a boy named Bob Mann giving a party and I went to it.

I had come too early. I looked through a window and saw I had come long before the party was to start so I went for a walk.

It had begun to snow. I had told mother I might stay at Bob Mann's all night.

That was what raised the devil—just walking about. When I had grabbed the money out of the cash drawer I did not think there was a soul in the store. There wasn't. But just as I was slipping it into my pocket a man came in.

The man was a stranger. What a noise the silver made. Even when I was walking in the street that night, thinking about the man, it made a noise. Every step I took it jingled in my pockets.

A fine thing to go to a party making a noise like that. Suppose they played some game. In lots of games you chase each other.

I was frightened now. I might have thrown the money away, buried it in the snow, but I thought . . .

I was full of remorse. If they did not find me out I could go back to the store next day and slip the four dollars back into the drawer.

"They won't send me to jail for two dollars," I thought, but there was that man.

I mean the one who came into the store just when I had got the money all safe and was putting it into my pocket.

He was such a strange-acting man. He just came into the store and then went right out. I was confused of course. I must have acted rather strangely. No doubt I looked scared.

He may have been just a man who had got into a wrong place. Perhaps he was a man looking for his wife.

When he had gone all the others came back. There had been a rush before the runaway happened and there was a rush again. No one paid any attention to me. I never even asked whose horse ran away.

The man might, however, have been a detective. That thought did not come until I went to Bob Mann's party and got there too early. It came when I was walking in the street waiting for the party to begin.

I never did go to the party. Like any other boy I had read a lot of dime novels. There was a boy in our town named Roxie Williams who had been in a reform school. What I did not know about crime and detectives he had told me.

I was walking in the street thinking of that man who came into the store just as I stole the money and then, when I began to think of detectives, I began to be afraid of every man I met.

In a snow like that, in a small town where there aren't many lights, you can't tell who any one is.

There was a man started to go into a house. He went right up to the front door and seemed about to knock and then he didn't. He stood by the front door a minute and then started away.

It was the Musgrave's house. I could see Lucy Musgrave inside through a window. She was putting coal in a stove. All the houses I saw that evening, while I was walking around, getting more and more afraid all the time, seemed the most cheerful and comfortable places.

There was Lucy Musgrave inside a house and that man outside by the front door, only a few feet away and she never knowing it. It might have been the detective and he might have thought the Musgrave house was our house.

After that thought came I did not dare go home and did not know where I could go. Fortunately the man at the Musgraves' front door hadn't seen me. I had crouched behind a fence. When he went away along the street I started to run but had to stop.

The loose silver in my pocket made too much racket. I did not dare go and hide it anywhere because I thought, "if they find and arrest me and I have four dollars to give back maybe they'll let me go."

Then I thought of a house where a boy named Jim Moore lived. It was right near Buckeye Street—a good place. Mrs. Moore was a widow and only had Jim and one daughter and they had gone away for Christmas.

I made it there all right, creeping along the streets. I knew the Moores hid their key in a woodshed, under a brick near the door. I had seen Jim Moore get it dozens of times.

It was there all right and I got in. Such a night! I got some clothes out of a closet to put on and keep me warm. They belonged to Mrs. Moore and her grown-up daughter. Afterward they found them all scattered around the house and it was a town wonder. I would get a coat and skirt and wrap them around me. Then I'd put them down somewhere and as I did not dare light a match would have to get some more. I took some spreads off beds.

It was all like being crazy or dead or something. Whenever any one went along the street outside I was so scared I trembled all over. Pretty soon I had got the notion the whole town was on the hunt.

Then I began thinking of mother. Perhaps by this time they had been to our house. I could not make up my mind what to do.

Sometimes I thought—well, in stories I was always at that time reading—boys about my own age were always beginning life as bootblacks and rising to affluence and power. I thought I would slide out of town before daylight and get me a bootblack's outfit somehow. Then I'd be all right.

I remember that I thought I'd start my career at a place called Cairo, Illinois. Why Cairo I do not know.

I thought that all out, crouching by a window in the Moores' house that Christmas eve, and then, when no one came along the street for a half hour and I began to be brave again, I thought that if I had a pistol I would let myself out of the house and go boldly home. If, as I supposed, detectives were hid in front of the house, I'd shoot my way through.

I would get desperately wounded of course. I was pretty sure I would get a mortal wound but before I died I would stagger in at the door and fall at mother's feet.

There I would lie dying, covered with blood. I made up some dandy speeches. "I stole the money, mother, to bring a moment of happiness into your life. It was because it was Christmas eve." I remember that was one of the speeches. When I thought of it— of my getting it off and then dying, I cried.

Well, I was cold and frightened enough to cry anyway.

What really happened was that I stayed in the Moores' house until daylight came. After midnight it got so quiet in the street outside that I risked a fire in the kitchen stove but I went to sleep for a moment in a chair beside the stove and falling forward made a terrible burned place on my forehead.

The mark of Cain. I am only telling this story to show that I know just how a criminal feels.

I got out of the Moore house at daylight and went home and got into our house without any one knowing. I had to crawl into bed with a brother but he was asleep. Next morning, in the excitement of getting all the presents they did not expect, no one asked me where I had been. When mother asked me where I had got the burn I said, "at the party," and she put some soda on it and did not say anything more.

And on the day after Christmas I went back to the store and sure enough got the four dollars back into the drawer. Mr. Willmott gave me a dollar. He said I had hurried away so fast on Christmas eve that he hadn't got a chance to give me a present.

They did not need me any more after that week and I was all right and knew the man that came, in such an odd way into the store, wasn't a detective at all.

As for the kite—in the spring I traded it off. I got me a pup but the pup got distemper and died.

LAST WEEK OF
DECEMBER

Gil Stephenson
EDITORIAL

Gil is an old workman who has been all his life in this one Virginia town.

He worked in a factory when he was a small boy. That was just at the end of the Civil War.

They were getting barites out of the hills here then. There was a long dark building. A crusher crushed the ore. It rolled down a long chute. The boys picked out the stone and other impurities.

Afterward Gil began working at the printing trade. He has been at it forty years, has set enough type to go across the State.

He started a little paper of his own—The Marion Democrat. I publish it now.

In those days everything was done by hand. All the type was set by hand and the press was turned by hand.

Gil's wife helped with the paper. His children helped. There was never a man in this world who has more loyal children than Gil Stephenson. They have all been a help to him and he has been a help to them.

On press days they went out into the street and got a "nigger" to come in and turn the press. He turned out an entire edition for fifty cents.

Mrs. Stephenson addressed the papers by hand.

Advertisers didn't pay much for space and subscribers often paid their subscriptions with potatoes, cabbages, loads of wood, corn for making corn meal.

Tramp printers floating in.

"Well, have you any work?" "No."

"Here's something for breakfast though—and a cup of coffee."

The printers shuffled out to a little restaurant.

Presently they came back and all began to set type. They set enough to pay for the firewood and the breakfast.

Some of them were fast as lightning too.

There were old fellows, worn out, cast aside—old drunkers.

Then there were young fellows—going on their trade journey.

Sometimes—along in the morning—they caught a freight out of town.

"Well, good-by—good luck."

Gil still sets type at his case every day. He is a grandfather now. His body is as well and strong as that of a young man.

He likes his trade. "You can't cheat or fake at it," he says— "every defect shows."

Of course defects show everywhere, in all trades where workmen are slipshod but people do not know the difference.

Sometimes, when the presses are going in our shop and Gil is feeding we find a defect.

"Oh, let it go. Who cares?"

"Who cares? Who cares?"

"Railroad it."

"We got to get this paper out."

The press runs on. Suddenly it stops. Gil climbs down from his press-feeding platform.

"Oh, it will only take a minute," he says.

Well he had to stop—he couldn't go on.
"That's Gil all right," the others in the shop say, and laugh.

FROM THE PAPER

Rain

Rain drums on the roofs, drums on the ground
Drums with a dull monotonous sound;
  Out of the west, the thundering west, it comes
And drums . . . and drums.

The black frowning clouds rumble and drone
Over the wind's low monotone,
  And the rain comes down, down on the town,
Down on the slumbering town.

Now in the solemn tantalizing gloom
The town is a musty dismal tomb,
  And the houses huddle close in the night,
In the dark, funereal night.

OLIVER JENKINS

Concord, N. H.

O, Joy

NEWS

Mr. Otto H. Kahn, famous international banker, backer of the
Metropolitan Opera, music enthusiast and philanthropist, has already listened to our appeal for the Marion Band. Our idea was
that Marion, always having had a fine band should continue to
have one. We believe that a good band is of indefinite importance
to a town.

The band represents the town on its gay days, when the fair
comes, when there is a celebration, Fourth of July, any kind of a

jamboree, when every citizen becomes a boy again, then a good band, stepping gayly out, the drums beating, flags flying—what is a town without a good band?

You cannot have a good band in debt. You cannot expect the boys to blow gayly, step out with real gusto, when they are in debt. To have a good band requires nights of steady practice, it requires sticking to it. What can you expect when the boys have to come to band meeting and plunk down a dollar just for the privilege of working to be good when we want them good.

And there is something else. There is a kind of fineness in giving. Through the columns of our Marion papers, we are asking people who love a band as we do, to give the amount of the dues of one band boy for one year. That would be twelve dollars. Mr. Otto Kahn started us off by sending us a check for $100. The check is here in this office. If the treasurer of the band will come in it is ready for him.

A Letter
EDITORIAL

A young boy writing from Chicago. He has just gone to live in the city. From his letter I gather he is a rather high-strung sensitive young fellow.

There he is in the city. He knows no one. It is Saturday afternoon and he has been out walking in the crowds. Many town and country people have never known the feeling this boy has been having. They are born, live and die among people they have always known.

But a surprising number of young Americans do go to the city. They get a job there, perhaps in some great office or in a factory. It is all very well, while they are at work but after work evenings come. There is Saturday afternoon and Sunday to be got through.

The boy has come to know a few others in the office or factory where he works. When the place closes at night or for the week-end they scatter. It is easy to get lost in such a place.

On every side crowds of people. Once a woman told me of an experience she had when she was a young woman. She had gone to work in a city where she knew no one. One evening she grew so desperately lonely that she went out and walked along the street. For an hour she walked about looking at men. "I wanted to speak to one of them, had all I could do not to try to make a pick-up of some stranger," she told me later.

She didn't. She went back to her hall bedroom and cried with loneliness.

But to return to our boy. He is a stranger to me but has read some book or story of mine. I get a good many such letters. The boy has had experiences he does not want to write to his father, or dare not. He writes telling me of his loneliness and of the feeling he has had. "May I write to you now and then," he asked. When he has got better acquainted in the city he will quit writing to me.

Anyway there he is in his hall bedroom. I can see the place. Outside there is the roar of the town. He has been walking in the crowds until his legs are tired. It is lonely in his room and more lonely outside in the streets. He has a small cheap iron bed, not too comfortable, two cheap unsightly chairs, a small uncomfortable table.

It was Saturday and he came home from his work at noon. He walked a little in the afternoon but later went to sit in his room. Lascivious thoughts came. He writes me that he is often filled with lustful desires.

He went out to walk and felt his loneliness as that woman once said she did. He might have tried to flirt with some girl but being a small town boy, newly come to the city, was afraid and shy.

He became afraid of the crowd. Suddenly a feeling of terror swept over him. The city was too big. So many thousands of people. How would he ever get to know any one there?

There were organizations to take care of such boys. He says he might have gone to the Y. M. C. A. or some other such place but that was not what he wanted. He did not know what he did want.

He went into a park. There were people all about. He was still afraid. He began to run along a path. People might have thought him a young athlete out for training. He took off his hat, held it in his hand and ran until he was tired.

Later he went back to his little room and slept for a while. When he woke up he happened to think of my name. He had seen in his city newspapers that I had bought a weekly newspaper at Marion.

He began to write, telling me all he had felt during the day. I have not put down here all he said in the letter, it was too long.

This I do know, that writing the letter gave him a great feeling of satisfaction. Just writing down all you feel often does that. It is the way innumerable writers begin being writers.

After a time this boy may begin putting his experiences down as having happened to another. That will lead to writing tales. The modern writer is much concerned with what goes on inside of people. There are always innumerable little dramas going on inside people who on the outside look quite calm and steady. Some of our most vivid experiences in life are unknown to any one. By telling me of his strange lonely day in the city this small town boy may be learning to understand not only what has happened to himself but something of what is always happening to others.

Buck Fever Says

NEWS

I was not invited to the grand reception at the General Francis Marion Hotel when the beautiful Miss Rhodes was meeting her friends and admirers after she married Dr. Willis Sprinkle, but I went in anyway. I figured, if they would not let me in to have a look as reporter I would try passing myself off as a traveling man come to the hotel to spend the night.

There were a lot of beautiful girls there. I never saw so many in one room in my life. I always thought it a shame when the girls looked so beautiful like that, the men looked so homely.

Well when I was standing there I heard that Miss Mazy Copenhaver was going to the wedding but the man she was going with fooled around and didn't get himself any pearl-handled shirt studs until the last minute.

Then he came running for Miss Mazy and when they got to the house the wedding was already going on and they were shut out. Tough luck I call that.

I don't know why it is but I never get enough of looking at all the pretty girls I see at a place like that. It sure eases up the eyes fine.

Gee, but that Doctor Sprinkle is a lucky man.

I saw Mr. Charles Lincoln down in the hotel lobby. A week or two ago he was in New York and went to a hotel. Well he put his name on the hotel register, Mr. Charles Lincoln, Marion, Virginia.

Just then, I heard, Mr. James Tate who lives over at Chilhowie came in the same hotel.

Up he came, signed his name on the same register.

Mr. James Tate—ten miles from Marion, he wrote. I wonder why he did that.

I tell you what, if I lived in Chilhowie I wouldn't never renig like that.

I was up in Coon Hollow for Christmas and Pa got pretty drunk. He gave me ten dollars. He was pretty drunk you bet, or he would never have done a thing like that. I wish my boss would take to drinking more than he does.

I heard they took all the hinges off the garage doors up at the Rhodes'. I guess if any one wants to eat any rice in this town they'll be in tough luck. I don't care. I never did like rice.

I smelled a good many moth balls and gasoline up at the dance in the hotel the other night.

Alas, Poor Nellie

NEWS

Nellie the print-shop cat is gone. She was but a young thing. Some two or three weeks ago Gil Stephenson picked her up one day in the street. She had been dropped or had jumped out of an automobile, a tiny gray thing with soft friendly eyes.

Gil picked her up and carried her to the shop and we all at once fell in love with her. Every man in the shop was ready at any time to go out and buy her food. She fared well while she was with us, perhaps too well.

One day she had a fit. It was just as the paper was being run off the press, a mad little thing whirling about the floor under our feet.

The fit passed. One of the boys picked her up and laid her on a pile of print. She never had another fit. A consultation was held. She had been given too much food.

A diet was decided upon and Nellie prospered. Her affection seemed inexhaustible. All day she sat on the bookkeeper's desk, on Joe's lap at the lino-type, on Gil's make-up table or on Jack's type case. Now and then she arose and poked her gray head up under some one's hand. "Well, quit working a moment and pay a little attention to me," she seemed to be saying. Nellie was very feminine surely. She seemed to live for affection. In the morning when I came to the shop she was always on Zeb, the print-shop devil's lap. "Why don't you sweep up, Zeb," I said, "the boss will be here pretty soon and he likes things clean. He'll be sore at you." "I can't," Zeb said. "Can't you see Nellie is here in my lap."

And now Nellie is gone. What happened no one knows. Perhaps the absent-minded boss left the door open. Nellie walked out to get a bit of mountain air. It may be that Pat Collin's dog got after her. Later, after she had quite gone and we all began to be a bit anxious, all sorts of rumors came floating in.

Such and such a gray cat had been seen, in such and such a place. It might have been any gray cat. How did we know it was our Nellie? We all went home that night saddened and chastened. There was little sleep. All the print-shop crowd waking up in the night to think of Nellie.

Perhaps pursued by dogs, cold and hungry. Hands reached out of beds into the cold darkness, looking for that soft living little ball of fur and affection.

And the next day, Christmas day too. Members of the staff wandering one by one down to the cold silent shop. They all did the same thing. They unlocked the door went in and called.

Nellie. Nellie. Nellie.

How useless it was. All knew she was not there. She would come back all right but no doubt is lost. She may be dead.

On the other hand she may be huddled up in some corner somewhere, cold, frightened, starving.

Well, some one may have picked her up. She may have found another warm comfortable home, other hands to stroke her soft young body.

That hope clung too. No one here wants any other cat. We want our Nellie back.

BUCK FEVER

FIRST WEEK OF

JANUARY

∾∾∾

News from the Sheriff's Office

One of the most elusive men in Smyth County is Jim Bolling. Jim can slip through the hands of the law as handily as any man in all this section. He has been out for a long time now, with a warrant in the sheriff's hands against him. Unfortunately there often is a warrant out against Jim. He has been known to climb mountains and trees, jump through windows, run over roofs and swim rivers for the sake of freedom.

Just now he isn't free. It came about in this way. He was over near the poor farm having a little social chat with a relative of his named Mrs. Osborne and Sheriff Dillard went over there. The Sheriff crept over toward the house, got up close, approached the door and then, knowing Jim, made a jump for it. He jumped right in on Jim who was washing his face, preparatory to eating breakfast. He was even a little afraid Jim might dive into the wash bowl and disappear. He got him that time though. There is one thing about Jim. When he is caught he doesn't fuss about it. He is accused, we understand, of making and selling, having and holding, etc.

Andy Caldwell, son of Wiley Caldwell and Roy Testerment were to have been in court the other day to appear as witnesses

94

THE BAND

against Harrison Caldwell and John Simons, also accused of making, selling, etc. They didn't come. No witnesses. Nothing else for the court to do. Wiley and Roy are as free as the robins again.

Sheriff Dillard took S. B. Price and B. G. Thompson with him and went on a little trip over to Walker's Mountain. Evidently the Sheriff had his suspicions. Besides he needed exercise. He got it all right. Walker's Mountain is no cinch to climb. The sheriff got up there all right. Some of the boys up there were trying to warm themselves these cold days with a nice thirty-gallon copper still. Also there were gallons of other warmth sitting near.

Some men running through the bushes to get warm too. Mr. Thompson got Manche Chapman, also Manche's shotgun. The other ran too well. Any one who can run as those fellows did, over such ground as can be found on the side of Walker's Mountain, can get away from almost any one or anything.

Manche is down spending some time with us, and expresses himself as liking it so well he will stay until court convenes in February. On the other hand some one may bail him out. The sheriff says that the view from top of Walker's Mountain is magnificent. He thinks that it would make a grand blue grass country up there.

Kiwanis High Jinks
NEWS

The members of the Kiwanis Club put on their best duds and stepped out for the installation of new officers on the evening of Friday, December 30th. It was ladies' night at the club and the ladies were there. A fine dinner was served and for a crowd that has just come through the holiday eats we'll say they did well by them. Our correspondent, young Buck Fever, who turned in the report of this meeting, says he never saw better people to eat in his life. He says that ever since he has been down here from Coon

Hollow he has been admiring the way Marion people eat and the good things they have to eat.

After the meeting the other evening, Buck says, there was to be some speeches but all the regular public speakers in town, except Mr. Goolsby had stayed away. He says he doesn't know why they didn't let Mr. Goolsby make his regular speech about the roads, but they didn't.

And so, there being no professional speakers there and everything being eaten up, they put on their High Jinks.

Mr. Bill Allen, Wilson Scott, Quincy Calhoun, Beattie Gwyn, Tom Greer, Dr. Baughman and Bascom Copenhaver were sent out of the room together and told to think up something entertaining to do. Buck says he never saw so many heavy thinkers in one crowd before. He says there was a heavy sucking sound, like drawing all the water out of a bathtub, when the crowd went out of the room. We deny responsibility for this statement. Buck made it.

Anyway he says they came back soon and warmed up the room again. They had decided to be a calliope, or a brass band or something like that. Buck didn't know which it was. He said no one guessed. Mr. Copenhaver would touch one of them with his finger and he would make a sound as though he were about to die. It might have come, Buck thought, from all that thinking they did outside. Buck also thought maybe they were trying to pass themselves off as Otto Kahns.

And after that was all over and the worst had passed the ladies decided they would do something too. Mrs. Goolsby, Mrs. Sclater, Mrs. Peery and one or two others went out and when they came back put on an imitation of an old Ford.

Buck said it was good but he left. He said he couldn't stand any more than he had stood. He said that when ladies like that wasted their time being old Fords when there was a swell new Ford, just out, such ladies could have imitated just as well, it made him tired.

For Sports Only

Not to Be Read by Any One Under Twenty-one or by Women or Children

The sporting fraternity of Marion and vicinity gathered at the Court House theater on Saturday evening to see the bout between Lefty Harris and Battling Buck, sometimes called "Bouncing Buck, the pride of Rural Retreat."

The name Rural Retreat certainly suggests to the mind a soft and silvan spot, into which are gathered perhaps tired and harried souls from some of our modern industrial cities. What I mean is that upon hearing the name some such picture as that floats up into the mind, but—

But yourself no buts when you speak of Battling Buck. This young gentleman will never suggest to your mind anything silvan or soft. Dismiss that idea. Why, when he was mauling Mr. Lefty Harris in his best style, Cecil Wolfe of Adwolfe and father of some pretty nifty boxers himself—suddenly got excited, jumped to his feet and yelled in a loud voice that Battling Buck was the best little man that had ever stepped across the corporation lines of Marion.

Some praise that, I'll say, coming from Cecil Wolfe of Adwolfe.

Anyway Mr. Battling Buck made our own Lefty Harris look more and more bewildered as the evening wore on. Fists were coming at him from all directions and what a lot of fists. Every once in a while Mr. Harris got up off the floor and looked about. "Is it hailing or is there a cyclone or what?" he innocently asked a bystander. Then he retired to the floor again. If there had been a cyclone cellar he would have got into that. We can't say we would have blamed him for it.

Your own faithful correspondent was thinking that—well he

was thinking that if this Battling Buck turned out to be not so good we would challenge him in the name of Jim Blood of Coon Hollow but after he saw what happened to this Lefty Harris he kept quiet.

Why, this Battling Buck was so good and pranced so that he even pranced the carpet right off the floor. You ask any one who saw him. He was one of the few people I have ever seen who could prance like that at both ends.

Boo Harris sparred with Buster Cox, Bully Steele took on Bob Harris and a young man named Yancy took a nice trimming from one of the Wolfe boys. Yancy might have done better with a hair cut.

As for Bully Steele he is one of my favorite fighters. I look for him to get into the big league in a few years now.

BUCK   FEVER

Nellie Home

THE ADVENTURES OF NELLIE, THE
PRINT-SHOP CAT

"I am back home. I tell you it pays to advertise. To tell the truth I never thought my getting away from the print-shop the way I did and getting lost would stir up the town of Marion the way it did.

"Well, I've got to say, the people of Marion are mighty nice people. I've had a big adventure all right but I'm none the worse for it.

"So now I think I'll put the story in the paper and tell just how it happened. So here goes.

"First of all it was the bosses fault. He came to the print-shop Saturday afternoon before Christmas, when every one was gone, and started writing some more of his stuff. He pounded away at the typewriter awhile but pretty soon he got cold, not having much fur on him and went out. I went out with him. Well along the street he went, his head up in the clouds, and I was at his heels. Then I saw a dog. The dog got after me and I lit up a tree, a little one in the corner of the courthouse yard. It wasn't Pat Collin's dog. I don't know whose dog that was. I saw a lot of dogs while I was out on this party.

"And so the dog went away and I got down out of the tree. Constable W. W. Farris picked me up. He petted me awhile and was going to take me home with him. I wished he had. It would have saved me a bum night.

"The Constable took me down near the print-shop and there were some young kids playing in the sand pile down by the city machinery building—the beautiful one the boss gets sarcastic about sometimes. I guess the Constable thought I belonged to the kids. He put me down. Night came.

"A night of dogs, of bad dreams, of cold. It was Christmas Eve too. I kept following people along streets. I mewed a lot. Every time I thought some one was going to take me home and feed me up, I saw another dog. Finally I got so afraid and discouraged and hungry and cold I gave up and went into an old shed. Lordy, what a night. Bells ringing, too, people laughing. I never slept a wink.

"And then morning came at last, Christmas morning. I tell you what, I'm a print-shop cat. I can smell printer's ink a mile off. It was my instinct for printer's ink saved me, I'll tell you that.

"I had come out of the shed and was standing in the street. I smelled something in the air, far off, so I trotted along a street.

"Do you know what I smelled. It was Marvin Anderson. I understand he isn't a print-shop man now, but he was once. I can spot them all right. I can smell 'em I tell you what.

"So I trotted along and crawled through a fence and was in

Mrs. E. H. Higginbotham's yard. My instincts had led me right. This Marvin Anderson married a Higginbotham girl. He has some fine children all right. They picked me up and took me in the house. I got fed up fine. Christmas day went grand for me.

"I guess Mr. Marvin Anderson's children thought I was a Christmas cat. They thought Santa Claus brought me but they were wrong about that. If Marvin Anderson had stayed in the printing business I'd have stayed with his children.

"He didn't, so Zeb came from the print-shop and took me home. Thanks to Mrs. Higginbotham and the Anderson children for a fine Christmas dinner. I would have liked to stay with them but the paper has got to get out. They can't do a thing down at the print-shop without me.

"Folks of Marion, I'm home."

NELLIE THE CAT

SECOND WEEK OF

JANUARY

Nellie Is Dead

THE PRINT-SHOP CAT PASSES AWAY
QUIETLY IN A SHOE BOX

The many friends of Nellie, the print-shop cat, will be grieved to hear of her death.

After returning from the escapade of Christmas Eve when, if you will remember, Nellie had to spend the night abroad in a cold empty shed, shaken by fear of dogs, hungry and miserable, she found a warm home and a good Christmas dinner in the home of

Mrs. E. H. Higginbotham and was later returned to her home in the print-shop, she seemed all right and quite happy.

For several days she was her old self. However the terrible experience through which she had passed had left its mark. Nellie was as affectionate as ever but did not seem strong. After several days she became really ill.

By the middle of last week her case was serious. Her disease was diagnosed as pneumonia.

There is something terrible about seeing such a little animal suffer. During the three days' illness before her death she never complained. A shoe box had been provided for her and it had been filled with soft white cloth.

For three days Nellie lay quietly in the box, refusing all food and breathing with difficulty. Her little body shook with spasms of pain. Jack, Gil, Joe and Zeb went quietly about the shop with serious looks on their faces. It was rather odd to see a young fellow like Buck Fever so upset. He wouldn't go near the box to look at Nellie.

Nellie died on Friday, the 6th, at 2:09 in the afternoon. We were late with the News last week. It was just going to press.

Gil, who was feeding the paper into the press, got down off his pressman's stand and went to look at Nellie in her box. We all saw him put his hand down upon her. Then he looked at his watch. "She's dead," he said and went back to feeding the press. The machinery, that had been stopped, started again. There was a sharp little feeling of relief all through the shop. At least the little animal's hours of suffering were at an end.

It is a little odd, dear readers, to have so much fuss made about a cat.

Nellie was a tiny thing. She was never very strong. It will be easy enough to get another cat.

But it will be hard to find another cat that will be such a little bundle of affection as Nellie.

Another Son

A LETTER

A young man writing from a western University. Some of my readers may remember a statement made in this column about youth.

"What is the use trying to make my son or daughter think I have led a pure life when I haven't. I know I haven't," I said.

That brought down upon me a hot letter from a man named Miller of Knoxville, Tenn. I will say Mr. Miller wasn't so modest about himself. He rather intimated that, for purity, no mountain stream ever had anything on him.

He also went on a lot about pig pens, flower gardens and buzzards. He may have been calling me a pig pen or buzzard. I'm pretty sure he never intended to call me a flower garden. Anyway I'm not one.

Here is a letter that just came in from the son of some other man:

"I liked what you said about a man's relations with his son. I've stood a lot from my own Dad. Mine is one of the kind too that is always talking about the pure life he leads.

"Maybe he does. I'll say this. I never actually got anything on Dad.

"I remember though, one night when I was about twelve years old. Mother was away from town and Dad had some friends in. I had been out in the country at my uncle's and got homesick and walked home that evening. The back door to our house was open and I went in. Dad had some of his friends in there and they were smoking cigars and talking. They were telling stories and that night I heard some that would curl your hair.

"I suppose the same stories wouldn't shock me now. I've been to college and last summer I worked in a factory.

"Do you know, that time, I didn't have the heart to let Dad

know I had overheard the conversation between him and his friends. And I'll bet it wasn't a week later I heard him getting off a lot of talk about a pure mind.

"What is the use always putting up a bluff, particularly with your son who is just bound to get on to you after awhile."

A SON

THIRD WEEK OF
JANUARY

Romance on the Highway
NEWS

A dark and rainy night. Mayor Dickinson had come home and had got out his book. The Mayor is a great reader. He was in a soft easy chair. Outside it rained. Nothing nicer than sitting in an easy chair under a good light with a good book. The rain pounding on the roof overhead.

Suddenly the telephone rang. The mayor jumped up. Floating over the phone an alarmed voice.

A man who gave the name of Nelson was driving east along the Highway toward Marion. At the overhead bridge three men, he said, jumped out and confronted him, demanding that he throw up his hands. For a moment the man named Nelson said he had hesitated and then had taken a chance. He had stepped on the gas and had managed to make a getaway.

Then he had gone to a nearby house and had phoned to our mayor. His voice trembled so he could scarcely speak.

Well, it was a bad night to go out but duty is duty. The mayor got out Sheriff Dillard and Jailer Hopkins and getting into a car they set out. They had decided to get themselves held up by the three desperate men. They rode up and down the highway for an hour. Not a soul in sight. The rain beat on the roof of the car. The mayor was thinking of his easy chair and his book.

The Great Dog Case

NEWS

The great Clay Sawyer, John Cassell dog case has at last come off. Mr. Clay Sawyer's dog was well known up at Attoway. He was apparently a good dog. Many a morn and oft did he go to bay the fox.

On an unlucky day, December the thirteenth, he was abroad early and got up a fox. Accompanied by another hound, he was hot on the trail from five in the morning until perhaps two in the afternoon.

And then the fox went to hole. Mr. Clay Sawyer's hound started home. To get home he had to cross over the land rented by John Cassell.

Mr. Cassell, it seems, does not like dogs. And in addition he says dogs had on that day been worrying his sheep.

Mr. Cassell had been out killing dogs. He had killed three that day, all apparently with good non-sheep killing records up to that moment.

He did not kill Sawyer's at once. What he did, apparently, was to shoot the dog and then let him go off and die in the road. It was his claim that when he shot the dog there was a lone sheep there and that the hound was worrying the sheep.

Mrs. Sawyer had, however, seen the killing and swore she had seen no sheep. She and many other witnesses seemed to suggest, by their testimony, that the affair had been a rather malicious killing of a good dog. The dog was so good that when a lawyer asked one venerable witness what such a dog was worth he hesitated a moment and then said, "well, I guess he's worth more than most anything else on earth."

That's what they think of good fox dogs up at Attoway. This correspondent gathers, from what happened, that Justices Farris, Frances and Johnson feel something the same way.

Mr. Cassell conducted his own case and lost it almost as well as any lawyer could have lost it for him. Mr. Preston Collins took advantage of the occasion to make one of the best dog speeches we have ever heard. All in all Mr. Clay Sawyer's dog, good in life, had a good sending off. The witnesses and the justices were apparently all for him and his owner. Mr. Sawyer won his case. The damages, assessed against Mr. Cassell, were seventy-five dollars.   BUCK FEVER

A Bitter Pill
A COMPLAINT

This paper has just had a sad, sad experience. In last week's paper we thought we had achieved that most toothsome of all things to a newspaper, a clean "beat."

You know, when it comes to news we weeklies are at a disadvantage compared to the dailies. As a matter of fact we do not expect to be right down to the minute on "News."

We had stumbled upon what we thought a grand story about Mr. John Dix of Pulaski. Perhaps you read the story—how Mr. Dix picked up an old woman on the highway and looked at her hands. Then the coming of suspicion, and how he cleverly let his hat blow out of the car window. After he had escaped Mr. Dix had found, in a bag left in the car by the old woman, a set of burglar tools.

A marvelous story truly. The Roanoke *Times* handed us a bouquet. "Marion Paper Scores Clean Beat." O sweet words. The editor of this paper loves to think of himself as essentially a modest man. When a thing of this sort happens he doesn't brag to any one but his wife. Before his wife, when he is alone with her, he does throw out his chest. "My dear, did you see what I did? Did

you see the Roanoke *Times* cracking me up as a newspaper man?"
O sad, sad bereavement. The John Dix story wasn't true. Mr.
Dix now says it never happened at all. Well, some one we trusted
told us the story. This wail is partly addressed to our informant.
O, Mr. C—why did you betray our young faith? Did you make
that story up, were you spoofing us?

And Mr. Dix. Why did you not back us up. We never had a
newspaper beat before. If it never happened to you on the highway
why did you not lie a little? Really we had made you out as very
clever, had we not? If you, Mr. Dix, had been running a newspaper and had scored a newspaper beat a small thing like the
truth or falsehood of the story would never have stopped us. We
would have lied for you to the limit.

Well, alas and alas—the story evidently was not true. Our only
newspaper beat has vanished into thin, thin air.

FOURTH   WEEK   OF

JANUARY

Foreclosed

An alien plow will cut this loam
    When spring comes trooping back:
He will not sow the clean seed oats
    Nor put the sheaves in stack.

He will not watch the sickle drop.
    The swathes of clover hay:
Some other hand will plant the corn
    The warming days of May.

His draught span soon will feel the whip
    And drag his meager goods:

Over the frozen, rutted roads
Along the burroak woods.

But he will cast a backward glance
His sombre mate may weep:
And he may dream those first few nights
Of cattle and of sheep.

How soon the dingy corn-town streets
Will seize him as their prey:
And make him plod at deadly tasks
Which spirit hope away.

But when he haunts the village store
He'll draw his chair beside,
The man who claims the fullest barns
And one whose fields are wide.

JAY G. SIGMUND

Winter Day in the Country

EDITORIAL

Extraordinary days, coming in the midst of winter. In town this writer was reminded of winter days in Mobile and New Orleans. But what a different country this from the low swampy flat lands of the gulf states.

On Sunday to Wytheville by the highways and the afternoon spent exploring many side roads among the hills. The hills and fields along the road all aglow with soft rich colors.

For every country its own prevailing color. Years ago I used to try to paint. I had never learned to draw but color always excited me.

There are few enough people who see color, just as there are few people who hear sounds.

To be sure, obvious sounds are heard. You hear the scream of a railroad engine or a factory whistle. But what of the multitude of little sounds, overlaid one upon another, the sounds that come to the ear of a finely trained musician? Such a man would hear a hundred sounds that altogether escape our ears, would separate them just as a well-trained hunting dog separates scents.

To see color the same training, the same care and absorption in the subject over a long period, is necessary. I never got very far with it.

When I was living for a winter on Mobile Bay I used to go in the afternoon and lie for hours on the beach, studying the shades of color in the bay, in the surrounding country and in the sky. The bay absorbed something of color out of the sky, the sky out of the bay and both borrowed from the land.

The land down there was red. Often at evening the sky and the bay both became blood red.

In Grayson, where I lived recently, the prevailing color is blue. It is almost the blue of the skies of Paris. There is the same clear light.

And we have the same extraordinarily clear light here in Smyth. It is partly because of the altitude.

The land here is inclined towards a tawny yellow. Skies are often a clear pale blue. The sky lending its color to the land produces a strange coppery landscape. It is always touched with spots of red and bright yellow.

This Southwest Virginia has always seemed to me an ideal painters' land but if there has ever been a painter here I have never heard of him. I do not mean painters of flowers, mere daubers. Fine painters are rare. America has produced but a few of them. I mean a man in whom the sense of color is highly developed and who has that other rare thing, a quick sense of line.

To a painter of this sort the winter here would be even finer than the summer. In the winter, because our hills here are sharply outlined, the very bones of the country may be seen and felt.

And what a rich structure this Southwest Virginia has. How sensual all the lines here. Passing over into the Rich Valley, for example, on any of the roads I have been on over Walker's Mountain, in all the scene that rolls out before your eyes that combination of the sensual and the solid so often seen in old Italian paintings, done by the old masters.

People in general have an odd idea about the art of painting. They think it means merely getting down on canvas, very cleverly, a pretty picture. Well, it means much more than that.

There have been men in some countries—all of the great landscape painters have been like that—who have felt for some particular section of country much as a lover might feel for a woman he loved. He comes into the presence of a scene, in the country he loves, much in the spirit in which he might come into the presence of a beloved woman. His painting becomes in fact a form of making love.

There is something deeply stirred in him, purified. One of Von Gogh's greatest paintings was of a single great sunflower in full bloom. When he made that particular painting he was so exhausted, with the depth of his emotions, that he was a sick man for days afterward. He hung the picture in his room. Gauguin, another great painter, came in and stood before it a moment. Then he shouted with a loud voice. In a moment he saw the marvelous thing the man had done.

And what is it that makes such a painting marvelous. At the core of it it is love. In spite of all progress, all talk of progress and civilization, love remains the only truly powerful force in the world. The Christians have that clearly defined although there are few enough men and women, who call themselves Christians, who would dare face the challenge back of their faith or who know much of love.

There is love of a particular thing. It might be just a sunflower. The same man Von Gogh, a Dutchman, made one of his greatest paintings with his theme a kitchen chair. To-day that little painting, of a chair in a workingman's cottage, is worth more, even in money, than the finest farm in all Southwest Virginia.

Why?

It takes a long time and training of the senses to know why. I sat for hours before the painting once. Gradually, as I sat there, I came to realize that the man who painted it had put into that simple painting a kind of wonder that as you look steals over your own senses. He has got the bones of what he felt, the delicate shades of color, the meaning. The man had felt something toward all other humans and had, in that simple painting, condensed the feeling of an entire lifetime.

But I am off the track again. I was talking of our own hills, the delicate colors to be seen here, the fine strength combined with softness in the turn of our hills. A drive into the country on a fine winter day here is a treat never to be forgotten. Just now, at this season when the plow has been at work in some of the fields, turning up new earth, when the dead burned grass of last year lies on meadow hillsides like tawny hair, when the clear streams reflect the soft pastel colors of our skies there is a richness to the days that should make us all glad we live where we do.

Winter Day in Town

Snow on the sidewalks, in the streets. The time of cold rains, cold winds. How nice the houses are now. The editor of this paper likes to walk in the streets alone at night. He goes down one street, crosses over and goes along another. The houses are all lighted. There are fires burning.

People sitting in the houses, men, women and children. Houses are like people. I beg you all when you walk thus, when your minds are not occupied with your own affairs, to begin thinking of houses.

The houses have faces. The windows are eyes. Some houses smile at you, others frown.

There are some houses that are always dark. People in them crawl off early to bed. You hear no laughter from such houses, no one sings.

Other houses are proud. They are well kept. As you pass they seem to look at you with a sort of "keep off the grass" expression. You hurry past such houses.

I know houses that always seem to be whispering to me. There are secrets hidden in such houses. They plead with you not to disturb them. Alas, I am an inveterate hunter of tales. Odd things happen to people behind the walls of houses. Many people are one thing inside their houses and another on the street. Sometimes the secrets, hidden away behind the walls of houses, are merely sad but sometimes they are exciting too.

There are evenings when I walk thus and see houses that they all seem to be talking to me. They are trying to tell me what I cannot understand.

I go past a dozen houses, two dozen. There are the glad houses, the gay ones, the one where all the doors seem ready to burst open. Some houses shout at me. "Come in," they cry.

The man who loves life and people shows it in the way he walks along the street. His house would tell us his secret if we could only understand.

FIRST WEEK OF

FEBRUARY

∽∽∽

I am back in the shop now after three days in New York. The city drunkenness has passed. Gil has been working in this one shop for forty years. Perhaps he has never been to New York.

Nor has Joe, the lino-type man. Jack has been there. He has been a wandering workman. Zeb will go there some day.

The paper is to be got out again. What a persistent thing it is.

Who Are the People?
or
Who's Ground-hogging?
NEWS

On the evening of Friday, January 27th, the town council held one of the hottest meetings in its history. Fire was snapping from a dozen directions at once. For a while it looked as though there would be at least a half dozen fist fights. As every one knows we are looking for news so we just sat there smiling and being glad we didn't belong to the town council. What are a few black eyes to us? We love action.

The whole fight started about this amendment to the town

THE PRINT SHOP

council business. A month or two ago this correspondent went to a meeting of the town council. During the week before a correspondent of this paper had written an article advocating the city manager plan for the town government. The council took it up and discussed it at the meeting. We wrote another article about the discussion.

Later at another meeting it was decided to amend the city charter. The proposed amendments were printed by us last week. Here they are again:

PROPOSED AMENDMENTS

"To Honorable B. F. Buchanan, Senator, and Honorable C. M. Shannon, Member of House of Delegates:

"We, the undersigned citizens of the Town of Marion, respectfully request that you introduce and have passed by the General Assembly an act providing for the amendment of the Charter of the Town of Marion as follows:

"Separating the offices of Sergeant and Collector, and giving the duties of Collector to the Town Treasurer.

"Providing for a Council of six members, with the Mayor as presiding officer, members of Council to hold office for four years and three members to be elected each two years.

"Providing that all officers, except Mayor, shall be appointed by the Council.

"Giving the Council power, in its discretion, to appoint a police justice to try violations of town ordinances in place of the mayor."

THE TOWN COUNCIL

When these amendments were decided upon and it was also decided to circulate a petition there was evidently a good deal of confusion. Rumors went flying about town. A rival petition was circulated by Arch Snyder and Strap Mitchell.

By the time the council met on Friday evening, as we have already suggested, fire was cracking in the underbrush. The town political woods were all on fire.

The meeting began with a passage at arms between M. M. Seavers, of the council, and James White Sheffey, speaking for Gordon Snavely. That warmed things up a bit. After that the council decided to hear from citizens present. Arch Snyder got up and said some one in the council was ground-hogging. Strap Mitchell told the council he thought they were all wet and did not know what they were doing. Sheriff Dillard spoke and said that he had been informed that, in the circulating of the petition, word had been passed that he, the sheriff, was not exactly giving the town a square deal.

The council squelched that in a hurry by passing a motion of respect and admiration for the sheriff. We didn't blame them for that.

Other people made speeches. Jack Menerick spoke on the power of the press. Various councilmen spoke. It seemed to us the waters were getting rilier and rilier.

There was much said about THE PEOPLE, and the proposal was several times made that there be called a mass meeting of the citizens.

To an outsider it was just a bit difficult to tell what it was all about. It was evident that, if the voice of the people was being heard the people were as confused as any one else.

At last out of the confusion a definite proposal did emerge. It seemed that the town council wanted to separate the office of town sergeant from that of town treasurer.

Mr. Snavely was not opposed to that, Arch Snyder did not care. He even said he would go in with any one on a petition-tearing-up party. As Senator Buchanan is in town at just this moment and as all were apparently agreed that the two offices mentioned should be separated it was proposed that Mayor Dickinson see Senator Buchanan and ask to get from the legislature permission to make the change.

Guns were slipped back into pockets, the waters grew clear and quiet. All is well on the banks of the lovely Holston.

Kiwanis

NEWS

A dark, gloomy, evening with slush underfoot. Mr. George Cook gone to Florida. Everybody else wishing they were there or in some other warm place. The food cheered everybody up. The Methodist women furnished the food.

Tom Greer got up and announced gloomily that George Cook would not be back until the robins began to sing. That was pure pessimism. George Cook told us he would only be gone two or three weeks. There won't be any robins here that soon. Mr. Greer wasn't thinking of the Kiwanis at all. He was thinking of some warm spot down on the southern seas. In fancy he was sitting there with his feet dangling in the warm water. If we were only running a herb place and not working on a snappy newspaper, the way we are, we would be in some warm spot these days. People don't need herbs the way they do a paper. All Tom Greer can do is doctor up their bodies. We doctor up their eternal souls in this paper, at least the boss says we do. I haven't noticed it any myself.

But to get back to Kiwanis. Mr. Marvin Copenhaver brought his father who made a nifty little talk. He said he thought the Kiwanis was a church organization until he saw us there.

Mr. B. E. Copenhaver, W. R. D. Moncure and C. Brown Cox who are engineering the idea of getting some grand publicity for our town and are going to get up a snappy book about it reported that plans are being made for a grand hullabaloo to raise the money about February 20th. Mr. Moncure got up and said I was going to speak a piece at the show. Who told him that? If it was boosting Coon Hollow I'd do it all right. My sister, Miss Spring Fever, might come down and sing them a song. She would if Quincy Calhoun asked her.

Mr. Fleet Wolfe was to furnish the entertainment at the meeting but got up and said it was the beginning of February and he didn't feel like entertaining any one. We didn't blame him a bit. It was a rotten night. He said he looked around and looked around but couldn't think of anything gloomy enough to do. He said he thought of inviting an undertaker in, but they were all busy. There was a gravestone salesman over at the Francis Marion. He might have got him.

Anyway, the Rev. F. B. Shelton, who is the power behind the Red Cross movement in this section, got up and helped Mr. Wolfe out. He introduced Miss Lucy Coleman of Roanoke, a field worker for the Red Cross, and she gave us a fine talk about people sick and dying other places with a lot of figures in it I can't remember.

I got this, however. We are going to have a county nurse here yet. Mr. Robert Goolsby got up and said he would shell out personally if the rest would. However, Mr. Tom Greer said it wasn't regular and parliamentary to just lay money on the table. Not, he said, that he suspected any one.

However, it was decided to send Robert Goolsby, Will Lincoln, Doctor Holmes, Doctor Sherrill, Jack Sheffey, George Collins and me before the county board of supervisors and try to make them give up. Everybody thinks we will get it if Geo. Collins is in good form.

BUCK FEVER

Trouble on Shooting Creek

NEWS

Monday evening was a busy evening up Shooting Creek. Well, it was a dark, gloomy afternoon. Neal Gullion was having a little party all to himself. Then he met Jack Hutton and took Jack along. They went to Claude McCarter's house up Hook's Branch and Neal went inside while Jack stayed down in the road.

Neal says he got a pint and drank that up—then another pint and drank that up.

By that time Neal was ready to talk to the stars. "Stay up in the sky there, stars. Don't you bother me."

Word got down into town about Neal's little party and Sheriff Dillard, Sergeant Snavely, Mr. Hayes and Mr. Hopkins went and got him.

They turned him over to Mr. Hayes, but he suddenly leaned down and bit Hayes' hand and lit out. With three pints of Shooting Creek stuff in him the average man could bite through a brick. Neal's teeth went right to the bone and Mr. Hayes dropped all holds. He turned him loose.

He had the night free all right, but Sheriff Dillard and Sergeant Snavely got him in this morning. He was up in Mayor Dickinson's court on Tuesday morning and told where he got his stuff. He was fined $19.75. The town got that.

Claude McCarter's troubles have, however, just begun. Last night Sheriff Dillard, Sergeant Snavely, Mr. Hayes and Mr. Hopkins went up to Claude's house with a search warrant, and they found some of the biting stuff up there. There was a keg, empty but smelling suspicious, a five-gallon can, the same, an innocent empty five-gallon can, a quart jar half full of the real stuff.

Mr. McCarter will be bound over to the grand jury. Questioned as to whether or not it was McCarter's house to which he went with Neal Gullion, Jack said he didn't know. "I wasn't in any shape to tell one house from another," he said. BUCK FEVER

In Washington

NEWS

In Washington, where I have been sent to interview the Secretary of Commerce, Mr. Hoover. I do not like the job much. Why did I take it?

I am always undertaking something the Lord never intended me to do.

I have arrived in the city in the early morning and am not to see the man until late afternoon. It is bitter cold. When I saw Washington last, some fifteen or twenty years ago, it was merely a great straggling town. Now it has become a modern city.

I have been at a big hotel and have left my bag. I begin wondering what I shall do with my day.

We who live in country towns miss certain things. The radio and the phonograph can bring us music by the best orchestras—if there are any bests—we can hear speakers talk, but there are things we cannot get.

We cannot see the best players on the stage and we cannot see paintings.

I decided to go to a museum.

There are days for everything. Was this a day to see paintings? I should, no doubt, have gone to talk to some politician, but I knew no politicians as politicians. No one ever talks politics to me. I went to the new Freer Gallery.

The Freer Gallery, named for its builder, was built by a rich man of Detroit and was intended primarily to house the paintings of the American painter Whistler. In it are housed as well, many old and rare objects of Chinese and Japanese art.

I went to the gallery in the morning and it was quite empty but for the attendants. There was a hushed quiet over the place. The walls and the attendants seemed crying out at me "be careful, walk quietly, this is a sacred place."

Sacred, indeed. What a strange thing is the life of the artist.

Standing in the gallery and looking at these paintings, conscious all the time of the uniformed attendants watching me, afraid perhaps I might steal some of these sacred objects, an odd feeling of annoyance creeping over me.

Such a man as Whistler lives. His work is condemned or praised by the men of his own time. It has been the fate of some men, who have produced the greatest art, made the greatest discoveries in science, the greatest contributions to scholarship, to live and die unknown. They are perhaps the lucky men.

Such a man as Whistler, fighting for fame. He was always a great fighter. Once he wrote a book called "The Gentle Art of Making Enemies." He knew how to do that all right.

Much of his energy must have been spent in fighting for fame. Well, he has won. He has fame. Fame, in the end, does not always mean worth. If you keep insisting that you are a great man after a time people will believe. It doesn't necessarily mean you are great.

James McNeill Whistler was not one of the great painters of the world. His fighting and his personality got him somewhere. A rich patron of the arts, Mr. Freer, became devoted to him. He has spent hundreds of thousands of dollars, his time, his own energy, in making Mr. Whistler's fame secure. Mr. Freer, because of his devotion to another, may possibly be a finer and a greater man than Mr. Whistler.

As for myself, I could not get over the feeling that much of Mr. Whistler's work is vastly over-estimated. Many of these paintings, carefully guarded by paid attendants, housed in this great stone building, are commonplace enough.

I went out of the famous Peacock Room and into the room where the older art treasures are housed. There were the old Chinese and Japanese things.

Objects of art come out of a day when there is no such thing as publicity—paintings by reticent, devoted men. Whistler has been rather widely advertised as having brought over into his own day much of the fineness of these older painters. He has not brought over so much.

Such a short time ago, some fifty years, and Whistler's house in London was being sold over his head. Many of these paintings, so sumptuously housed now, were sold then for a few shillings. Have they increased in value so much?

The value of the older Chinese and Japanese things is fixed. Money cannot express it. There is "The Waves at Matsushinea," painted by some unknown man called "Satatsu" in the seventeenth century. In another painting the Chinese Emperor Ming Huang is with his concubine Kuei-fei in a garden. What a charming lady! It is spring. She is singing to make the flowers bloom for her emperor.

And there is another painting. The Emperor Weu, of the Chow Dynasty, is meeting the sage, Chiang Tzu-ya. The two men are meeting on an island in a winding lake. All nature seems hushed and quiet. Clouds are standing still in the sky, as though intent on the scene below. There is a sense in the painting of infinite time, space, distance.

Mr. Hoover and I did not meet on an island in a winding lake. There were no fleecy clouds floating in the sky; no sense of infinite time, space, distance.

It may be that Mr. Hoover has in him the making of an emperor, but I am no sage.

If I had been a sage I would not have been where I was.

I was in a great office building in the modern city of Washington. Before me sat a well-dressed man of perhaps fifty. Like myself, he was a bit too fat. He had leaned too long over a desk, over figures and plans, and I had leaned too long over a typewriter. Besides that Mr. Hoover had just been to a dentist.

And he did not want to be interviewed.

"Are you an interviewer?" he asked. "Yes," I said doubtfully. I had never been such a thing before. I am a writer of books, sometimes a teller of tales. I run a country weekly. Country weeklies are not newspapers. We do not interview people. I am not a politically-minded man. Always I am asking myself the question, "Why does any man want to be President? Why does any man want power?"

By my philosophy power is the forerunner of corruption.

To be a bright, intelligent newspaper interviewer, I should have asked Mr. Hoover some embarrassing questions. He was a member of the cabinet of Mr. Harding, sat cheek by jowl with Mr. Fall and Mr. Daugherty. A stench arose from that sitting. What about it?

The question trembled on my lips.

Other questions crowding into my mind. "What of the League of Nations, our attitude toward the small republics of Central America?"

Better that I should not ask such questions. The man would twist me about his little finger. "It is just possible he knows something about leagues of nations and all such things, but what do you know?" I was now asking myself.

A fragment of song floated up into my mind, even then, at that unfortunate moment. The song was like the clouds floating above that island when the Emperor Weu went to meet Chiang Tzu-ya.

"My freedom sleeps in a mulberry bush.

"My country is in the shivering legs of a little lost dog."

"I am not going to be interviewed," Mr. Hoover said again. "I don't care," I said. As a matter of fact, I did not care two straws. I had made a futile trip to Washington. Well, it was not futile.

I had seen the Emperor Ming Huang with his concubine Kuei-fei walking in a garden.

The Emperor Ming Huang had walked in his garden with Kuei-fei in another age than my own. There were no factories in that age. Men did not rush through the streets in automobiles. There were no radios, no airplanes.

Just the same men fought wars, men were cruel and greedy, as in my own age.

My mind full of things far removed from Mr. Hoover and his age, I was going out the door, having got nothing from him, having failed as a modern newspaper correspondent—a task that no such man as myself should have undertaken—when Mr. Hoover called me back.

"I will not be interviewed, but we can talk," he said. Mr. Hoover was being kind. He must have felt my incompetence. I understood what he meant. He meant only that things were to be in his own hands. We were to speak only of those things that Mr. Hoover cared to discuss.

He began to talk now, first of the Mississippi problem. It was a huge problem, he said, but it could be met. There was a way out.

There was the river cutting down through the heart of the country, twisting and winding. Had I not spent days and weeks on the great river? I told him I had. "It is uncontrollable," I said. "The Mississippi is a thing in nature. It is nature." But did not Joshua make the sun stand still? I remembered a summer when I took the Mississippi as a god, became a river worshiper.

I was in a boat fishing on the Mississippi when a flood came. I felt its power, it put the fear of God into my heart.

But Mr. Hoover had been down there and was not afraid. He spoke of spillways. There was to be a new river bed creeping down westward of the Mississippi—all through the lower country.

Then when great floods came rampaging and tearing down and Mother Mississippi was on a spree, she was to be split in two. Two

Mother Mississippis, gentled now, going down to the sea. "What a man," I said to myself.

And could he also handle like that the industrial age?

There was the question. That also had become to me like a thing in nature.

I had after all got down to the heart of what I wanted to ask Mr. Hoover.

The industrial age has been sweeping forward ever since I was a boy. I have seen the river of it swell and swell. It has swept over the entire land. The industrialists may not be Ming Huangs but they are in power.

They have raised this Mr. Hoover up out of the ranks of men as perhaps the finest Republican example of manhood and ability in present-day American political and industrial life. He is, apparently, a man very sure of himself. His career has been a notable one. From a small beginning he has risen steadily in power. There has never been any check. I felt, looking at him, that he has never known failure.

It is too bad never to have known that. Never to have known miserable nights of remorse, feeling the world too big and strange and difficult for you.

Well, power also, when it is sure of itself, can gentle a man. Mr. Hoover has nice eyes, a clear, cool voice. He gave me long rows of figures showing how the industrialists have improved things for the common man. We spoke of Mr. Ford and he was high in his praise of the man. "When I go to ride in an automobile," he said, "it does not matter to me that there are a million automobiles on the road just like mine. I am going somewhere and want to get there in what comfort I can and at the lowest cost."

That, it seemed to me, summed up Mr. Hoover's philosophy of life.

When you have a man's philosophy of life, why stay about? Why bother the man?

Mr. Hoover spoke of the farmers. It is quite true that, in the distribution of the good things the industrial age has brought, the industrialists and the financiers have got rather the best of it. Labor has been able to take good care of itself, Mr. Hoover thinks. The farmer is another problem. Here is one place where the modern system has not quite worked.

It is a matter, he said, of too much waste between the farmer and the consumer. I gathered that the whole system of merchandising would have to be brought up into the new age.

"Something like the systems of chain stores," I suggested. He fended me off there. I presume any man in political life has to be cautious. The merchant class is a large class. There are votes there. My mind flopped back to my own town. Voters gathered in the evening at the back of the drug store, the hardware store, the grocery store. The small, individual merchant, who is, I gather, at the bottom of the farmer's troubles, has power, too—in his own store.

There had been something hanging in my mind for a long time. I thought I would at least take a shot at it. All of this industrialism and standardization growing up in my day. I had seen it grow and grow. A whole nation riding in the same kind of cars, smoking the same kind of cigars, wearing the same kind of clothes, thinking the same thoughts.

Individualism, among the masses of the people, gradually dying.

You get a few men, drawn up and become powerful because they control the mass needs and the mass thought. No questions asked any more. All doubting men thrown aside.

Young men, buried yet down in the mass, squirming about. They not liking too well the harness of industrialism and standardization. Men coming into power, not as Lincoln came, nor yet as Napoleon came.

At the bottom of it all, a growing number of the younger men feeling hopeless boredom.

Is the heavy boredom of a standardized civilization true for Mr. Hoover as it is sometimes true for me? I asked Mr. Hoover that question and for the first time during our talk he did not seem comfortable.

But power is power. He fended off again. After all, the age and the system of the age that may destroy one man may make another. Mr. Hoover has been made by his age. Apparently, he is satisfied with it.

I got out of Mr. Hoover's presence feeling we had got nowhere. Surely it wasn't his fault. I went walking for a long time in the streets of Washington. The more I walked the more sure I was that Mr. Hoover is the ideal among Republican men to be the present-day President of the United States—if he can make them see it.

Other men feel that. I asked several men I had never seen before.

I asked a man who drove a street car, one who opened oysters, another who scrubbed the floor in the lobby of a hotel.

"He is the ideal man," they all said. They were afraid the politicians would not give him the chance. The reason given was that he has too much brains.

But these men's opinions have also been made by the standardized newspaper opinion of the age in which they live. Their expression of doubt was merely resentment. Mr. Hoover is the blameless man. In Mr. Hoover's head has developed the ideal brain for his time. Are the other leaders of his party afraid of him? Surely theirs are not the nameless fears of such men as myself.

It would be a little odd if, the age having produced a perfect thing, a man who does so very well and with such fine spirit just what every one apparently believes they want done—should be thrown aside, being too perfect.

There is no doubt in my own mind. I am convinced Mr. Hoover would make the ideal Republican President.

No one will ever sing songs about Mr. Hoover after he is President—if they decide to give him the chance. There will be no paintings made of him walking at evening in a garden while a lovely lady sings to make the flowers bloom.

But it is not an age of painting, not an age of song.

And so there was I walking in the streets of Washington, having made a failure of my day. I had tried to be smart and had not been smart. I had got myself into a false position. What happens to the age in which a man lives is like the Mississippi, a thing in nature. It is no good quarreling with the age in which you live.

I had come to Washington, I think wanting to like Mr. Hoover, and had ended by admiring him. He had not warmed me. I went over past the White House and tried to think of Lincoln living there. Then I went back to the Freer Gallery for another look at Ming Huang walking in his garden and listening to the voice of Kuei-fei—but it was closed for the night.

SHERWOOD ANDERSON

James Overbay Goes Back
NEWS

James Overbay, who has been at the reform farm and who has recently been out on a furlough, is going back. If you will remember Sheriff Dillard went out to the Overbay place some time ago and found a still there. Jim DeBord was with him. This was early on a Sunday morning. The still was all ready to operate, the mash all there and everything. The nearest house is the Overbay house. It is surrounded by woods.

And so there sat the Sheriff and Jim DeBord in the still house, waiting for some one to come. Three very small children came up the path through the woods. They were the younger Overbay children, all little fellows. One of them had a small pail in his hand. Evidently they were coming directly to the still house, but one of the little fellows had sharp eyes. Through a crack he saw the sheriff sitting in there. That was the little chap that was carrying the pail. His mother says he was going to water a calf. No reflections on any one.

Anyway, the little chap ran and the other children surrendered. There was the sound of some one else cutting out through the woods and there is a suspicion that it was James Overbay, but there isn't any definite proof. He was to have gone on trial, defended by Mr. Bill Birchfield, but decided to go back to the reform farm instead. No reflection on Bill either.

So there wasn't any trial. Justice Dickinson gave the younger children a fatherly talk about walking toward still houses when they went for Sunday morning walks and that was all.

BUCK

THIRD WEEK OF

FEBRUARY

A Play

In the kitchen of the Hotel Lincoln, Buck Fever comes in.
Buck: "Why don't you fellows bake more kinds of pie?"
First Cook: "What do you mean pie? What's the matter of our pies?"
Buck: "I want more apple and pumpkin pie."
First Cook: "We don't make that Coon Hollow stuff here."
Buck: "What about a little spoon bread then?"

George of Covington, coming in: "Yum, yum, that ham, that ham."
Both Cooks: "What ham?"
George of Covington: "That Virginia ham. Yum, yum, that Covington ham."

First Cook: "Do you mean that old time spoon bread?"
Buck: "Yes, yes, that's what I mean."

Waitress (coming in): "That fat traveling man wants more of the ham."
Buck and George of Covington sing:

> *"That ham, that ham,*
> *That Covington ham."*

All begin to dance and sing, Buck Fever, George of Covington, two cooks and waitresses dance and sing.

> *"That Coon Hollow spoon bread,*
> *That Covington ham."*

Mr. Walker, the manager, comes in. Throws a ham at Buck Fever. George of Covington, waitresses and all duck through doors. Voice of Buck Fever from an alleyway:
"I want my spoon bread."
"I want my Coon Hollow pies."

Sports Mourn

NEWS

The latest report is that the County Supervisors have refused permission for the boxing bout, as advertised in this paper, and that was to have been held in the Court House Theater on Saturday evening. Cecil Wolfe of Adwolfe says they are making a great mistake. He says boxing is being taken up these days by all the higher educational centers.

"Now how are we going to get a proper education," he says.

Well, well, there is something in what Mr. Wolfe says. Is this not an age of money and did not Mr. Tunney make a million in

Chicago in a few minutes, just by mauling Mr. Dempsey? Suppose now—as the saying goes—we get a good, strong boy growing up in this section, with a chance to be heavyweight champion of the world and refuse to him these early cultural influences that do so much to mold the young.

With Mr. Tunney going in for literature, etc., and all the ladies of the cities crowding into prize fights it looks as though Marion and Smyth County were taking a step backward.

It is too bad but evidently the county supervisors are determined.

Roosevelt Bear Does Quick Step on Konnarock Road

NEWS

Roosevelt Bear quick-stepping down the road from Konnarock to St. Clair Bottom. The evening light growing dimmer. Jailer Sir Oliver Hopkins from Marion and Squire McClure after him. The famous old jurist from the St. Clair district can do a step, too, when he wants to. They make a mistake when they think they can get away from that old man and from Jailer Hopkins.

But we had better give you the story. Roosevelt Bear, who was up for chicken stealing some time ago, was accused of stealing a calf. He is supposed to have got the calf at Konnarock and then he took it down into the St. Clair Bottom and sold it to Bud Blevins. From all reports it was a good-looking calf, too.

The story got out and Jailer Hopkins was sent for. He went down there and got Mr. Bear. Every one knows that Teddy, the immortal Roosevelt, hunted bear in this section. Well, he had nothing on our own Sir Oliver. Hopkins got him too, and haled him into Squire McClure's court.

And there was the court quietly convened, as one might say, papers being made out and all, and then, getting to his feet, Mr. Roosevelt Bear slipped through the door and lit out.

The evening light was falling fast. A figure fading into the gloaming. Hopkins, Squire McClure and some half dozen of Konnarock's citizens in full chase.

They got their man and hog tied him. Then they brought him back into the squire's court and the squire slapped him into the Marion jail. He is among us here now and will get his chance to tell what about that calf when court convenes later in this month.

FOURTH WEEK OF
FEBRUARY

The boss ran a piece in the paper about chicken stealing, how to do it and all, and there has been so many chickens stole since that he don't dare go on Main Street.

BUCK

Thanks

Some time ago Jack Sherwood of the Chilhowie Milling Company brought some of the print-shop boys a bag of flour each. It was a good-will offering and the boys took it home and used it. They want now, through the paper, to thank Mr. Sherwood and to say that the flour worked up into as good bread as they ever ate.　　　　　　　　　　　　　　　　　　　　　　　　　　GIL

Conversing With Authors
EDITORIAL

For a long time now I have been thinking that something should be written giving some rather formal rules for conversations between authors and common people. As the matter stands both authors and people suffer a good deal through lack of understanding of each other. There are, I am told, some thirty thousand clubs in America that hire authors to come and lecture to them. Authors go to these places when in need of funds and must be met at trains and, as you can see for yourself, the field is pretty rich. Even at a dollar a club, thirty thousand clubs should bring in thirty thousand dollars—a lot of money to an author. I myself have a plan I would like to propose to a few of these clubs. I will lecture in any town on the following understanding, that is to say, twenty-five cents to hear me lecture—a dollar for the privilege of not hearing me.

But we were speaking of the matter of conversations. Authors, as everyone knows, naturally pine for solitude but they do go about a good deal. I was in Kalamazoo, Michigan, one day, and met ten in the hotel lobby during the afternoon. Authors are becoming so large a part of our population that we should all try to understand them better. On shipboard they usually manage to conceal themselves in some obscure place, say at the captain's table, but ashore they are more in evidence.

They are, of course, very sensitive people. I, myself, have noticed that—when I have lectured somewhere—people, after the lecture, realizing my sensitive nature, are very reluctant about giving me money. As I stay on and on they grow more reluctant. When the matter becomes pressing they do not walk up boldly and give me the money but put it in an envelope. They act as though I were a preacher and had just married some one—or had done something else of which I was ashamed.

It is because they think I am sensitive on the subject of money—and, of course, I am.

But, as I just said, an author, pining for solitude in a strange town, at once goes and tells some one he is there and that he is an author. "I am the man who wrote 'Buckets of Blood,' " he says to the taxi driver who takes him to the hotel. "Do not let any one know. I am very sensitive and love solitude." He says something of the same sort to the hotel clerk.

At once people, feeling how deeply he loves solitude, come to see him. There is need of a technique. Even among ourselves we authors hardly ever know what to say to each other.

In the first place I think it would be better if the subject of money were not mentioned. Those of us who make very little money are sensitive on the subject and those who make a good deal are ashamed. The subject had better be left alone. The main thing to bear in mind is our extreme sensitivity.

Also, if he happens to be an American author, I would not ask him who he thinks is the greatest American author. That is also a subject that causes extreme embarrassment. How many times I myself have been asked that question and how it does upset me. I swallow hard, grow a little red in the face and do not know what to say. Some time ago an editor had the bright idea of having an American poet pick, each month, the man or woman he thought had written the best poem. I was in Chicago at the time and I remember that Mr. Carl Sandburg, when it came his turn, picked a man whose poem had appeared in a newspaper in a small town, of interior Arkansas if I remember correctly. No one could get the paper to read. I thought it very clever of Mr. Sandburg. Since that time I work something of the same kind when people ask me about short-story writers or novelists.

Authors are very, very sensitive. You would never believe how sensitive they are. They may not be quite as sensitive as actors but they run them a close second.

In general it is a bad thing to speak at any great length of an author's work unless you have read a little of it. He will almost always catch you. Critics often do it very well, but they have had a lot of experience. If you haven't much time quotations may usually be had out of newspapers. In passing an opinion do not use the critic's exact words. Give them a turn of your own.

There is one thing you may always do with safety. This may be worked successfully, even if you have never read a word your author has written. First of all suggest that the mind of the author is too deep for you. Say something like this—"your mind is too deep for me, but I always carry away with me a feeling of power and beauty. It is because your sentences are filled with haunting beauty. You do write such beautiful sentences."

If you will but say something like that I am sure it will be enough. Bear in mind that no author ever thought himself capable of writing a bad sentence. If you want to win his entire gratitude, not to say fervent devotion, and have an opportunity to look into one of his books, you might commit one sentence to memory. The happiness you will bring to your author will repay you for your trouble. It does not matter what sentence you choose. Choose any sentence. Surely, that will not be very much trouble.

I am only making a point of this because authors are becoming so large a part of our population. We might get into another war. We need to stand together. We should constantly be saying to ourselves—"see America first."

But I was speaking of conversations. Or was I telling you how sensitive authors are? They are really very sensitive people.

In going into a room where there are several authors do not try to please them all. It would be better to pick out one author and devote yourself to him—or her. The others may be left for another time. If you try to speak kindly to two authors on the same occasion and they catch you at it you will only cause hard feelings. If you can praise the one author at the expense of another you will bring home to him in the most forceful way the fact of your own discernment. That is because he is so sensitive. For all you know he may make you the hero of his next book.

It is very nice to ask an author whether or not he takes his characters out of real life. He enjoys that.

It is very unfortunate to approach an author and say to him that you cannot get his books out of the library, that they are always out. This brings home to him the matter of money, it touches, that is to say, upon the question of his income. But it has been agreed that the money question is to be altogether avoided.

If I had more time I would say something about the sensitivity of authors, but you may have noticed that yourself. O, the sensitivity of authors—particularly in the matter of money.

Authors in general do a great deal of swearing under their breaths. That is other people's fault. It is because they are compelled by circumstances to associate so much with people not as sensitive as themselves.

When it comes to the morals of authors . . . Well, after all, this is a matter that, like money, had perhaps better be left alone. It is a delicate subject. It is so easy to make a mistake. Too many people are likely to go up to an author and suggest that, although many other authors may be immoral they are sure he is not, that he is, in fact, a good man. Something of that sort, carelessly said, may make an author unhappy for months.

I have seen old friendships destroyed by such carelessness as that. An author I knew very well committed suicide after hearing something like that. Whatever you do never question the immorality of your author.

Do not go to an author and tell him that you are too busy to read very much. When you decide to quit drinking you do not call up your bootlegger to give him the glad news. But this brings up again the question of income and we had already decided to let that subject alone.

It is always very nice, when you are in the midst of a conversation with an author, to suggest to him that his work reminds you strongly of the work of some other man. It makes him very happy. Say to him that, when you read his books, you always begin thinking of Mr. George Moore. Then tell him how much you admire Mr. Moore. Watch the glad, sweet light come into his eyes.

By all means, when you are where authors have congregated, do not speak of anything but books. To speak of the weather, things to eat, horse races or any topic other than authors and their work is very rude. Who wants to be rude to an author? It is the one thing we are all trying to avoid.

You are in a room with an author and there he is. Look how handsome he is. As likely as not, if you speak of ordinary things, you will disturb his thoughts. He is sure to be thinking. You may be quite certain that, as you go about your ordinary affairs, he has been consorting with the gods. When you have been in bed and sleeping he has been among the stars. Authors hardly ever sleep.

The main thing to bear in mind in carrying on conversations with authors is that they are no ordinary beings and do not think ordinary thoughts. If your author is a good author, and I take it for granted you would not associate with him at all if he were not great, the whole purpose of his life is to live quite separated from ordinary people.

He loves the heights and, therefore, wants to be constantly thinking of books, O, how he loves conversing of books, thinking of books. And how, in particular, he loves thinking of and conversing of other men's books. Do not ever let this thought go out of your mind.

Authors really want so little and there are so many of them. They are very, very humble, and as I suggested but a moment ago, O, how sensitive they are. All we need to do to get along better with them is to be a little more thoughtful. I am quite sure that, on account of the growing number of our magazines and the eagerness for intellectual stimulation, so characteristic of Americans in general, the race of authors will grow. That is why the subject is so important. For a long time I myself had the notion that like the negro race the race of authors would tend to breed out, that they would in short become whiter, but I am losing hope of that.

Authors become thicker and thicker. Hardly any one can tell when he may be put into the position of having to hold a conversation with one of them. We should all try to learn how to do it.

I have tried to make some suggestions that may be of help. Perhaps you can think up some for yourself.

The main thing is to be prepared. As I have said we Americans should stand closer together. Perhaps some one will shortly write a book on this subject. I hope they will. We need more books. That is one of the crying needs of our life.

Some lecture manager or some one who has worked a good deal in a publishing office or has had a good deal of experience at an editor's desk might by a little effort do something on this subject that would be really good. A book might be compiled telling how to converse with each particular author.

We might begin with visiting authors.

However, I dare say it would take too many volumes. It would cost too much. There I go—speaking of money again. You can readily see that I, who am an author myself, do not know how to handle this matter.

Really I would suggest letting authors alone but that I am very fond of some of them. I do not want to see them commit suicide. And then besides we are in such crying need of books.

Something will have to be done. Some one with more keenness will have to teach us all how to converse and live with our authors.

Segregation might be a way out of the problem.

HENRY MENCKEN PARK

FIRST WEEK OF

MARCH

∽∽∽

Style

EDITORIAL

To illustrate why much newspaper writing is better than the so-called highbrow stuff about which so much fuss is made, take this from the New York *World*. Why, it is as good as George Borrow, beyond which, in the praise of writing, no man can go.

"In one of the most vicious battles the New Madison Square Garden ever has seen, Tony Canzoneri, youthful New Yorker, last night clinched full claim to the featherweight championship by whipping Benny Bass of Philadelphia, in fifteen rounds.

The crowd literally stood in its chairs as the youngster smashed to head and body without a let-up through the fifteenth. Tony ripped cleanly to the head, short jolting hooks, but Bass hammered tellingly to the ribs.

In the banner crowd was an unusually large number of women, who always like to see the little fellows box. The old guard was out, too, for, be it said, they never miss the crowning of a new champion.

Bass was the first to appear, in a maroon and gray robe, while Tony meandered in wearing a dark brown satin "hoopla." Benny was pale and determined looking, the local boy just

137

a grinning kid. Tony raced across and mitted his opponent.

Bass was the first to score after the bell rang, with a right to the body. But Tony doubled the count, with two to the ribs. A right to the jaw was repaid with interest to the same spot by the Quaker. Canzoneri saw stars when rocked by another telling right to the button. Bass was flinging his right as wickedly as a mule does a left hind foot. It was the Quaker's round.

Mickey Connolly lost the first "duke" to Sammy Faber in the opener, Benny Schwartz defeated Johnny Green in the first of the eight-round bouts. Green was dropped to his knees in the eighth round by a blow to the jaw. He was up immediately.

Joe Kaufman defeated Armando Schekels of Belgium in the second eight-round bout. The crowd didn't seem to like the verdict and set up a dreadful din. It was manifestly a fair decision.

In the semi-final, Al Winkler of Philadelphia outpointed Bobby Burns in eight rounds. It was a rough and close battle."

Economy, the proper use of the argot, to fit the occasion. I have a distinct notion that the future of writing in America lies with the newspaper boys who do not know they are writing.

It is like this: if you get a reputation as a highbrow writer you are doomed.

Well, the literary ladies take you up. Look at me if you want a dreadful example. Do you know that, this year, I was offered five hundred a week, and all expenses paid, to go around lecturing to literary ladies?

Why, in the name of God? I am not naturally that kind. It doesn't take so much to keep me alive. Of course I like fancy clothes, loud ties, loud suits, but I can get along without them.

In Grayson County, Virginia, I can get good biscuits and gravy for nothing, in any house in the whole county.

The newspaper boys are out after the stuff of life. Of course a lot of newspapers cramp their style. Highbrow notions, respectability, have swept the country. The average man on the street thinks he knows a lot about writing when he doesn't know a thing.

He thinks good writing is something he doesn't understand and doesn't much like.

Schools have a lot to do with that. A school teacher will take a lot of youngsters and make them read, say Dickens. Well, they read it. "Now you write an essay about Dickens' style," says the school teacher. Of course Dickens hadn't any more style than a mud turtle but the school teacher doesn't know that. She is probably a pretty woman thinking about how to get a good husband, or should be. What does she know or care about "style in writing"?

She has got a book in which some college professor tells her, "now you ask them to define Dickens' style."

Why style in writing is a thing as subtle as women's clothes. You know how women dress. If a woman has good legs she wears clothes to show them off to the best advantage. Suppose her eyes or her hands are her best points. It's a poor woman who does not know her own good points.

And how subtle she is in bringing them out. That's her style. How are you going to define it?

A while ago I spoke of George Borrow. More people ought to read that man. There was a subtle fellow for you. Beside him fellows like Dickens and Thackeray—the school men's favorites, were mere amateurs.

George Borrow wrote as, say Eddie Collins at his best, played second base. He was a life lover. Read him some day. See how all kinds of people sift through his pages.

And what gusto he has, what love of queer characters. There was a writer for you.

Cats—and Other Things
NEWS

We have a new cat. Mack Morris sent her to the shop. It is a very interesting thing about pets. There was Nellie, for example. You will remember that Nellie died. It is just possible that Nellie a little exhausted the store of affection of Zeb, Jack, Gil, Joe and the rest of us.

I am talking to men now. Do you remember, when you were a boy, your first love. Mine was a red-haired girl. As I remember it I never did speak to her.

At that time I was living in a town about the size of Marion. I had a job, driving a delivery wagon for a grocer. I might have been thirteen or fourteen.

One day I was driving along the street and saw this red-haired girl. How unspeakably dainty she was to me. It seemed to me that my heart stopped beating.

Well, she breathed, she ate food, she lived in a house. Alas, her father was not in such an inspiring position in life. In that day towns like Marion still had saloons. Her father was a bartender.

They lived in a little frame house on a certain street. To get to the end of that street and pass her house I had to go to the end of the street and turn. It was a cul-de-sac. How I wished our store had more trade on the street. As I remember it, we had none.

I was driving, to the grocery wagon, an old black horse. Poor old thing. A dozen times a day I drove her (the old mare, I mean) to the end of the street and turned. Other boys laughed at me. They knew all right.

O, the suffering of the young heart.

That red-haired girl knew too. Sometimes she let me see her, sometimes she did not. She used to come out and stand on the porch of the house and pretend not to notice. I never did get courage to speak to her. When she spoke to me my cheeks burned with blushes.

It is a bit odd about women. We strong men are inclined to like and even love weak-looking women. Let a woman be too big, too strong and broad-shouldered and we turn from her.

It is because weak, dainty-looking women make us feel strong and commanding.

What a joke life is. The weak, gentle-looking women so often bully us men a thousand times more than strong, healthy women ever would.

We fall for them just the same.

But we were speaking of cats. Nellie, our first Marion cat-love, is dead. She has gone to her reward. The new cat is a handsome lady, as strong as Nellie was weak. She is a true cat with at least nine lives.

She is very affectionate too. But look you now. She hasn't even a name. Won't some big, strong woman, among our subscribers, who has in her heart a secret sympathy with this new lady cat, knowing her strong as I have said, an independent fine-spirited cat, knowing the disadvantage she is under, following Nellie, won't she send in a name for her. No need to reveal yourself. Send it on a postcard. You don't even need sign your name.

Do this as a rebuke to the men in the shop, who love the weak, rather than the strong.

SECOND WEEK OF

MARCH

Our old friend Will Privett, from over near Grant, was in to see us the other day. Will is a real bear hunter and big-time wild-cat shot. He has a son named Roby Privett who goes out into the woods and catches wild animals with his hands, and gets them, too. Will has a brother named Harrison Privett who is the champion horse trader of Grayson. Will is going to put out a few acres of corn for us this summer.

The boss pulled a boner all right. Did you see what he had in last week's paper about that new cat? Well, he went on about her, making her out a rather masculine cat. He said she was affectionate but not as gentle as Nellie.

You know how a man like that is. He gets to writing and can't stop. He wanted some woman to send in a name for the cat.

Here are some of them:

"Miss Marion Virginia"—from Berea College.

"Queen Elizabeth"—Chilhowie suggestion.

"Charlotte Corday"—Seven Mile Ford.

"Susan B. Anthony"—Saltville.

The terrible joke is that she isn't a she. That's one on the boss O.K. I guess every one in the shop but him knew it.

BUCK FEVER

Pound Party

NEWS

There was a pound party at the company store the 29th of February for the benefit of Geo. Tipper for bravery in defending the honor of his family, by whipping John C. Ockrel.

Mr. Tipper is a peaceful man, aged 69, but when he goes into action he is a regular war horse. Which he has proved with great honor.

Everybody was invited to be present at the party and to get Mrs. Tipper one pound of something in the eating line. This was a worthy cause and the people came up with pounds amounting to over one hundred. They tried to give him as many pounds as he gave blows to the man he whipped.

Tom Greer

OUT OF TOM GREER

A slow-speaking, sensible man, with a thousand friends. He loves wit and has a keen sense of humor. Men respect him for his solidity. When he tells you something you believe it.

His business is one of the most interesting in town.

As a business man "Tom" Greer, Riley Thomas Greer—to be exact—reminds you more of a European business man than an American. The modern American idea of "bigness" at any cost has not caught him. He is in business now with the same associates who have been with him almost from the beginning. The business is not a corporation but a partnership and associated with Mr. Greer is his cousin, George W. Greer, who conducts a branch of the business at Pikesville, Kentucky, and Mr. C. C. Stafford of Kentucky.

To a writing man there is a touch of romance to the business of dealing in roots, herbs and barks. Walking through Mr. Greer's big warehouses, where there are bales of goods on all sides and here and there spread out on the floor to dry, fragrant roots, barks and herbs, there floats through the mind visions of high mountain valleys, lonely spots along mountain streams, dense mountain forests.

Mr. Greer is a dealer in roots, herbs and barks, the largest dealer perhaps in the country. Products from his warehouse go to cities all over the world.

Here are some of them:

Virginia Snake Root, Stillingia Root, Senega Snake Root, Slippery Elm Bark, well rossed, Shonny Haw Bark.

One hundred and fifty such items on Mr. Greer's price lists. Who would not be a Stillingia if they could, and well rossed, too?

Or a Shonny Haw.

Well do we remember the last time we were well rossed. What a headache we had. But that is neither here nor anywhere else.

Would you know any of these things if you saw them in the forest? Would you know a Pipsissewa? How about a Bugleweed Herb?

People do know them, mountain people, women and boys.

Tom Greer was a boy over in Watauga County, North Carolina. His parents did not have any more money than we have now. As a boy he used to go around gathering Shonny Haw and Pipsissewa. He sold it to a little country store six miles away.

In that country, at that time, they had school only three months a year and then the schoolhouse burned down. Tom Greer missed most of the disadvantages of modern education.

No one ever told him that he was anything special or that Italy lay over the Alps and so he grew up to be the nice quiet man we all know.

It was, from all accounts, a rather hard growing up. There he was, with Marion, Virginia, the nearest railroad station, sixty-five miles north. He went to work in a country store. Already he knew the practical side of gathering roots and herbs and now he learned something about the commercial side. He had got together two or three hundred dollars. You know how that boy had to work and save and go without to get that.

He had, however, got something else too. There was a little company formed, Tom Greer, his cousin George and two or three others, all mountain men. He had got the confidence of his neighbors.

They sent Tom and his cousin George out to scout the land. Tom landed in Marion and his cousin George in Pikesville, Kentucky. They were both the same kind of men. When they had made up their minds they had made up their minds.

And so they went back and got their families and came out to the railroad in covered wagons, Tom to Marion and his cousin on to Pikesville.

Tom Greer began business here in a small way—very, very small in fact. He had to teach the mountain people in the hills about Marion the medicinal roots and herbs. Many of them he gathered himself. There was little or no money. Mrs. Greer helped. In fact, Mrs. Greer has become an expert in certain branches of the business now.

Besides roots, herbs and barks, pollen is now used in some of the modern treatments of diseases such as hay fever and asthma.

Pollen is gathered from the blossoms of all sorts of weeds, flowers and grasses. It is delicate, particular business and must be done by an expert. This has become Mrs. Greer's line.

And in the meantime, all over the hills, people, largely women, go out into the woods to gather the medicinal herbs and barks that are sent into the Greer warehouse and prepared for shipment. The growth of the business has been slow but sure. From a few thousand dollars a year it has grown so that there is now annually shipped from a quarter to a half million dollars worth of goods.

The business is run as it was first started. When it was new and at a period of financial stress Mr. Charles C. Stafford, a well-to-do farmer from near Pikesville, Kentucky, put into the business some six thousand additional working capital and did it against the advice of his banker and merely because he liked the looks of Tom Greer and his cousin George.

For that little act of generosity and keen judgment of human nature Mr. Stafford has been getting back each year about the full amount he put in and has been getting it for many years. There have been years when he got two or three times that much.

As I said at the beginning, Mr. Tom Greer is like a good many European business men. Many temptations have come to him to spread out, to spread-eagle, to plunge into this or that. However, they have really not been temptations at all.

He has always been interested in his own business. He likes it, never loses interest. To-day he is the same quiet unassuming man he was when he came to Marion—some say, laughingly—barefooted out of the hills. He is a man going about his affairs quietly and efficiently, rolling a bit of wit under his tongue, enjoying his town, his neighbors and the business in which he has been so successful.

THIRD WEEK OF

MARCH

Negro Singing

THE HAMPTON QUARTETTE ENTERTAINS LARGE CROWD

NEWS

It is something inherent in the negro race. It comes to the surface in singing and in dancing. The Hampton Quartette sang here last night. It was fine song singing, having the peculiar quality of song singing, a thing different than any other kind of music making, but I have heard infinitely better negro singing.

Who can doubt that the negro race has something the white race has lost. I mean an unconscious giving of himself to the song by the singer. The average white woman who sings, for example, gets up before an audience and is conscious of her clothes, of her physical beauty, if she has any, of a thousand things other than the song she is singing.

Surely education is all right, but education, in the white man's sense, does something to the black and the brown man.

I remember a hot night on the Mississippi at Baton Rouge. Negroes were carrying bags of evil-smelling fertilizer up a steep gang plank and singing a song called "The las' sack."

Another night, years ago, up the Mobile River. The boat tied up on the river bank. Lonely forests all about. The song that time was a work song of some sort. "O, my babe. The banjo dog." A queer medley of words, meaning nothing. I sat in a dark part of the boat with the pilot. It was hot. The song of the workers suddenly caught something lost when the negro came out of his native Africa.

These were real black boys. Not a man could read or write. Suddenly the song seemed a real part of the lonely forests, of the river, the night. To describe its quality is impossible to me.

Organizations like the Hampton singers are at their worst when they think they are at their best. They are good, surely. But when you have heard negro singing, as I have, in lonely places in the far south—

Negroes on lumber rafts in the turpentine forest or on the lower Mississippi.

There is a quality to negro singing going out fast. Music is the most primitive of all the arts. The negro, in coming into the more cultivated arts, the singing and creation of classic and semi-classic music, and the other arts, has a long trail ahead. In spite of his native voice quality, a thing also that will go from the educated negro—the white man will beat him a thousand miles at all of the sophisticated arts.

The Hampton Singers still sing well. They do not sing beautifully as do some of the negroes of the fields and rivers who have not tried yet to swing into the white man's world. I can soon forget the admittedly fine singing of the trained negro singers. I will never forget some of the negro singing I have heard from the lips of so-called ignorant negro workers.

In the arts you have to lose all before you begin to gain anything. The arts are like religion in that.

Just Walking
A REMINISCENCE

What I was doing in that particular town I can't remember. There was a murder trial on. It must have been a county seat.

Maybe I was trying to sell something or get advertising for some newspaper or magazine. I worked at a lot of things about that time and lost a lot of jobs.

That evening I was coming along a rain-washed street and saw Fred Downie. Fred was working as reporter for one of the Chicago dailies. He was down there with three or four other men on the murder case.

It was one of the kind of murders that gets spread out, all over the pages of all the papers. Why some murders get all the attention they do, while others get none, I do not know. Fred and the others talked about it that evening. I remember a fellow named Jim Gore getting all worked up. "You take a guy that goes to all the trouble to commit a murder now," he said, "a guy like that, furnishing all the good reading he does, and maybe getting hung for it, and then they pass him up. He don't get any publicity at all."

No one knows why some murders get all the attention they do. I suppose they are worked up. There must be at least some uncertainty. "Uncertainty whether they can get a conviction or not," I remember Fred's saying. He said that a murder story, to make a really good spread for the dailies, must be one in which the public is pretty well convinced the authorities have got their hands on the right people. After that it becomes a game. Can the authorities prove their case? Now let's see who has the foxiest brains, the defense or the state. "What the murderer did is pretty much forgotten," Fred said. If the murderer gets convicted and hung, every one is shocked. They had forgotten everything in their interest in the game.

But I did not start to speak of murders but of nights. I remember some of the nights in Southern and Middle Western towns. I may have had a dozen such nights as that one, perhaps not so many. It was in the late fall that time I saw Fred, but the nights were still warm. In those days, when I was traveling about, trying to pick up a living, my real interest was in writing, just as it is now. I would get myself sent to some town. Some firm would give me a job and expense money. Very likely I would get into a room in a hotel in the town and begin to write. A lot of stuff I wrote wasn't any good but it excited me. I would stay in the town until I was broke, forgetting what I had been sent for. Perhaps the firm that had sent me out had sent also several telegrams and I hadn't bothered to open them. That's the kind of fellow I was. It isn't any wonder I lost jobs.

And then sometimes, when I had been in a country hotel, writing away like that, there would come an evening. I would go out of the hotel room and walk.

Something in the air, in the faces of the people passed in the streets. If I went out of the town and walked on a country road something happened to me. It is pretty hard to describe.

There was a kind of sweeping acceptance of life; something inside you at such times. It is the same way when you are in love but in a love affair there is a woman involved. With a woman you are likely at any moment to get too definite—if you know what I mean.

But when you are alone, or with another man who feels as you do—

I remember once being in the city of New York. That was in the winter. I went to a party. There was some drinking but that had nothing to do with what I am talking about.

That night in New York it snowed, a soft, clinging snow. I had never seen New York like that. It excited me almost unbearably. The soft snow had clung to everything. I had come out of the party at three o'clock in the morning. There was a tall man who came out the door at the same moment. It had been a large party and if I had met the man during the evening I did not remember.

I didn't even know his name. Anyway we came out together into the soft quiet of that night. There was an odd blue light. As by a common impulse the tall man and I began walking together.

I remember his long face and the peculiar long stride with which he walked.

We walked for hours, not saying much to each other. Here was a strange city indeed. Everything was absolutely white, the city outlined in white against that blue night sky and unbelievably lovely.

The man and I walking thus in the quiet city, saying nothing to each other, feeling the same thing—just the beauty of the night I presume. We went far uptown and then downtown to the Battery. I do not believe we said a dozen words to each other during the hours we were together.

But to go back now to that time I saw Fred Downie out in the Middle Western town. He took me to his hotel. There were other men there, friends of his. I do not remember their names so I will call them George and Frank and Tom. Oh, yes, there was that Jim Gore.

Of course Fred introduced me and there was talk of how we should spend the evening. A poker game was proposed. We might have done that. I hardly know why that poker game never started. We might have spent the evening in a hot little hotel room, sitting around a table, the air full of tobacco smoke, drinking strong liquor too. We didn't.

One of Fred's friends—it was the one named Jim Gore—said, "Let's go walk." It might have been nine o'clock. We started.

It was just one of the kind of nights that excite a man. There had been the rain in the late afternoon. It was, as I have said, late fall but the night was warm. I was walking with a man named Tom and the others were coming along behind. First we walked for an hour in the residence streets of the town. Although it wasn't late, as things go in larger places, a good many of the houses were already dark.

The night itself was lovely. After the rain the air was peculiarly clean on the lips and up in the sky there were great banks of dead white clouds, hurrying along. Between the clouds spots of clear blue.

There was an insane asylum in the town. I had not known it until that evening. I knew very little about the town. I presume I had been staying in my hotel room, writing—nonsense more than likely.

The five of us were walking and came to the buildings of the asylum on a hill. There was a small river ran along the edge of the town. Beyond the river and the hill, on the far side, an open country. You could see quite a long ways across country in that light.

There were a lot of great brick buildings. We were all curious and as the grounds were open went in and stood quite close to one of them. The one we came to first had bars over the windows. I remember now that in the murder case, the men I was with were down there covering, a woman was trying to get herself clear by proving she was insane. If she succeeded she would be brought, I fancied, to the very building we were now standing before.

As we stood there some one inside laughed. It was a nerve-shaking laugh, heard thus in the night. It went on and on, a seemingly endless outbreak of clear girlish laughter. It broke finally. Then a gigglish voice began to chatter. There was something being said about an organization called the B. P. O. E. What it is I don't know. The voice just kept saying—"and so you were at the B. P. O. E. He was at the B. P. O. E. Do you hear that? He was at the B. P. O. E."

A senseless lot of words surely. The voice said them over and over. Then the laughter came again. We were all huddled together in silence on the lawn. We had unconsciously drawn close together thus. Some one walked down a corridor inside the building and a man's voice spoke. The laughter came once more. It was low and sweet now.

We all went silently away.

We had been feeling something and I presume that thing happening made us feel it more. A man couldn't of course help having thoughts about the woman in that place and some man—a lover or a husband. What had he done? What had she done? "And so you were at the B. P. O. E., eh?" Every man has had bad moments with some woman. There are plenty of President Hardings in this world.

We went walking out into the country. We were silent. There was a road running along the crest of the hill. It was a nice road to follow because there was the flat land spread out before our eyes. After the rain the road was muddy. It was a road not much used. Down below, in the flat land. there was a highway. We could see the white thread of it running away into the darkness. It went the same way we were going but was beyond the little river. Now and then we saw the moving lights of automobiles.

Why we were walking like that no one knew. Where we were going no one cared. No one offered to turn back. What I think is that the fellows I was with were just fed up, being day after day in a crowded courtroom hearing a murder trial, seeing the game going on that Fred had talked to me about, later writing and sending in their murder stories for the newspapers. They had all done it that evening before I saw them.

We walked and walked and the man named Tom, I had never seen before that evening, was beside me and we must have got some ways ahead of the others. Suddenly he began to talk. His talk was about another walk he had taken on another evening. He began to talk about it. He said he was in Chicago and it was spring. He had been sent out on some assignment. Why he had so hated to cover it he couldn't remember. It was some messy affair, a divorce or something, if he remembered rightly. It was late afternoon, he said, and he was walking along State Street in Chicago.

First, he said, he met a man who was the father of another reporter he knew. The man was an old Jew. This fellow, named Tom, had met him with his son. That, he said, was at State and

Madison streets in Chicago. He said he was going along the street when this man, the old one, suddenly plucked at his coat and when he turned around the old man put a hand on his arm and pulled him over against a building.

Nothing special about the encounter. It, however, upset Tom. He said hearing the old Jew talk was like hearing the woman laugh in the building for housing the insane.

The man in the street with Tom pressed him against the building and began to talk. He was a cutter for some big tailoring establishment. He wanted to tell Tom that he was an artist at his trade. He kept telling him that, insisting on it. You understand Tom had seen the man but once before and then quite casually. He knew nothing of the man's ability, didn't care, he said. It was an odd thing to have happen in Chicago, on State Street, you'll admit that. At first Tom thought the man was drunk. He wasn't.

After he got away from that one Tom went along the street and met another man. It was a fellow he knew but slightly. This one, he said, worked in an office where he had once gone to get a story. The second man suddenly made a proposal, "I'll tell you what," he said, "let's you and I get out of town."

It was an odd proposal surely but Tom said he took it up. What induced him to do it he did not know. He said he and the man went to a railroad station and got on a train and that they rode until dark and then got off.

They began to walk. That was all to it. The man named Tom told me he had never spoken to any one of what happened that night. It had all seemed too queer and crazy.

He and the man he hardly knew had just walked and walked. He said the man could sing. They kept passing through little industrial towns, such as are scattered over the prairies, about Chicago. When they came to a town the man with him began to sing in a fine baritone voice. Once they were stopped by a policeman in a town, who asked them what they were up to, and the man with Tom laughed and said "just singing."

They walked all night and in the morning took a train back to the city. Tom almost got fired because he hadn't tended up to his assignment. He did not know what else to say so he said he had been drunk. He said nothing else happened.

As for our crowd, we had a singer with us too. I am talking now of the evening I walked with the newspaper men, the time we walked in that road along the crest of the hill. The road kept getting worse and worse. Pretty soon there seemed to be no road at all. We stopped.

It was then our singer began to sing. By that time it might have been twelve o'clock. There was a small house just below us at the foot of the hill on which we stood and on the bank of the little river. At first we did not know the house was there.

We stood on the hill and the man with us—it was the one named George, a little, red-headed man I hadn't noticed before—began to sing in what seemed to the rest of us a really lovely voice. I don't know how long he sang but as he sang we all became conscious of the house below at the foot of the hill.

We became conscious of it because people began coming out of the house. Whoever they were, and they were no doubt farming people, there might have been some five or six of them.

You know how a man's eyes become accustomed to the light when he is out at night like that. First we, standing on the hill and listening to our man sing, saw the house and then we saw the people come out and stand and look up the hill to where we were.

George quit singing presently and there was silence. We began drifting off along the hillside road toward town. I hardly know how far we went.

Then the thing happened that put a sort of finishing touch to our walk. There was a singer down there among the farming people too, a woman singer. We could still see the group of people standing before the house and then the voice of their singer came up to us. Whoever it was sang only one song, and then we all walked back along the road and past the insane asylum and to the hotel where the newspaper men were staying. I went to my own hotel. It was just a night and a walk, such a thing as sometimes happens. Why it seems important I can't say. The next day when I went back to Chicago I had lost my job. The newspaper men stayed on their jobs. They went right on finishing up that murder trial. I can't even remember whether or not the woman who was on trial, and who was trying to get out of killing some man by proving herself insane, did it or not. When I saw Frank Downie again I never even took the trouble to ask.

FOURTH WEEK OF

MARCH

Hello Towns

EDITORIAL

Nations are, I think, like people. It takes a long, long time for one of them to grow up. Most people, I am sure, never get to be beyond about twelve years of age. No one gets very old or very wise. The great problem is to get intellectually and emotionally beyond twelve.

Thank Heavens we in America have begun to hear less and less of the good old days, and of the spotless virtue and wisdom of the makers of America. In Abraham Lincoln's day you had to breathe softly when you spoke of "The Fathers." Certain men, being ambitious, managed to get up a row between the American colonies and mother England. For a long time our historians had to be very careful in speaking of all that period. Such a sacred lot of men, doing such a sacred thing. Every one noble and grand—doing noble, grand things—outnobling all the rest of mankind.

It makes your bones ache to think of it. Nowadays anyway we can be a bit more careless and human when we speak of the early days of the Big Boy, America. It is being done. First-rate histories are now being written about the whole affair. We are finding out something of truth about the Adamses, the Jeffersons, Madisons and the rest. I think we respect them none the less but they get a bit nearer our own level. That's a help. We are what we are and we aren't so bad. No need to twist the British Lion's tail any more. The Irish vote doesn't cut the figure it did. When you quit being afraid you can be more gentle, more human. America is far and away the strongest and richest nation in the world now. If we can learn to be gentle without being too patronizing we'll be O.K. A hundred and fifty years since we pulled that little party on King George—well, well. How the time passes. If we hadn't pulled it how many grand titles we might have had over here by now. Think of it—Sir Charles of Kalamazoo, Count Albany, Duke Schenectady, Viscount Reno, Lord Pittsburgh and Wheeling. It makes your mouth water to think of it. Thinking of it almost makes a royalist of a man. I have several friends who think there should be a royalist party in America. And it isn't a bad idea. I like a parade myself. If we only had a pretender I believe I'd get in line.

Well, we got started, running our own house and of course we had to go on. There was another little scrap with England later but we were lucky to get out of that as well as we did. She came near slapping us good—that time. What we got out of it was the beginning of the reign of the people.

There was one Andrew Jackson who fought a battle in New Orleans after the war was all over and no battle needed—and won it too. It was about the only thing we did win, that time.

It made Jackson, made the common man politically conscious. When Jackson went in, the old Eastern and Southern crowd, who had been running things, were in a bad way.

It's rather dangerous business this talking all the time about what a wonderful fellow the common man is. He may believe you.

After the second war with England we got a trial of the common man in power. That ended in Lincoln. A lucky ending. No nation ever gets a poet in power more than once.

But I am not trying to write, even briefly, of the political history of America during these hundred and fifty years. I am trying to think where we have got in another way. After all being politically minded may be but a sign of immaturity.

Such faith in politics and in politicians all during that long middle period of our history, after we had fought our way through to recognition as a nation. For a long, long time the State was to the average American what God was to the man of the Middle Ages.

Pass laws and make men happy. Solve the problems of life by passing more laws. Ten thousand new laws by 1935. Onward and upward.

For a long time Americans thought the power of the state would work down into individual lives—remake individual lives—but that faith is being lost now. No one hangs on to it but the anti-saloon league, the Watch and Ward Club and the K. K. K.

A big, fat, rich country, the country stretching away westward, on and on. Great rivers, forests, mines to be opened, railroads to be built, emigrants pouring in. Had England managed to hold on this might have been an English country now. We do speak that language, after our own fashion. That is a confusing fact.

What a conglomeration of peoples from all over the old world, coming here, raising their sons and daughters here, speaking our American language, making songs in it, writing stories in it.

It must be confusing to the English mind. You still hear an occasional Englishman referring to us as one of the Lion's cubs. We aren't, of course, anything of the sort. In any American town or city nowadays there are more descendants of any one of a dozen European nations than of England. After we kicked loose the young bloods of England began going out to their own colonies. Why not?

We got out of our row with England the chance for making something new in the world. Who wants another England this side of the water? That's been done once.

You see I'm only trying to sum things up after a hundred and fifty years in my own way as a present-day American man, a man glad he is an American.

Surely we don't deserve so much credit, being so rich and grand and all. We do deserve some credit for being so amusing, and we are amusing. We have made of America a lively, amusing place in which to live, at least they must give us credit for that.

It must have been a long time to wait here for something to begin but it did begin.

Sophistication began, civilization began.

From the point of view of the arts, and I am speaking somewhat from that point of view, being one of that sort and being very American; from the point of view of the arts, I say, we are beginning to get on a bit. There is evidence of it on all sides, in the buildings in our cities, in the cities themselves, in the rapidity and boldness of our development, in all forms of expression.

As a nation we are still young. It has only been a hundred and fifty years. What's that? Well, we may still be wearing short pants but we are walking down past the clothing stores on Main Street and looking at the spring styles in long pants almost every day now.

Such a job we tackled!

The only reason we ever hung together as one nation was because the mechanical age came along at the same time we did. The machine is the only thing that made it possible for us to be one nation, spreading ourselves out over an entire continent. The very thing that made us is what stands in the way of our development as a civilized people.

The machine itself isn't a civilizer. As a people, and for a time, it looked as though we were going to be a nation of machine-worshipers, but I've a hunch we are going to escape that.

Civilization, sophistication, depends, I should say, upon the opportunity offered in a country for the development of individual expression of life through work. The machine and the natural wealth of the country did away with much drudgery but it tended also to destroy individuality. We had a lot of that at the beginning. In the early days when the towns and cities were widely scattered, when it was a difficult slow job to get from one place to another, when the forests spread away on all sides, men lived in comparative loneliness and were thrown back upon themselves. Those who were able to bear such a life at all became strong individuals. They were bold half mystics, believing divinely in themselves and their own dogmas, thought out in lonely places, infected other men with their dogmas, because they were strong men.

Then the machine, the herding of men into towns and cities, the age of the factory. Men all began to dress alike, eat the same foods, read the same kind of newspapers and books. Minds began to be standardized as were the clothes men wore, the chairs they sat on, the houses they lived in, the streets they walked in.

For a long time here the only individualistic expression of life in the arts or in architecture were European fragments, accidentally overlooked in the swift march of the standardizing machine. There was the Vieux Carré in New Orleans, fragments of Spain on the West Coast, English and Dutch fragments in New York City and in New England.

The machines had promised America a lot and had delivered. All of American life is unbelievable, more comfortable, more livable, than it was in the days of our more rampant early individualism.

And individual life here, being more comfortable, has also ascetic values it did not have before the machine came. The crass, tobacco-chewing, cock-fighting, quarreling life led by the men of the middle period of American history is unknown now except perhaps in a few isolated regions of the South, where the railroads, the automobiles, the radios and the airplanes have not yet done their work.

You get all of this standardization of the trappings of life— cheap comforts—and you pay for it. We are paying for it.

Democracy is itself, I am sure, but an expression of the notion of the standardization of life. The majority are right. It is the duty of the minority to conform. What an absurdity—really. We see the absurdity very clearly in the effect upon us all of the passing of our prohibition amendment—the state more and more losing its grip on men's imaginations, the state as a controlling factor in lives becoming constantly more and more ineffective.

Is this loosening of the grip of the state necessarily a destructive sign? I think not. To the men of the middle period of our hundred and fifty years it would have seemed terrible. It may be only a way of putting the state in its proper position in our scheme of living. Putting it somewhere near where the French put it after their debauch of state worship. Surely, for citizen Anderson, the state should be a servant, not a master. It should clean and police the street in front of his house, arrest violent men who disturb or annoy him. The state should never be permitted to say what he shall eat and drink, what he shall think, what he shall say to his fellows.

My own central interest is in human life, getting all I can out of my own life and the lives about me—not in the growth and power of the state. I believe that with the coming of civilization comes also the international mind. Nationalists are primitive. I admire some primitive arts but I do not want to be a primitive. I believe also that I am a pretty typical American.

However, I am talking in the dark now, being pretty heavy and serious. This is the first time I ever tried to talk about such a big thing as America. I am confused and a little puffed up. I feel like a president, writing a state paper, and really cannot think politically. There was a man I met once. His name was Randolf Bourne and he had a perfect scheme of government, had all of the functions of government properly arranged in the scheme of lives. I used to sit hearing him talk and his words were like music to me but he is dead now and I cannot remember any of the details of his scheme.

I am just a man going about. Since I was a child I have seen that life was unfair to some men, more than fair to others. I'm a lucky man myself. All the old negroes tell me so. I've got the power of making passes. I cure warts. I have no idea that laws will change anything. Life has always been like that. There is a kind of natural compensation always at work.

What I conclude is that in America life is better now for the individual man than anywhere else in the world. And that isn't due to any special virtue in us, as Americans, but to the fact that our country is so big and so rich.

We present-day American men live in flush times, and I'm glad we do. I consider myself lucky, being born when I was. In another three or four hundred years we may be as crowded and hard up here as men are in older lands.

By that time, I dare say, our tone as a nation will have become fixed. The French, the Germans, Italians, English, Spaniards, all of the older peoples of Europe were once a mixed people, as we are now, but none of them ever had such a grand garden to play in.

They became fixed as a type, as a people because new people from the outside quit pouring in and because, gradually coming to know each other, living a long time together in one place, accepting themselves for what they were, they developed artists who gave expression to their lives.

As I have already gone so far as to suggest, a nation is at the beginning like a newborn child. If England was the mother of the Big Boy America, she was, I fear, a woman of questionable virtue at the time. No one knows for certain who the father was. The child got out of the mother's arms and tried to walk and talk for itself. For a long time it talked the mother's tongue, rather unchanged, thought the mother's thoughts.

The child had been left alone in a big place and was afraid. It is the frightened child who brags, blusters. That was the tone of American thought and of American art for a long time. Boasting of our own inferior efforts at national expression and secretly imitating the very people we pretended to scorn.

All of our early literary efforts, our painting, architecture, music was imitative. When I was a boy there used to hang, in almost every Middle Western house, framed pictures of Whittier, Longfellow, Holmes and Emerson. None of these men expressed anything distinctively American. They were not motivated by the life in which they lived.

Whitman came, a windy, gusty, sweet singer but his voice was not heard.

Followed Poe and such men as Bret Harte and Howells.

To the modern man there seems in all of these men except the young Whitman a kind of death. They were like men living and working in a vacuum. O. Henry was in the same mood.

Twain broke away. He wrote Huckleberry Finn but they caught him and suppressed him. Boston and respectability put him to sleep.

What went on in writing went on in all of the arts. One might have thought that life in our own towns and cities meant nothing. It did not mean much.

The fear was on us still. We had an inferiority complex.

Fear of what England would think, of what Germany and France would think. The arts are for older peoples. Younger peoples should be seen and not heard. It was not so very long ago that the most second-rate of English novelists, coming to our shores, was met down the bay by representatives of all the big metropolitan newspapers. "What do you think of us? What do you think of America?"

People everywhere reading what such men had to say as though it mattered. If we have been brutally patronized by many such men it was our own fault. We surely laid ourselves open.

We have begun getting a somewhat different feeling in America now. Of course we still bend the knee some but not as abjectly as we did. We are beginning to build our own cities, love our own towns, respect ourselves as artists and as a people. When I was a boy there used to be a saying, "when he dies every good American goes to Paris." Now he goes to New York and I don't blame him. It's a better town, more majestic, terrible and wonderful.

San Francisco is something too and New Orleans and Boston and Chicago.

What has helped more than anything else is the dying out of the old belief, held so strenuously by the so-called Fathers, and carrying on through all the middle period and until well after the Civil War, the belief that in America all the problems of mankind were to be solved because this was a special God-made country, inhabited only by men up to a special mission to show mankind how to solve their problems.

You can't get over that belief until you have artists who spring up naturally in a country, who get their inspiration as storytellers, painters, singers and builders, out of the life of their own country and the people directly about them.

Artists who look upon themselves as men with missions are, of course, pests but they are poor enough artists if they do not serve a purpose indirectly.

Believing in the life directly about them, these men begin to give it forth so that all may love a little and believe.

My notion is that things do not begin at the top and work down. Things work the other way. My own life begins in the house in which I live. It goes from that out into the street, begins a little to comprehend the life of the street, of many streets, of a town, a city.

What nonsense for me to say I love my country if I do not love my own house, my own street, my own town. If I am not interested in the life of the neighbor across the fence I am not interested in life at all. Living, emotionally and imaginatively, in Europe or in some place far away, living in books or pictures primarily, I am nothing. When I want to reform or change the life about me, because of some fancied superiority in myself, I am a pest and a bad citizen.

Personally I think that America is getting somewhere and has been getting somewhere in my time. I like it here. The Puritans, the Reformers, are still with us but they are on the defensive now.

We get on. To-day, in America, no man does good work in the arts without it being recognized as good work. He may not be widely acclaimed but good work never was very widely acclaimed very quickly anywhere.

We get enough. Being Americans we are lucky dogs. It may not be any special merit in ourselves that we live in the most prosperous country in the world, in what is perhaps its most prosperous period, but I am not one who dislikes the good things of life because I do not deserve them. I rather like things better for not deserving them.

I may not deserve to be an American, in America, in 1928, but I'm surely glad I am one.

JOE

FIRST WEEK OF

APRIL

The Gypsies

NEWS

They lie and steal, they laugh and sing. The morality of modern society means nothing to them. But they have their own morality. Who ever heard of a gypsy woman going on the town. The gypsy woman sticks to her man. She will lie and steal for him. She obeys her lord.

And so the gypsies came to town on Wednesday. Nowadays they do not drive bony old horses but drive cars and it is said are as slick in fixing up and trading an old car as they formerly were in getting rid of an old spavined horse. The women ran about, telling "dukkerin," which in the gypsy tongue means telling fortunes and the men were trying to get on a trade.

But night was coming on and knowing that, with gypsies in town at night, nothing was very safe, Rush Hayes escorted them out of town.

He escorted them out along the highway as far as the bridge, this side the railroad station and left them.

They did not get out of town at once though. They went over to see Tom Wassum, at the Peery Grocery Company. "Give us some candy for our children," one of the gypsy women said, and Tom gave her some.

She said she wanted to show her gratitude. Gratitude indeed. Did ever gypsy feel gratitude toward a gorgio. She pretended to drop a nickel into Tom's purse but really slipped out a twenty dollar bill.

And so they faded away and were on the road when Tom missed the twenty. He told Rush Hayes who, calling a citizen to help, got in a car and lit out after them. He overtook them and got Tom's twenty back. It was that or go to jail and work and what gypsy wants to work.

The daffodils in Mrs. Robert Goolsby's side yard look like young girls tripping down the lawn over the green grass these days. When I woke up Sunday morning and, looking out, saw a snowstorm raging I shivered with dread thinking of what might happen to them. By noon the snow was all gone and there they were, as fine as ever.

To lunch at Mrs. Wolfe's boarding house with our county agent. The best traditions of Virginia cooking. Ate myself into a coma. Afterwards walked about with Andy Funk and got caught in a rain. Saw giants and fairies and fawns dancing on top of Stayley's Knob. Saw a new pink house against the clear green light of the western sky. Andy said it wasn't pink. He spent the time bragging about his mechanical knowledge.

Snowy Nights

A PIECE

I don't so often wish I were rich but sometimes I do. I am always seeing things I want—fast red automobile, a grand house to live in. I would like a string of running horses. Also I would keep a few fast trotters and pacers.

I would like to wear silks. Once I had a grand idea. You know how the performers dress at the Grand Opera in the cities. Kingly robes. I thought I would go and get me a lot of second-hand kingly robes and wear them about. Wouldn't I look grand going down Marion's Main Street in a kingly robe?

If I could only have remained always about thirty-three or thirty-four. A lot of people talk of being tired of life. I am not tired of it. It makes me sick to think I can't go banging about for the next three hundred years.

Watching the show—watching the wheels go round.

You know that negro song, "There is a wheel, within a wheel, away up yonder in the sky."

I like to walk around trying to think why people do as they do, why some are what is called, "good" and others what is called, "bad."

On Sunday night, the 17th of March, year of our Lord, 1928. The town was very quiet and still. It had been snowing all day and all the night before.

The snow began with a rain, wetting everything thoroughly, so that the snow, when it came, all stuck.

It was still snowing when I set out from my house. The world was white.

In my mind a line, just snatched out of a book of poems I had been reading. The book by Miss Marjorie Meeker of Columbus, Ohio.

"This wary winter that was white so long."

Winter of life, eh.

"This wary winter that was white so long."

I kept saying the words over to myself as I walked, loving them.

Loving too the memory I had of the woman who wrote the lines. I saw her once sitting in her big fine house.

Every one who lives here knows how white and beautiful that Sunday night was in Marion, Virginia.

I walked out Main Street to where the houses end to the east and then back again, through town to where they end at the west.

It may have been rather late. There was no one abroad. When I had got out west of town I climbed over a fence into a field.

A few people driving closed cars on the highway. The lights of the cars were nice, playing over the fields and among the branches of trees.

Every limb and twig of the trees outlined in white.

I wishing suddenly and crazily for a horse to ride, a white clean-limbed galloping horse. Thinking of that old painter Rider's galloping horse in the mysterious night. Have you ever seen that painting?

"This wary winter that was white so long."

A white horse, galloping across fields, in and out of white forests.

Or a sleigh with a fine team of trotters or pacers hitched to it, eh.

Such a team as I once drove but never owned. Fiery boys they were.

I was working for their owner then—a mere groom—not a proud editor as I am now. Alas, you see, there is no aristocratic blood in me.

Once, on just such another wonder night as that of last Sunday, the owner of that team was away from home. In the barn there was a sleigh with white swan's heads thrust out in front.

I was in love with a little country girl just at that time.

And so, on that night, I stole the team and the sleigh out of the barn, not putting on the sleigh bells, not wanting any one to hear and tell my boss.

Fiery blacks, the team were. The owner was a grand man, such a man as I would like some day to be but can't quite cut it.

I had managed to slip the team out of town and presently there I was, in the country before a farmhouse, the house in which that girl lived. I hallooed to her. She came out to my call but her father came too. He said she couldn't go.

The whole world was white that night. There must have been something white and swift and nice in me, in the team and in the girl. There were warm robes in the sleigh.

So the girl stood in tears on the porch of the house. Growling her father went inside. I said nothing and the girl said nothing.

Suddenly she made a little run down to me and climbed into the sleigh. Her face was white like the night. "Quick," she said and we drove off.

That was a ride. Once the black horses ran away. We were crossing a bridge. The sound of their own hoofs on the floor of the bridge frightened them. I let them run until they were tired of it but did manage to keep them in the road and the sleigh right side up.

And so my country girl and I rode in the white night like a prince and a princess—in the grand manner. What the father said to her when I took her home I don't know. You may be sure I avoided him. I got one cold quick kiss in the darkness before the house and lit out.

And the man who owned the fine horses never knew. It was a lucky night for me.

"This wary winter that was white so long."

Wanting my youth back, of course. Walking in the white night in that field that Sunday night every little bush and weed stood up straight and white. The sky was bluish black overhead.

Thinking of youth, wanting my own youth to go on and on a long long time I began thinking how our town might be more gay.

It was then I wanted to be rich. "If I were only rich," I cried. Plans began to form in my mind. I would buy me a huge old house with a garden here in Marion.

The house would have big rooms all with big open fires for cold nights and there would be a swimming pool in the garden back of the house.

I would publish my two Marion papers in rooms at the front of the house.

And I would have a library with many books and a place to dance and the Marion Band would come and play for the dances on a Saturday night.

And there would be quiet nooks in the house and in the garden for old people to sit and for lovers.

And it would all be free.

And country people would come into town for the fun, and city people would come here to see us. I could think of many people I would like to have come.

Now and then perhaps a poet or a singer or a painter to spend a few days.

And I would walk around like a lord, and edit my papers and dance with the pretty girls and wear the loudest clothes I could buy and stay young forever.

If I were only rich now.

All of this in my head as I walked in that field and in the white road and no one abroad but myself and saying over and over to myself those words of the poet . . .

"This wary winter that was white so long."

SECOND WEEK OF

APRIL

Town Notes

I was in the office of another Virginia editor when he drifted in. He was a man of about fifty years of age with a gray beard and looked as though he had been drinking. Evidently he had spent the night sleeping in some barn.

"Have you any work for a good job printer?" he asked. "No," the editor said. He explained that job work was pretty scarce now. The old print sat down in a chair beside the editor's desk. He was chewing at an unlighted cigar. His eyes looked bloodshot.

He began to talk. He introduced his own subject for conversation. "I was a job printer in this section during the Civil War," he said.

"During the Civil War?" the editor asked. He winked at me when the man wasn't looking. He was a cheerful seeming man. He turned and smiled. "Yes," he said. "I was here when Lee came through."

"It was that time when he captured Abraham Lincoln. You'll remember that," he said, turning to me. "Oh, yes," I said. There was a picture of Abraham Lincoln on the editor's wall and beside it one of Lee. "They haven't changed so much, have they?" the old print said, getting up and going to look at the pictures.

"When Abraham Lincoln was Lee's captive we thought he looked a little thin. Lee was in a hurry," he said, "and to make time had tied Lincoln to his horse's tail. He had a rope around Lincoln's neck and the other end of the rope tied to the horse's tail."

The old print said that at that time there was a town pump in the street just before the place where the print-shop now stood. There was a pump and a horse trough. Lee hadn't any army with him. He looked tired and Lincoln looked tired, too. Lee had told the old print that his army was somewhere behind him. Lincoln, he said, had such long legs and took such long strides that he was always stepping on the horse's heels.

There was the horse, trying to keep out of Lincoln's way and Lincoln trying to keep up with the horse. They had lost the army and the heels of Lee's horse were all raw and sore. The old print sighed when he spoke of it.

"Was it Lee's famous horse?" I asked. "Yes, old Ironsides," he said. The editor got up and went away. "Here's one of your own sort," he said. The old print did not seem to mind his going, or his comment as he went.

The old print chewed away at his unlighted cigar and explained life in Virginia towns in the early days. "The boys were always playing long ball along the roads," he said. Long ball was a game played with cannon balls, he explained. Boys rolled them along the road. "There were lots of big boys in this country then," he said.

He remarked that every print-shop then had a half-dozen negro boys, slaves, in it. They were there to wait on the prints. They lighted cigars for them, handed them their hats, when they came in or went out the door. They kept the type lice off the type.

"But where were you before that?" I asked. He said it was difficult for him to remember all the places he had been. He remembered one place where he used to sing in a church choir. "I had a lovely tenor voice once." He gave me a sample of his voice. He sang *Jesus Saviour of my soul, let me to Thy bosom fly* in a loud, husky voice.

The print-shop in which we were sitting, in a neighboring Virginia town, has the editor's room separated from the shop by a partition made of glass. A young man was working at a lino-type machine and another at a small job press. The editor was walking up and down waiting for my visitor to go. They all stopped working to hear the song. The man at the lino-type and the fellow at the job press were grinning. When I turned to look they waved their hands at me.

The print began telling of an experience he had before the Mexican War. He said that war with Mexico was in the air. The North didn't want it much and the South did. "I am a Southern man myself," he said. He said that the great, the controlling impulse of his life was got just at that time.

He had enlisted, it seemed, in the army and with a lot of other men had been sent down to camp on the shores of the Sabine

River. That was in what is now Texas. "It was lovely down there but rather dull," he said.

There they were, the American soldiers, on the Sabine River, on the borders of what was then Mexico, so long ago. The men used to fish in the river all day long. There were little clumps of woods along the river and an abundance of game.

There was an old man, an American, who had a house on the shore of the river and before the soldiers came he lived there all alone. He was like the old print—that is to say he was an intellectual. He had, the old print said, gone off down there to live so he could have time to read books and to think.

Of course he and the print got in thick. When the others went off to hunt or fish or when they were just wandering over the wide green landscape the print and the recluse would get a book and go into the wood on the river shore and read aloud to each other, he explained.

"We would read and discuss all day," he said. "First he would read a sentence and we would discuss that, then I would read one and there would be some more discussion." The print said that he felt that most of his later intellectual development had its inception at that time. He said he could just feel his mind growing.

And he had got a great moral impulse too, just at that time. One day he was lying in the wood, on the shore of the Sabine, just as described, and the recluse, the intellectual recluse, was beside him. It was the print's turn to read aloud. A book was in his hand. He read a sentence. He said that he had never had such a feeling before. The words, he said, fairly burned themselves into his brain. "I have never forgotten them," he said. As a matter of fact they had been at the bottom of all his actions since that day. "Do right and fear no man," were the words he read. He said he had never done a wrong since.

"They were the making of me, those words," the old print said, getting up. He asked me if I could let him have a dollar and I did of course. He put it in his pocket. "Thanks," he said, "since that day on the shore of the Sabine I have feared no man."

He went out and the editor came back into his office. I asked him about the incident of Abraham Lincoln, tied to the tail of Lee's horse, and he laughed heartily. "I am just curious about one thing," I said. "I am curious to know if there ever was a town pump out there." I pointed into the busy street. "There was," the editor said. "There was a town pump and a horse trough, and the boys used to play a game called long ball in the road." "But that was long before our time," the editor said.

Small Town Note

There is a bachelor who lives in a small house on a certain street in a certain American town. He is a photographer, a long thin man with a big Adam's apple.

The ideal of his life is to be a professional ball player. He has never in his life played baseball, in fact has always been rather a sickly man.

He however takes two or three daily papers and reads nothing but the sporting pages. In the winter, when there is no baseball gossip in the papers, or very little, he is desolated.

He knows all of the players in all the leagues by name and can tell you their records. He lives in a town some two hundred miles from the nearest city in which he can see big league baseball, but during the year he saves enough to go to the city several times.

It happened that I was in his town writing advertisements for a manufacturer. We wanted some photographs taken and I went to see the man in the evening at his house. Some one told me where it was.

He did not know I was coming. It was a little house on a side street. There was a small lawn in front. I was crossing the lawn when I heard a voice.

The man was in his house alone and had become in fancy a ball player. I saw what happened through a window. The man was squatting, with his hands on his knees, in the living room of his house. He had become a shortstop and was all alert. I dare say some one like Babe Ruth was at bat. When the man had gone to the city to see the professionals play he had noted how the infielders kept talking to each other.

"Now, Ed. Careful now, Ed. Watch him, Ed!" I heard the photographer cry. He spoke sharply to the pitcher. "Get it over the plate, Bill!" he cried.

It was evident the batter had made a hit. "There he goes! Quick! Quick!" he cried.

It must have been a double play. I saw him dash across the room for second base. He had knocked over a chair on the way but he did not care. He had made the play.

I saw him receive the ball and throw to first. There was an intent look in his eyes. Would the ball get to first ahead of the runner? It did. "Ah," I heard him sigh with relief.

It goes without saying that I went away and returned on the next day to see him about taking the photographs we wanted.

Small Town Note

A man taught school in a town where I once lived. When he was a boy he was not very strong.

He lived in a street with several tough boys.

There was a boy used to lay for him and beat him. He made no resistance. The boy hit him in the face. "Hit me again," he said. The boy did. He kept saying it and the boy kept hitting him.

He got married later. How it happened no one apparently knew. His wife was large and strong. She was a handsome woman.

She bullied him. When he left the house in the evening she said, "You be home at eight o'clock, sharp." He always was.

The men of the town used to laugh at him and he joined in the laughter. Whenever any of the men of the town proposed anything to him, a fishing trip or perhaps a poker party, he said, "I don't dare, my wife won't let me."

You would have thought the wife would have hated such a man. When they walked along the street together she always walked a little in front.

He told every one he was afraid of his wife, boasted of his fear of her.

Once a neighbor told me that when the two were alone together, sitting together on the porch of their house in the darkness of the summer evening (they had no children), she used to take him into her arms sometimes and rock back and forth in a rocking chair, as though he were a small child.

The neighbor said that the wife, who had the reputation of being a bully, was in reality one of the saddest people he had ever seen, and that she was in fact a very gentle woman.

THIRD WEEK OF

APRIL

Will Culbert of Marion, Va.

"But where do rocks come from?"

"Why, don't you know? Rocks grow."

"I never seen any grow. I never seen one a-growen."

"I never seen one a-growen neither, but they grow all the same. You pick up all the rocks off this here hill and in a year there's as many out again. I lay there'll be a stack to pick up right here again next year."

"I can't seem to think it. Rocks a-growen now. They don't seem alive. They seem dead like. Maybe they've got another kind of way to be alive."

"Maybe they have. All I know is they grow."

"Rocks have got shells printed on the sides and some have little snails worked on their edges and some have got little worms like worked on them. But once I found a spider with a dragon beast in a picture on its back. Some rocks, now, are shaped like little silos and some are all marked with little snails and waterbugs and some are open fans and some have little scollops on the edges. Rocks grow in ways that are right pretty now. It's a wonder, really."

"I wish I could see a rock grow," she said again. "I can't think how it is. You could watch a rock for a whole year and you'd never see any sign of it growen."

Elizabeth Madox Roberts—in, "The Time of Man."

A man's life is a strange thing. There is Mr. W. F. Culbert of Marion. He isn't young any longer now. A delicate sensitive looking man dealing with the stones that come out of the ground.

From any hill about town you can see the great gash in the hill where he has been taking out rocks for twenty-five years now, in that one spot.

It has made a great hole. Go up into it some day. There will be men working in the quarry high up there on the hillside. Above the men the hill goes up and up all solid rock. The men look small, like flies up there. A man is shoveling stone into a little car. It seems like the old woman, trying to dip the water out of the sea with a teacup.

But a man can do a lot during a life by sticking to it. A college man, who I presume knew what he was talking about, said that not more than one man out of a hundred ever used more than about 20 per cent of his possible energy.

A man can dig a great hole in solid rock, he can make money and he can build a character. Mr. Will Culbert has done all of these things. He is one of the most respected men in our town. Men feel him like a rock hill, a little gray, strong and honest.

It wasn't much of a start he had. He came from over in East Tennessee, was a Royal Carter man. When he was a boy, just after the Civil War, there wasn't but one Democratic vote in his whole district.

They believed what they believed, those East Tennesseans. It wasn't easy, before the Civil War and right afterwards—for a man to be a republican in the South. Andrew Johnson, who was Vice President in Lincoln's second term, and President after his death, came from over there.

And he was a sturdy man too. History has never done him justice. Lord Charnwood, the famous English biographer of Lincoln, says, that after Lincoln's death, Johnson was the only man in government who did keep his head.

And came near getting impeached for keeping it too. It's hard luck being a wise man when all the rest of the world decide to be fools.

Will Culbert when he was a boy used to walk bare-footed along a country road past the big fine farm and house Andrew Johnson built after he got through being President. "I am going to own that farm and that house some day," Will said to himself. He did too. That is the strange part of it.

At that time there were iron foundries all through this country and over in East Tennessee and for the iron foundries they had to have charcoal. Will became a charcoal burner in the hills. He was helping burn charcoal as soon as he could walk and at sixteen became an independent burner over at Ore Knob in North Carolina.

He worked at that for a time and then worked on the railroad. Then he decided to go west.

The far west was calling and calling to young men in those days. Will had to work his way through the west too.

He went slowly along from state to state, working, saving his money and then going on until he got into the far western mining country.

It was a wild country in those days. That will be nearly forty years ago now. Mining towns, flush with gold, great copper mines being opened up.

The towns full of eastern men gone west and gone bad too. All restraint was shaken off. There were gambling houses along the main streets of all the towns, the dance halls were thick, men reeled through the streets drunk, prostitutes abounded, men quarreled and shot each other. At nights the town was noisy with profanity and the sound of brutal revelry.

And Will walked straight in all that too. He went to see it all, looked at it all and made up his own mind what kind of a man he wanted to be. There is a kind of iron and stone quality to Will Culbert. He may have got it into him out there.

Three years of that and then home. When he was at work in a mine near Anaconda—the famous Marcus Daly mining town—a great stone slid down on him and nearly crushed him. His leg was broken in two places and the bones of his chest crushed in.

They carried him in a spring wagon twenty-six miles over deserts and mountains to Anaconda and he tells how a few days later a miner came in and poured a handful of gold on the bed. It was the money made up by his fellow miners to see him through the trouble. They must have liked Will even if he didn't carouse with them.

When Will Culbert came back into this country he went to work on railroad work, helping make the grade for the Clinch Valley Railroad. That led him into quarry work to get commercial stone for grading—at first under a contractor and then independently, on his own.

Mr. Culbert has had various quarries, at Big Stone Gap, at Clinchfield, Ga., Foster Fall, near Wytheville, and finally near Marion, starting here with the old quarry on the Henry Copenhaver place.

He has been taking stone out of one quarry now for twenty-five years and if you want to know how much he has taken out go up some day and see. It is a thing to stir you, standing up there in that great hole and knowing what one man has done.

As for the quarry at Marion, now owned by Mr. Culbert, it has perhaps the largest straight deposit of high grade calcium carbonate stone in America. For years vast quantities of it have been used by the Mathieson Alkali Works at Saltville and for eight years they worked the quarry on a royalty plan.

Besides the quarry at Marion Mr. Culbert has developed other high grade stone deposits, one at Clinchfield, Ga., afterwards sold to the Clinchfield Portland Cement Co., and others in various parts of the country.

And all handled capably. A stone man, knowing as much of stone perhaps as any living man.

And a good man too. A man who has built a character while he was building a fortune and making that great hole in the solid rock that tells you whenever you look at it what one man of character and perseverance can do.

The Black Hole of Marion

EDITORIAL

This town of Marion, situated as it is in the very heart of one of the most lovely stretches of country this correspondent has ever seen—a fair town in a fair valley with softly rounded hills about it and full of good people, has in it a black hole that makes the nerves shudder to contemplate.

I refer to our county jail. It is a veritable pest hole. Go into it some day. Look about you. See what the prisoners in our jail are up against.

Well, you may answer, it is a place for criminals.

Not quite that. I myself was raised in a poor family. It was a family of boys. At a tender age we had to get out and scratch gravel. One of my younger brothers—he is dead now—went eastward from our middle western country town, seeking work in one of the factories of the east. He had little money when he set out and had to beat his way on freight trains. Many a mile have I myself traveled in that way.

The point is that in a New York town he was arrested for vagrancy and kept in just such a pest hole as is maintained by Smyth County and he was kept there for over two weeks.

He didn't want to send home for money because there was no money to spare at home.

Once, at Marion, Ohio, I was myself arrested as a suspect in connection with a diamond robbery. I had never heard of the robbery until the moment I was arrested. Some of our county officials may wonder why my sympathies are always with the man in trouble. The men at Marion, Ohio, sat and shouted at me. "You lie and you know you lie." I got out of that because, at that time, I had risen a bit in the world and had some friends.

To return to our county jail. Do not blame our county officials for the hole. There are two rooms downstairs and one up. Mr. and Mrs. Hopkins are doing mighty well with what they have to work with. The prisoners like and trust them. Our jailer and his wife are both kindly human beings.

There are two rooms downstairs and one up. One of the downstairs' rooms is for women prisoners. It has two little cubby-hole windows and an open toilet, right in the open room. The women prisoners must sleep, eat and make all of their toilet arrangements in the one open room. Hardened women prisoners, syphilitics, tuberculars, dopes, etc., must go right in with the rest. Very often young girls are confined in the place.

Remember that not all the prisoners thrown into jail in a county seat town are guilty. Many are merely suspect. They are cleared when they come to trial.

Of course they are let out on bail if a responsible bondsman can be found but suppose you are poor and unknown.

And now let us go into the men and boys' department. The law provides that these prisoners are to be kept in cages. The cages are some eighteen feet long by fifteen feet wide. In one of these cages at the present time there are eleven men. Some of them have been in there, they tell me, for months, twelve months one of them. There is one open toilet in the cage and no bathing facilities. The boys tell me that at this time there is a syphilitic in there. They must use all of the facilities for bare brutal living he uses. A tubercular case may be thrown in at any time. If there is no one to offer bail, guilty or innocent, he must stay until his case can be brought up in court. You know about the delay of courts. Suppose the delay went on while you waited in there.

Day after day no place to exercise, diseased men, criminals, etc., in there with you. Eleven of you in a little cage eighteen feet long. Step it off on your parlor floor. Eleven of you in there jammed together, mind you.

In a cage upstairs the same condition. The state delaying about coming and getting men already committed to the penitentiary.

A few boys and men, in for minor offenses, wandering about the narrow room outside. Boys are put in there from the age of twelve years up.

It would sear your soul if you went to see it.

Oh, of course, it would raise taxes a bit if the county built a decent jail with decent toilet arrangements, a place to isolate diseased cases, a bit of a yard for exercise and a peep at the sun.

They have such places in penitentiaries, where men, convicted of crimes, go.

And don't be so sure you or your boy won't get in there. A prominent young man was thrown in there recently for being drunk and disorderly. It can happen to any one any time.

The county that permits such conditions to go on is as guilty as the men who commit the crimes and are thrown in there for committing them.

To Drive 100 Hours Without Stopping

NEWS

The exhibition will take place on the streets of Marion starting on Tuesday, the twenty-fourth. A driver will be sealed into a car which is not to stop running night or day for 100 hours.

Gas and oil must be taken while the car is in motion, if there is a puncture the tire must be changed without stopping the car.

The exhibition is an endurance driving test to be put on in Marion and will be a severe test to car and man.

Dooney Hester, an old Marion boy who has been through several of these tests, will put the exhibition on. It will start from in front of the Court House at eleven in the morning on Tuesday and end at three Saturday at the Sprinkle Motor Company, Chevrolet headquarters.

FOURTH WEEK OF

APRIL

Henry Mencken Park in Marion

A TOWN EYESORE

Since we have been editing the two Marion papers and all the time getting better and better acquainted with the town we have been hoping that something would be done with what we have from time to time called "Mencken Park."

It is the prize eyesore of the town. Standing as it does just back of the courthouse, with a green pleasant lawn in front, this lot is at present occupied by a building that would make a poor excuse for a cow shed.

The building itself is used to house the town machinery. In the yard beside it are piles of sand and crushed stone, iron pipe, empty tar barrels and other junk. Since we have been here we must say that Mr. W. H. Wheeler, the street commissioner, and his helpers have been very nice about keeping the place as orderly as is possible.

It cannot be made a very pleasant place while it is used for its present purpose.

And it has seemed to us that another place, not so conspicuous, might well be found for this stuff.

Having something of the sort in mind this editor recently made a proposal, in a conversation with some of his friends. He proposed that, if the town council would find some other place for the stuff now kept in this conspicuous place, he, or these papers, would spend some money to try and make this little plot of ground more pleasant and agreeable to the town.

Already some of our citizens are having pleasant hours in the park pitching horse shoes. It was the notion of this editor that if the town would clear this space and give permission, this editor would level off the little park, put green benches about it and perhaps a strip of lawn around it and some shade trees.

If the papers cannot pay for it then I'll write a story for some magazine and pay for it that way. It would be a more worthy cause than most of the story writers are up to most of the time.

It is our understanding that Mr. Charles Funk put this idea up to the Kiwanis Club but there was some misunderstanding. They seemed to think we were talking about a children's playground and the town, it seems, already has one.

And anyway the place isn't large enough for that.

We were thinking about a pleasant place, here in the very heart of town, instead of an eyesore. The present place is in full sight from Main Street. It gives a bad impression of the town. Incidentally a good many visitors come to this office—about every one in the county at some time during the year. A lot of outside people come here too.

If the town wants to take us up on this we are ready to put up for our part of the job. What do you say, town council?

Dooney Hester Still at It

NEWS

He went whizzing past the shop this morning looking as we used to look on many a morning, before we became an editor and therefore virtuous.

That is to say—looking a little bung eyed. Even in our palmiest days we never were on a hundred hour drive but once up in Wisconsin. Marco Morrow and Frank Dunn of the Topeko Capital and the Chicago Journal will remember.

But this isn't a confession. It is but to say that Dooney Hester, in a Chevrolet, is still at it, making his 100 hour drive and burning up the good Texaco gas.

He started on Tuesday morning, April 24th at 11 A.M., and will finish, in front of the Sprinkle Motor Company next Saturday at 3 P.M.

Marvin Anderson, who seems to be the Tex Rickard of this drive, tells us that rain washed off all of the signs painted on the car during the first night of driving and that water-proof signs—imported by airplane from Waterproof, Louisiana—were put on to take their places.

On Saturday, starting at 1 P.M., an ambulance containing a doctor, a nurse and Tex (Marvin) Anderson will begin to follow the driver.

Dooney is being given two massages daily by Mr. M. C. Ham, of the Curtis Beauty Parlors. That sounds more like one of our parties I must say.

Doctor A. B. Graybeal is taking care of the driver.

When he has finished the drive he will be put to sleep, we understand, in some one's show window—it isn't yet decided whose. We doubt whether he will have to be "put to sleep." He ought to just "go."

That time I was speaking about we put Frank Dunn to sleep in a barn and a farm hand inadvertently ran a pitchfork through his leg, but that is neither here nor there.

Don't miss the grand final. In front of Sprinkle Motor Company show room on Saturday at three.

Brains and Morals

EDITORIAL

The whole object of education is, or should be, to develop mind. The mind should be a thing that works. It should be able to pass judgment on events as they arise, make decisions.

There have been few enough good minds in the history of the world.

People have mind confused with learning. There have been more learned fools than wise ones.

Many people develop one sort of brain. For example, the man who can make money and is a fool in other things is not quite a fool. He isn't a fool about money.

And that is important. The trouble is that a one-sided man makes it too important. He judges everything by a money standard and gets everything crooked.

And morals also are largely a matter of brains. We are all driven through life by lusts. Why deny it. There is sex lust, food lust, lust for luxuries, for power.

The man with good brains simply recognizes his lusts as a part of his life and tries to handle them.

If he is an artist he tries to divert the energy arising from his lusts into channels of beauty. If he has any brains he knows what he is doing. Every artist worth his salt has always been full of lusts. Pretty little poets, lady authors, etc., may have no lusts but they remain "pretty."

Your son goes and gets drunk. He raises the very devil, perhaps smashes his automobile and is lucky if he escapes killing some one. You crowd repentance on him. Try to make him think he has disgraced you forever. Well why did he do it?

To be sure he was driven on by some kind of excess energy within himself and the chances are he did not have brains enough to direct his energy. Life grew dull to him. He was bored, wanted excitement. The trouble with most of your moral preachments is that you become a bore when you are getting them off.

And you are insincere, too. Your own lusts may just take another form. You eat, not like a man but like an animal.

Or you have a lust for money or power. To get it you will do anything. You see plenty of such men—in politics for example.

Men who will lie, cheat, steal, sell out their friend—politically, and who in other walks of life are fair enough men.

Well, that is just a form of lust too. It is political drunkenness. There are various kinds of drunkenness in this world.

The man of brains has found out that he has to adjust himself to life and most of all to himself. Take the matter of drink. I should think the man of sense would see it as not a moral question at all.

It is a matter of good sense. If a man cannot drink without making a fool of himself and hurting others he should let drink alone.

He should let alone anything he can't handle.

Few men ever get far enough with the development of mind to quite realize there is one thing they have to stay with always, as long as they live—that is themselves.

A man may move to a new town, get a new wife, a new house, a new suit of clothes. He is still himself.

I have myself learned to look at my body as a house in which I must live until I die. I want it to be a fairly clean, comfortable house. I do not like making a muss in the house. I have to sleep there. My thoughts dwell there.

If I let my body get too gross, if I gobble too much food, drink too much, get too fat, my house is an uncomfortable place in which to live.

I do not like it nor do I like myself.

To be sure there is a challenge in all this. Keep your house as clean as you can. Wash the windows and the doorsills. You cannot live well in a filthy place.

And do not be sick. The sick man is more than half a rascal. He may only be sick because he hasn't the courage to clean house. Many sick people are bullies—they use sickness as a club to beat others.

The house is a body in which the mind, the spirit and the imagination must dwell until we die. A little decent paganism wouldn't hurt most of us. We ought to try to be a bit less mixed about morals and a bit more clear about mind.

A little more decent faith in the house in which we live—the house that is the body—less thinking about death and more about living, more self-respect.

If that be paganism make the most of it.

W. F. CULBERT

TOM GREER

FIRST WEEK OF

MAY

~~~~

Uneasy Job

NEWS

Jerry Smith, a colored man, has been living on a certain strip of land over on Walker's Mountain. This particular piece of land is under controversy as regards its ownership.

It is a piece of land we wouldn't want to live on.

Jerry Smith, we are told, has been shot at several times.

Tom Flannigan shot at him and I guess hit him too. He was brought up in court on Monday morning on the charge of felonious assault and plead guilty. He got two years. That ought to ease Jerry Smith's night sleep for a while. No reason given. Sounds like Coon Hollow.   BUCK

Daring Dooney Gets Done

In spite of the terrible weather of last Friday night Daring Dooney finished his 100-mile endurance test drive in good shape. In fact, he ran some over seven minutes overtime.

To see the finish of the drive a crowd of several hundred people gathered at the Sprinkle Motor Company show rooms and in the street outside. Boys climbed upon buildings and men and women struggled to get closer.

189

As for us, we were perfectly willing to stay in the background. We never did specially enjoy seeing a man do himself up.

It is hard to see how a man could have picked a worse time for a drive. Here it was, almost the first of May. All day Thursday it rained. Then on Friday afternoon it began to snow.

As the night wore on the snow came thicker and thicker. At one time, during the night, the fall of snow was so heavy and blinding that it was impossible to see the electric lights on Main Street.

Do you remember Joaquin Miller's famous poem, "Columbus"?

The good ship sailed into the night.
Beyond him not the ghost of shores,
Beyond him only shoreless seas.
"What shall we do?" the sailors said.
The captain cried, "Sail on, sail on."

After Dooney had finished his drive a crowd followed him to the Hotel Marion, where he was put to bed. As nearly as we can learn no one got into bed with him.

He slept. No question about that. Dr. Graybeal came in and looked him over several times, and Mr. Ham of the Curtis Beauty Parlor came and gave him an electric massage.

Then they let him sleep until that night when they woke him up and gave him some soft-boiled eggs.

Back to sleep again until noon Sunday. He got up and sat down to table. Rumor has it he ate a whole turkey. Well, well. With all these beauty treatments Dooney ought to be making a hit somewhere these days.

"What do you want?" some one asked him when he woke up, after sleeping some twenty-four hours. "Something to eat," he said, "and then I think I'll take a little drive."

There are people in this world who never know when they have enough.

During the drive Mr. Hester drove 1342 miles up and down the same road. To prove what? God knows.

SECOND WEEK OF

MAY

O. K. Harris Free

A MURDER TRIAL

O. K. Harris, a gray-haired man of fifty, shot a man of sixty, named Sult, at the little railroad station at Groseclose near Marion late on an October Friday afternoon. Sult was accused of trying to start an affair with Harris' daughter. The girl had run off to Chicago with another man some months before· but had been brought home.

Harris went to the little country railroad station with his wife. Sult was standing there. Mrs. Harris went into a store and Harris approached Sult. There were some words, no one else heard, then Sult turned and ran. Harris followed, pouring shots into Sult's back. Sult fell down dead.

Not Guilty

Marked by five of the most brilliant speeches ever heard in Smyth County, the O. K. Harris murder case went to the jury at eleven-forty on Thursday morning.

The five speeches were all well thought out and delivered. W. R. D. Moncure was unemotional, a clearly thought out setting forth of the weakness of the defense and the strength of the Commonwealth.

Mr. George Cook was shrewd, emotional, eloquent. As he talked tears ran from his eyes.

Mr. John P. Buchanan was shrewd, smart, earnest, and his father, Senator B. F. Buchanan, was powerful. There was something of the old lion in the man, standing up there and pleading for Mr. Harris' life.

Perhaps the great speech of the day was that of Charles A. Funk, the prosecuting attorney for Smyth. It was logical, clearly thought out, put to the jury with simply tremendous force. Funk has grown during this trial. Because of the widespread sympathy with Mr. Harris the whole town and county is in a tense waiting mood. Every one sympathizes with the jury, too.

If ever twelve men faced a hard trying job these men did. The jury has come in. It is 2:40 P.M.—N O T G U I L T Y.

FIRST DAY

The trial of O. K. Harris, charged with murder, in the shooting of W. A. Sult, at Groseclose on Friday, October the 28th, began in Judge Stewart's Court on Monday. It was a wet, raw day and as many country people, who would ordinarily be busy at this time could not work, the court room was crowded.

There was some delay in getting started. Several jurors read themselves out of the case because they had conscientious scruples against the death penalty or because they had already discussed the case.

Mr. Harris is a fine looking man with a sensitive face and makes a good impression sitting in the court in his neat blue suit, with

snow white shirt and collar. His wife and daughters sit near
him. Buchanan and Buchanan and George Cook are the lawyers
for the defense, and W. R. D. Moncure and Prosecutor Funk are
representing the commonwealth.

For the case the defense has brought a court stenographer from
Roanoke, Mr. Victor Hugo Friend.

Mr. Hopkins, the jailer, is the dude of the court room. His silky
black mustache is the center of attraction.

The jurors in this case are: C. W. Lamie, T. F. Harjer, R. W.
Holmes, F. A. McCarroll, G. W. McNew, J. P. Bonham, M. T.
Pratt, J. B. Bonham, R. L. Rice, H. T. Lawson, J. T. Frazier, Jr.,
and Frank P. Moore.

In his opening Prosecutor Funk asked for a first degree conviction and Senator B. F. Buchanan presented the case for Mr.
Harris, indicating that the defense would be that Mr. Harris was
so upset and worried by his troubles that he was driven to the
act by a force within himself, an irresistible impulse he could not
control. He brought out the fact of the former escapade with
Joseph Deboe and spoke of anonymous letters and of other things
that kept Mr. Harris in a troubled, upset state of mind.

The first witnesses called by the Prosecution were: M. Medley
and James Anders, who identified the bloody shirt worn by Mr.
Sult the afternoon of the shooting. Dr. Huddle testified as to the
wounds and their location. Lilly Knoepfle did not see much and
said so. Roy Snavely, H. D. Simmerman, L. G. Welsh, Miss Silvia
Simmerman, L. I. Buck and Carl Walsh were all witnesses of the
tragedy. Geo. Gullion, deputy sheriff, made the arrest. Sheriff
Dillard, E. F. Sult of Wytheville, a brother of the dead man, said
his brother was sixty-one at the time of the killing.

With a simple presentation of the fact of the killing the prosecution rested and before court closed for the day one witness for the
defense, Mr. M. L. Harrison of Wytheville, was heard.

Mr. Harrison had no sooner begun to testify, telling of a conversation he had with Mr. Harris on a train after the Deboe affair, than a storm of protest broke forth from the attorneys for the commonwealth and the jury was led out of the room while the lawyers argued. In the end Mr. Harrison was allowed to give his testimony without the jury being present and under the protest of prosecution, the judge to decide during the night whether or not the testimony should be read to the jury.

SECOND DAY

The judge began the day by deciding against the introduction, by the defense, of all the matter concerned with Mr. Harris' troubles when his daughter went to Chicago with Deboe. The judge decided that all of this evidence was too remote. The defense is trying to prove that Harris went suddenly insane at the time Sult was killed. The judge held that, as he had appeared to be sane for two years after the Deboe affair what happened at that time could not be brought in.

Mrs. Harris was called and made a good cool-headed witness.

Miss Hazel Harris was called. She told about the letters sent her by Sult, while she was in school in Marion, and of her having told her father about the letters on the day of the killing.

G. W. Phillippi, from near Groseclose, was called and told about Harris' disturbed mental condition. Miss Annie Harris of Baltimore was called. Most of her testimony was thrown out by a ruling of the judge.

R. F. Parsons, E. W. Rhoades, R. C. Purcell and E. L. Byrd, all West Virginia friends of Mr. Harris, testified as to the man's changed mental condition after his troubles began. They told of his obsession with the subject, his constant weeping, talking aloud when alone, etc.

The testimony of the day closed with Mr. R. A. Anderson and

Mr. J. W. Sheffey of Marion and Mr. W. H. Hines, a deputy United States marshal—all of whom bore out the former testimony as to Mr. Harris' extreme agitation and mental disturbance as the day of the tragedy drew nearer.

THIRD DAY

The first witness called on Wednesday was Mr. H. B. Staley of Marion. Mr. Staley had known Mr. Harris for a long time and testified as to changes noted in him after the Deboe escapade.

Mr. J. A. Pruner, assistant postmaster at Marion, offered testimony to show Mr. Harris was much upset and distracted on the day of the tragedy.

J. D. Perkins saw him on the day of the tragedy. He thought Mr. Harris acted like an abnormal man.

He came to Lynn Copenhaver at the bank and talked of his troubles some two weeks before the killing. Mr. Copenhaver thought him abnormal.

Doctor C. Brown Cox of Marion Junior College saw Mr. Harris a few hours before the killing. He came to the college seeking information about a correspondence between the girl and Sult. The college knew nothing of such a correspondence, but Dr. Cox was glad to investigate. Mr. Harris would not take a seat in Dr. Cox's office. He stood and talked, "incoherently," Dr. Cox thought.

("Note it was after this conversation that Mr. Harris saw his daughter and apparently got a confession out of her as to her correspondence with Sult.")

Henry Box proved to be a relative of the defendant. The lawyers for the defense tried to get him to talk of the state of mind of the defendant over a long period. The court ruled the testimony out.

W. E. Copenhaver, a fine looking old man of eighty-five and a lifelong friend of defendant, spoke only as a character witness. He told of Mr. Harris' fine reputation as a man.

Dr. Wright, an important witness. Mr. Harris had been put under his observation at the state insane hospital shortly after his arrest. Dr. Wright thought that he was abnormal, particularly in an emotional way, when he came to the hospital. Could not stay on one subject, talked incoherently. Afterward, in the doctor's opinion, his difficulty cleared up.

On cross-examination the doctor testified that a man who, under emotional stress and with illusions of persecution, did such an act once might do it again.

The defense rested.

Rebuttal witness for the state.

Miss Ira Sprinkle was a stenographer in the office of Perkins and Funk. She was there when Mr. Harris came in, at the time Mr. Perkins had spoken of. She did not see anything abnormal or wrong with him.

Carl Davis of Groseclose. He went to Mr. Harris' house on the morning of the tragedy and arranged to buy some hogs. Then he went to Rural Retreat. After the tragedy, and knowing nothing of it, he returned to the Harris house and arranged about getting the hogs. He thought there was nothing abnormal about Mr. Harris.

Mr. M. C. Medley—called earlier to prove the crime. He saw nothing abnormal about Mr. Harris at the time of the tragedy.

Hope Hildreth, drug clerk at Rural Retreat. Mr. Harris came to the drug store to inquire about some medicine, designed to excite women, he believed Sult had got hold of and had given to his daughter.

Marvin Jones, telegraph operator at Groseclose. He saw Mr. Harris immediately after the tragedy. "Did he act abnormal?" Mr. Jones thought not.

The case is ready for the jury.

The verdict is, "not guilty."

THIRD WEEK OF
MAY

*The town has been deeply moved by the murder trial. Every-
thing else has seemed to stand still. Nothing else is spoken of on
the streets. The man accused had no case. Every one knew that.
Still he went free. Who is not glad of that?*

*During the trial the jurors came down at the noon hour and
pitched horseshoes before the print-shop. They came in the early
morning before the trial opened. How anxiously we watched their
faces.*

When the trial was over I fled to New York.

Exultation

Now I am in one of the New York literary hang-outs. How did
I get in here? There are leggy girls and women about. There is a
woman who knows me. She flies to me. Her eyes are shining. She
begins telling me, with obvious pleasure, that my friend, Mr. Theodore Dreiser, has been ill. "He is more than half dead," she says
happily.

There are other writers in the place. One of them rubs his hands
together. "Yes, yes, Dreiser. He is more than half dead. He is a
goner."

There is a young man present, the editor of a popular monthly.
He looks at me and I look at him. Well, well. A shadow passes over
his eyes. He is winking at me.

The woman is telling now of a young literary giant about to flash forth on the world. "O, he is wonderful." "You are dead Sherwood and so is Dreiser." How many people, I do not know so well, address me by my first name. They begin it immediately after the first meeting. At the second meeting they call me some endearing name. "Hello Sherwoodeo," they say gayly.

The woman addressing me is not so gay. She tells me that Dreiser, myself, Carl Sandburg, Mr. Cabell of Virginia—she names several others—we are all dead.

There is a new young giant emerging on the horizon. He is six feet four in height, has magnificent broad shoulders. Well, he is about to brush all other writers in America aside. Dreiser, I gather, is already a wreck. My own knees begin to tremble. I do not like giants. I am afraid of them.

"But where is he now?"

"He is teaching school somewhere." I am glad of that. School teaching may wear him out.

"Is he so wonderful? Does he write wonderfully?"

"O, he is so wonderful. You should see his shoulders. He has such vitality."

"And he is teaching school now?"

"How wonderful," the editor says.

"Will you come to my house to drink to-night? There will be a party there."

"Will you come to my house to drink to-night? There will be a party there."

"Will you come to my house to drink to-night? There will be a party there."

"Yes."

"Yeas."

"Yeas."

Conversation with a publisher I meet on the street. "Hello. Have you seen Dreiser? Is he well?"

"He is wonderfully well. He is working hard. I never saw the man looking better."

To walk. New York is New York. Was there ever anywhere else such a city? I dive down into a subway. Where else in the world will you see so many well-dressed women? I am enamored of the women of New York. They have quick, sharp, knowing eyes. Even the little shop girls know their own good points. They know how to play them up, how to conceal defects. Many of them have more style than the best dressed of our provincial ladies.

It is hot and stuffy in the subway. How many hours New Yorkers spend underground. You can go from the upper end of New York, downtown, dive under the river and emerge somewhere on Long Island for five cents. They are talking of charging seven. In the subways are many keen-eyed young Jews. I like them, like their sharp young voices and their sharp eyes.

Two young Jews are talking. "They put up a twenty-five story building right there by the park. They should not have put it up. It shuts out the air."

Second young Jew—"They should not have put it up."

Third young Jew—"Ah, what do you care. Let them put it up."

Imagined chorus of voices murmuring up from the subway. "Yes, yes, let them put it up."

"Let them put it up."

"Let them put it up."

I am out of the subway now, am far uptown. I am in the negro district, in a little narrow street filled with negroes. I remember once I was in love and had been raving to a friend about my love. He came to see me and my love. The man had read some of my books. "I am surprised she is not a black woman," he said.

In the little streets there are flower pots in the windows. Negroes are everywhere. There is the familiar soft laughter, soft voices. It is like an Alabama village. Negro women are good housekeepers. Windows are open and I see into bedrooms. The beds are snowy white.

I have gone in a taxi to see a friend I used to know in the far south. Southerners, both black and white, are drifting to New York. When I return to Virginia I will have a conversation with my wash-woman. "Why did you not see Nora, if you were in New York?" Nora is very black and handsome. She has a splendid job somewhere on Long Island. What a cook she is.

The apartment in which my friend lives is built about a great open court. If it were in New Orleans and were smaller, dirtier and in some odd way more beautiful, it might be called a "patio." It is very clean. There is a fountain.

A thunderstorm comes up. We have dined. When I lived in New York the radios had not come yet.

We sit down for conversation, but conversation is impossible. There is an outburst of voices. In the closed court the voices resound terribly. Mr. Coolidge is talking, perhaps Al.Smith and Mr. Hoover. There are jazz bands, orchestras, ordinary bands, vaudeville stunts going on. A little shrill voice is telling a go-to-sleep story. What an insistent little voice it is.

A young woman comes into the apartment. "O, what style." My heart jumps. "O, these New York women." Look, with what confidence she walks across the room. She is a glorious creature. Have I not often said—"you cannot match the women of New York."

Now I am whispering to my friend. "But, you fool, she is from Selma, Alabama. She was never in New York before. She came to-day."

The storm goes on storming. The radio voices are storming. The wind blows. A woman has crossed the Atlantic in a plane. Her name is Amelia Earhart. Before she went away she wrote a poem and sent it to a girl she knew in Boston. I saw it to-day in a New York paper.

"Courage is the price that LIFE *exacts for granting peace.*
The soul that knows it not knows no release
From little things:
Knows not the livid loneliness of fear,
Nor mountain heights where bitter joy can hear
The sound of wings."

O, livid loneliness. On the window-sill of the room where we sit, high up in the New York apartment house there is an antique vase. The wind blows it away. It falls far down to the court below and is shattered. What would you not give to be able to talk back to people on the radio, tell them what you are thinking, what you think of them. There is a couple crossing the court below. The vase is shattered at their feet. My friend and I are leaning out at the window. They look up and laugh. They wave their hands.

"O livid loneliness! O, mountain heights where bitter joy can hear—the sound of wings."

I am riding up and down the city in a taxi. Many streets are torn up. More subways are being put down. The ride is rougher than the one I might take on the mountain roads, near my home in Virginia. The streets are clean, though. New York is the only clean city I have known. It is cleaner than London or Paris.

The streets of the city are washed by the rain.

There is a river of motors in the streets in the rain.

My old hotel has been torn down and they have put up a new one in its place. That has happened since I was here before. When was that? Now it is two o'clock. I hug myself with delight, being in New York. I am in love with New York. I sleep.

I do not sleep long. They are building another new hotel. The electric hammers are going.

The day is cool. I go ride again in a taxi. It is driven by an Italian boy with nice eyes. We have a conversation.

"Are modern women more immoral than women of the past?" "Eh?" I repeat the question. It is a good subject on which to write for my newspaper. When I have nothing else to write about I can always write of that. "Eh?" He laughs. "Hell, no. They are O.K." We talk about it. It is a pleasant subject. "They try things in my cab. If the girls want them to get away with it they do. Otherwise no. It is 50 by 50."

"I like the girls."

"It is because you have nice eyes. They like you."

"It is 50 by 50."

It costs more to have my breakfast than I spend at home in three days. Well, I am a frugal man. I eat a lot. Once I told a Virginia hill man what eating cost in New York. "What, twelve dollars for a dinner. I would starve. I would shoot some one. Nothing to eat is worth that much."

I go to look at automobiles. It is glorious to see them in the windows of the stores. The glass is shiny. What shiny things are the cars. They are beautiful. They are gorgeously beautiful. Year by year they get lovelier and lovelier. If I had a million dollars I would spend it all for automobiles. I would put them behind glass and walk up and down. I would give an art exhibition.

Why are the newspapers not edited in the press rooms? It is the only place to be in a newspaper building. The lino-types and presses are as wonderful as automobiles. The editorial writers should sit there. Room should be made for them. As they write they should look up occasionally and see the presses. The editorial rooms and the city rooms of newspapers in the city are stuffy, horrible places. The pressrooms are beautiful. There is something going on, something magnificent. In the editorial rooms and in the local rooms nothing is going on. Buy yourself a morning paper and you will see.

I had a friend who had a great factory in the city. He used to buy paintings, being very rich. He asked my advice about buying. I begin wondering if he still has his factory. There is a great motor below the factory, below the street, in a great cement room.

I go in a taxi to the factory. The man is there. "Nowadays," he says, "I only come to the factory on rare occasions. I just happened to be here to-day. I am not well. My doctor told me I had to give up the active management of my affairs."

"May I see the motors in the cellar?"

The factory is in a street far uptown. It took a long time to get there. It is in a street filled with tall tenement houses. Fat women are leaning out at windows. Some of the young Italian women in the street are beautiful.

The motors are beautiful. "Yes, you may go there. You nut."

"Will you come to my house to drink to-night? There will be a party there."

"No, I am going out of town. May I go down and stand by the motors that run the factory?"

"Yes, you nut."

There is a man mending shoes in a shop window. He has on a coat made of bed ticking. It has broad red stripes.

It is more fun to run a weekly in a small town. The editorial desk is by the presses. An old lame print comes in. "Times are hard," he says. He gets fifty cents.

The make-up man is chewing tobacco. The "job" is printing a bill for a show. The machinery is close at hand. You may reach out your hand and touch it. The typewriter is a machine.

The body is a machine. Society is a machine.

"Do you want a drink?"
"Do you want a drink?"
"What do you drink when you are at home, in your Virginia mountain town?"

"But do you not see that I am already drunk? I am drunk with New York."
"Motors have made me drunk, and the subways, and the automobiles in the windows and in the streets."
"But I am giving a drinking party at my house to-night. There will be some swell girls. Will you come?"
"But I am drunk with girls seen in the streets. I am drunk with motors."
"You are a hopeless nut."
"I will tell the girls who you are. I will tell them you are a famous author."
"Will you come?"
"Sure."
"You lie."

I have driven to the harbor. O, to see the ships go and come.
People.
People.
People.
Alas, I live in the country. I am the editor of a country weekly in a Virginia town.
Thank God, New York is New York.
There is no city like it in the world.
"But you have not seen all the cities of the world. You talk like a city newspaper. What do you know of the cities of the world?"
"I know that the cities of the world are in the motors. They are in the automobiles."
"I know that you are a nut."
"Well, hurrah! I am a nut."

FOURTH WEEK OF
MAY

Murder everywhere in America. Virginia is an old state but there are many murders here.

Our own murder was committed by a man with a gentle face. He is a modern neurotic. Life has upset him. After the trial he came into the shop. An odd way he took out of his difficulties. Something in the nature of the man touched us closely. What a terrible way he took. He is free but as deeply involved in his difficulties as he was before Mr. Sult died.

Aftermath
EDITORIAL

The trial of last week had a strange effect on the entire community. It is seldom you see people so deeply moved. There are occasions of public calamity, a fire that burns half a town or a flood that sweeps houses away, when all of the people of a community become suddenly tender toward each other.

There was something of this feeling toward Mr. Harris. The attorneys appointed to defend him had apparently little or no case.

On the witness stand Dr. Wright spoke of "derangement in the emotional field." That is a technical way of putting the matter. As a matter of fact there was a profound derangement.

The jury that had to deliver this verdict was a fine one. It would be hard to get a better. They did not bring in their verdict defiantly. There were tears in the men's eyes. And it wasn't sentimentality either.

It was feeling.

They went into the jury room, it is said, and kneeling down, prayed together as Cromwell's army used to pray before going into battle. Then they looked into each other's eyes. "All those in favor of letting Mr. Harris go and live the rest of his life the best he can stand up," some one said. They all stood up.

Derangements, such as had come into Mr. Harris' life—in the emotional field—were. it seems, more common than any of us want to admit. A novel was really being written in our court house last week and most of us wanted to bring the novel to an acceptable ending.

We do not think that this verdict excuses murder. It does not mean that the next man who takes the law into his own hands will necessarily go free. There were elements in this case that did not come out in the trial, places where feeling went out beyond fact.

There was something in the personality of Mr. Harris. He is a man who inspires affection. The claim made by the defense—not proven—that he was swept forward by some power beyond his own power to control was obviously true.

During such a trial there is of course always a great deal of loose talk. "If some one dishonors my wife or child I will shoot him like a dog." When men make such speeches they swell up inwardly, feel big and strong.

As a matter of fact there are few enough men who take women without the consent of the women. There are sensual women as well as sensual men, evil women as well as evil men. The "spotless womanhood" idea, so much talked in the south, is nonsense.

It implies that, because a woman is a southern woman, she is an exception among all women.

There is evil in such a doctrine. It is provincial and stupid. The doctrine is hurtful to the men who declare it and profoundly hurtful to the women.

There are as fine women in the south as anywhere else.

And there are lewd women, domineering selfish women, silly empty-headed women. We all know some of them.

And some of them doubtless wearing the oldest and most honorable names.

And this is true. When men kill, as is so glibly said, to protect the honor of the family, they are not killing for that reason at all. Why not face the truth of such a situation. If I love a woman and she goes to another man do I help her any by killing the man?

If she loves another man let him have her. What happens if I kill him?

Very likely I drag the poor woman into a court room, make her whole life a public affair.

When it is not a matter of protection of life or property men kill to protect their own pride, or when driven forward by some force stronger than themselves. Usually they kill out of pure muddleheadedness. A situation is bad and they make it a thousand times worse. To love another, I should think, means to think of the best interests of that other. If I kill I help no one. I but serve a foolish personal pride.

And very often those who talk the loudest in public places about protecting their women are connected with women much stronger and more sensible than themselves. Such women are quite able to take care of themselves.

And surely the other kind aren't worth killing for.

The Hole in the Wall
NEWS

Willie claims the hole got in the wall when he had a partner in with him, in the barbering business in North Holston. Willie and the partner, it seems, did not get on the best in the world. One day the partner threw a stove lid at Willie and missed him. That is what made the hole in the wall.

Then Willie says he stuffed some old bags and things in the hole. He hung a picture over it. It was, if we are rightly informed, a picture of Patrick Henry himself, standing up there and saying, "give me liberty or give me death."

Anyway the report got around Saltville that you could get a little of the—well you know—by going up to Willie's shop and saying to Willie, "give me liberty or give me death." The report may be true or it may not be. Willie says it is plain defamation of character. Mr. Chapman, Mr. Halaway and others got up in the justice court at Allison's Gap on Monday morning and swore that Willie's past reputation was as driven snow.

Prosecutor Funk asked some embarrassing questions.

Here is what happened. Officer Thompson and Chapman of Saltville heard about the hole in that wall and went up there to Willie's shop and lifted the picture from the hole in the wall. It seems the picture had a crack in it—which was taken to indicate that it was lifted quite often.

Pretty thin evidence we thought. There wasn't a thing in the hole.

And when it comes to that we have seen some of the greatest paintings in the world all cracked up.

But nevertheless the officers went rummaging about Willie's shop and in a back room they found a glass fruit jar with some suspicious looking liquor in it. Why doesn't some one put a stop to the glass fruit jar industry? Seems to us that if they would only quit making glass jars the whole liquor business would go to pot.

There was the fruit jar and it had in it something that smelled— and tasted—like home brew.

Now they have been having trouble about home brew in Saltville and all up and down the Rich Valley. How were they to decide whether or not it had kick enough in it to be unlawful? Again and again the officers have captured some and sent it off to Richmond, to the state chemist.

And every time they did it simply blew up on the way. Bang, it went. No more evidence. Deep dark laughter among the home brewers.

But this time the Saltville officers and our own Mr. Funk had been more canny. They took it to a Saltville chemist. The story is that they took it to him in an iron safe, fearing an accident on the way. There was danger of the loss of human life.

Anyway, the chemist chemisted it and reported that it was all there. "That and more," they said. They intimated that it was horse trader stuff.

So Willie and his hole in the wall were up before Justices Jim Buchanan, W. H. Brickey and J. W. Hughes to explain.

And at that he was a fair explainer. A man, he said, had come into his shop on a busy day with a paper poke in his hand. He passed into a back room. "I left you a present," he said to Willie. If we had been Willie and some one had left that stuff on us we would have called him an enemy, not a friend.

Willie says he threw his eye up at the man but, at that moment, he was engaged in a delicate job of hair trimming for a young North Holston blood and really didn't recognize the man. Then afterward the rush in the shop quieted a bit and Willie went into the back room to see what the present was.

"O, goody," he cried, taking a sip. Then his expression changed. There were the two officers standing and looking at him. "But what was I to do?" he asked in the justice court at Allison's Gap.

After all a barber shop is a public place. If a man wants to leave packages in paper pokes in a back room what is a man to do?

"Well, you might leave fifty dollars with us," says Hughes, one of the justices. "And the costs," says Mr. Buchanan. That would make it $77.50. You have to do a lot of shaving and hair-cutting for that.

What I hope is that Mr. Thompson or Mr. Chapman or Mr. Funk do not get any notions about going up and rumbling about Paw and Mr. Ague's store, up in Coon Hollow.

If any one ever assessed us $77.50, working for this paper, it would be the same as getting sentenced for life.

BUCK

FIFTH WEEK OF

MAY

Buck and the Boss

The boss has been hot all this week on going ahead on that gloom number of the paper he has talked about before. I never saw cold, wet weather get a man the way it does him. People see him around the street and think he's a cheerful man. Well, he ain't.

When the sun don't shine for several days he thinks of nothing but getting out a paper full of deaths, crop failures, automobile accidents, etc. "Buck," he says, "go out and bring in a little more sadness." "How about a raise," says I. "Go to Wytheville," says he. "I can't be any sadder than I am on what I'm getting," says

I. "Well, you can cry, can't you," says he, "cry a little." "I been crying for a raise ever since I been here and it ain't done me any
good," I says.

That shuts him up for a while but he isn't the kind that stays
shut when you shut him. That's the trouble with him.

A Fire

NEWS

There was an early morning's fire, last Friday morning, in the
rooms above the Graham 5 & 10 Cent Store. The alarm went off
about a quarter to six. The boss and I have had several arguments
about these early morning fires. "You get up and go to them," says
the boss, talking as bosses always do. "Good Quebec," says I, "I
don't get paid for no such early getting up."

"Who do you think is building up this paper anyway?" says I.

"I am," says he.

"Just the same as you catch fish. Always going out all rigged up
and coming home empty-handed," says I.

I got him there. He shut up.

So this morning when the fire alarm went off I says to myself,
"Shall I get up or not?" "No," says I to myself. "You'd better," I
says to myself. After all I like this job here in Marion, in spite of
my tight-wad boss. That man can spend more money on himself
and less on any one else than any man I ever see. He's as tight as
my Paw.

Anyway I went back to sleep arguing with myself like that and
it wasn't hardly any fire anyway. A little blaze started in a store
room above Graham's store and our nifty fire boys got up out of
bed and run down in their pajamas and put it out and then went
back and had their sleep out.

BUCK FEVER

A Committee Meeting
NEWS

Was at the Kiwanis meeting and watched with joy the bosses face when that committee that was to take up his eyesore matter with the town council made its report. You know the boss offered to fix up the little park back of the court house if the town council would move the junk out of there. The town council will probably do it at that.

Mr. Funk was chairman of the committee to push this matter. "What was done," says President Cook. "I saw Jack Sheffey," says he. "Where'd you see him?" says Mr. Cook. "In the Clerk's office over at the court house," says Mr. Funk. "And what did you talk about?" asks President Cook.

"We talked about the frost—would there be one. I thought there wouldn't be but Jack thought there would. You know Jack is inclined, sometimes, to be a pessimistic man. I tried to cheer him up. "Jack, brace up," says I. It was a friendly talk. I have always liked Jack.

"But where was Doctor Sherrill, the other member of the committee?" "I don't know," says Mr. Funk. "Jack and I both looked out the window. He wasn't on the court house lawn or anywhere."

"Did it frost?" asked President Cook. "No, but it may yet, but don't say so to Jack. I don't want to make him sad," says Funk.

The whole club arose as one man to commend the fine work of the committee.   BUCK

Chicago in Coon Hollow
A LETTER

I used to know S. A. in Chicago, and before that back in Ohio. Well, I came to Marion from Chicago to see him. He turned me over to this young Buck Fever. He took me fishing.

First we fished the several forks of the Holston River. "What kind of fish are we after?" I asked him. He didn't seem to know.

His boss may have put him up to it. He led me up and down the sides of steep mountains and through tangled underbrush. "There can't be any fish up here," I said. "Come on," he said.

Then we waded through rushing shallows and over slippery hidden rocks. I kept getting my fish line tangled in trees and falling down. I tore my pants. I ripped my shins. I got sunburned. I fell down and got wet all over.

"Where we going?" I asked. Gee, I was tired. This young mountain man didn't seem to mind at all. What I wanted was to go to Coon Hollow. He kept promising me we would get there after a while.

We fished a little but not a thing in the world bit. O, yes. Once I caught a dog fish. We kept passing people who had strings of fish. "Where'd they get them?" I asked. "O, in Coon Hollow," he said.

We never got to Coon Hollow at all. I just wore myself all out for nothing. Two days of it. No rest at all. My legs never ached so in my whole life. At the end of the second day I asked him again: "Why don't we go to this Coon Hollow," I asked him. He is raising himself a mustache. He kept stroking the few hairs on his upper lip. He smiled, a cold tantalizing smile. "The roads are too muddy," he said. There hadn't been a drop of rain for a week. And anyway how did those other fellows get there to get all those fish?

I'm just telling you how it is, you understand. I'm sore. After two days of it, my bones aching like that, after I had climbed miles of mountains and waded miles of streams, I overheard this Buck talking to his boss, to S. A., when they thought I wasn't around.

"But, Buck, why didn't you take him up there," says S. A. "Not me," says Buck. "I didn't aim to do nothing but wear him out. I ain't taking no Chicago man into Coon Hollow."

He says, "Things are bad enough up there as it is."

A Chicago visitor to Marion.

Walker from the Hill

EDITORIAL

The editor is very fond of an evening walk. Sometimes he walks alone and sometimes a Marion lawyer, or a farmer, or a visitor from the city, or just some brother liar, goes out to walk and talk with him.

One evening recently he was walking the streets of Marion alone. It was a dark night with prospects of rain. Up near the fair grounds a stranger joined him. He was a tall man, very well dressed and with a brown beard.

"It is very odd," the stranger said. "What is odd?" I asked.

"It is odd about my automobile," he explained. "All the birds follow me when I ride in it."

He said it was a Rolls-Royce. When he drove it all of the birds came out of the forests and fields along the road. They flew alongside his car, singing madly. Now and then a bird alighted on one of the fenders or flew in at the car window and sat on his shoulder.

"How do you account for it?" I asked.

"It's because of Geraldine," he said.

"But who was Geraldine?"

"Geraldine was a queen," he said seriously. I gathered that the man I had met in the road had royal blood in him. Well, he was a tall, soldierly looking man and walked with a soldier's stride.

When he was a child, it seemed he lived in a palace. Some one stole him out of the palace at night. He had, he said, but the vaguest notion of it.

He remembered only long flower-bordered paths where he used to walk sometimes with a tall woman. She was a very beautiful woman—and sad too, he told me.

And then one night a man, with a black beard came and stole him away. "The man was Santa Claus," he said. "He came with a team of reindeers. We drove in the deep snow. It was the first snow that had ever come in that country."

"What country was it?" I asked. "It was Zenia," he said, "the kingdom of Zenia."

"But what of Geraldine?" I asked. "Who was she?"

"O, she," he said. "I had forgotten her. She went away with the stars."

"With the stars?"

"Yes," he said. "As for Santa Claus, he turned out to be an evil man. He stole my bees."

"Yes," he said, "my bees. He stole some of them at night. It was when the apple trees and all of the flowers were in full bloom.

"He would have got them all but Geraldine came down and helped me. We saved some. Geraldine put them in her hair. She went flying through the sky and some of them leaked out of her hair and became stars.

"She left me," the tall man said sadly, "and now I will have to leave you."

We had got down near Henry Staley's mill. There were clear places in the sky. I liked walking and talking with this man. His talk had playfulness in it. He had a fancy that reached out and played with flowers, kingdoms, stars, etc. We had got now to the foot of the hill that leads up to the State Insane Hospital. "I have to turn up here," he said. "I have a job up here."

"But what do you do up there?" I asked. "O, I take care of the stars," he explained. "I put them out in the evening and take them in again in the morning when the town is still asleep."

Bowing to me, the tall man walked off up the hospital hill.

Among the Drifters
THE KIND OF TALES THEY TELL

The workmen used to come into my room and talk and lie. It was a large, barn-like room on V—— Street, on the West Side in Chicago. There were a lot of factories out that way and a railroad ran along under my window.

Often enough in that house our talks were interrupted by freight engines shuffling cars up and down outside. The bell rang and sometimes the whistle screamed. Two freight cars went together with a bang.

The room in which we sat was on the second floor of an old frame house. Although the house was not ten years old, the floors already sagged. When a heavy freight train went by outside the walls trembled.

During the evening a half dozen pails of beer were brought in from a neighboring saloon. We drank the beer, smoked our pipes and talked.

We had our philosopher, our mystic, our politician, and there was a man who recited Bobby Burns. He was a Scotchman, of course an engineer.

The men loved lying to me, they would have liked to have me believe they were all dangerous men.

216

JACK

They were talking one time about death and murder. What do you feel at the moment of death?

How does it feel to kill some one? Suppose you get away with it. How do you feel the rest of your life?

A man used to come in from the next room down the hall, a tall countrified fellow. He was habitually silent. We were always sending him out for beer. You know how young fellows are—"I'll pay for it, who'll go for it?" The tall fellow—his name was Jake—was always willing. He bought his own share too but never drank much.

He never talked much either.

We had been talking of death and killings and all the others had gone out—to their own rooms.

It was a black rainy night and I was sitting by the open window watching the switchmen down below on the railroad tracks. I could see their lanterns in the darkness, the headlights of the engines, the way the rain cut through the streaks of light.

Something queer happened. A shiver ran down my back. When I turned Jake was standing and looking at me.

His face was a little drawn. There was something queer about his eyes. He had come into the room without making any sound.

When I looked at him he went and sat in a chair. He was making queer nervous movements with his fingers, opening and closing his fists.

He began to tell me something. Whether it was the truth or not, I do not know. Anyway, he talked.

"They were speaking of killing in here," he said. "I killed my wife."

"I didn't intend to do it," he said quickly. He had an odd little falsetto note in his voice.

"If I did not intend to kill, you ask me why did I have a gun in my hand?"

I had asked him nothing of the sort, had said nothing about a gun. If he had killed his wife and wanted to tell me about it, it was all right with me.

"It was very simple," he went on. You meet all sorts when you are an itinerant laborer as I was then. At one time I had been a hobo. You meet queer ones that way, too. They get up all sorts of desperate lies.

"I was in a field above the house," Jake said, "I was a farmer then." If he was trying to tell me a story of himself he was taking a lot for granted. He was taking it for granted I wanted to hear the story, that I knew something about him. To tell the truth, I wished he would go.

He had however got a start on the story and was bound to tell it. I listened of course.

"I was in the field above the house," he said again. "It was depressing weather. I was husking corn and it began to rain.

"When I had got through work it was almost dark and I started home. I was coming down a muddy lane beside a wood.

"The leaves had all fallen off the trees in the wood." When he told me that simple fact he smiled a sickly smile. What he thought was funny about it I don't know.

The leaves had fallen off the trees and there were wet leaves clinging to his shoes.

He said there had been dogs prowling about his farm at night. He had thought he saw one that night going down the hill. He said he was thinking of sheep-killing dogs. He mentioned also that during the previous summer there had been tall flowering weeds growing beside the lane in the shadow of the woods.

He seemed to be telling me these details, wanting to get at something and yet hesitating. Was he fending off telling what he wanted to tell or was he just working me up?

"My farming had gone to pieces," he said suddenly. "It was because I had married wrong." He said he had married a woman he despised. He began to tell me about her.

"I married her because I thought I had to do it," he said.

"It was what we called in our country, 'a shotgun marriage.' "

And now he was telling me about his courtship and his marriage. As looking directly at him seemed to make him uncomfortable, I turned my eyes away.

He said he was little more than a boy when he got mixed up with the woman he married and that his father and mother were both dead.

He and his sister were living together on what had been his father's farm. His sister was older than himself. She was engaged to be married, to a school teacher, he said.

One evening he had gone to a nearby town. He drove there in a buggy. There was a dance in the town, a public dance, but he did not go. He got in with some young men in town and had a few drinks. He thought he might have got a little drunk.

"I started home," he said. "It was about eleven o'clock. On the road, just after I got out of town, I met a woman walking and she was crying.

"Her name was Elsie Hardy."

My visitor explained that the woman he had met in the road belonged to a tough family.

She had ridden into town with her brother—a young fellow Jake knew, a notorious young rough—and when they got to town he found out there was a dance and told his sister to go on home.

She told Jake she had stayed about town hoping to find some one going out her way. She was afraid alone, she said.

Jake had got the woman Elsie into his buggy and he said they were both somewhat shy. The Hardys, he said, lived in a poor mean house over a hill, about a half mile back from the road and beyond where he lived. There was a short cut over the hill and through a wood. He said he felt a little queer being with her, as the Hardys had all been a rough lot and his own people had been all right.

He walked with Elsie over the hill and through the woods, and as he had described how the wet dead leaves clung to his shoes

on another evening so now he described the pattern of the moonlight on the path in the wood.

"I went crazy," he said, "and took the woman. She resisted
a little, not much.

"Afterward, and while I was lying with her, her brother came
up through the woods."

He explained that Elsie's brother had two young town men
with him and that they had tied their horses in the road near
Jake's horse. They were going over the hill to the Hardys' house to
get whisky. They were already drunk.

Of course they had seen Jake's buggy in the road and when
they got to the Hardy house Elsie was not there.

She was in the woods with Jake, behind some bushes. "I lit out
as soon as I could," he said, "but what good did that do?"

What he half expected to happen, he said, did happen. He was
working in the field one afternoon, a few months later, and looked
up to see Elsie coming across the field. Her brother and father
were down below in the wood and had guns slung over their
arms. Jake's sister was away from home.

Elsie, he said, came to him and told him her brother and father
had said that he, Jake, would have to marry her. "I'm that way,"
she said.

"All right," he told her.

He spoke of how thin she was. He said her neck was scrawny
and thin. "Her hair was thin, too," he said.

And so Jake had gone down to his barn, passing Elsie's father
and brother in the road without speaking to them and getting
out his buggy drove Elsie some eighteen miles to the county seat
where he got a license and they got married.

When he got home his sister had heard of what was up and had
packed her things and left. He said his sister made a pretty good
marriage. She married, he said, a school teacher.

And so, I gathered, there was Jake, on his father's farm with his wife and she had had a child and it died and he was discouraged and blue. He said the farm belonged half to his sister.

"I hoped to get away," he said.

He spoke again of the evening—after his marriage—when he had been husking corn. It was night, and rainy and dark.

He said there was a loaded gun in a granary near the barn. You will remember he had already spoken of having thought he had seen dogs when he was in the lane above.

The dogs, he said, were the Hardy dogs. They had already killed some of the neighbors' sheep. He thought they were hanging about his place because Elsie was there.

He took the gun in his hands and went silently around the house and into a neighboring field, wanting to kill one of the dogs. He ached to kill something belonging to the Hardys, he said. He only owned eight sheep and there they were. They were huddled against the fence at the edge of the field. There wasn't a dog in sight.

With the gun in his hand, Jake went from the field around the house to the kitchen door. The kitchen door was standing open. It must have been a warm night. His wife Elsie was cooking something in a pan on the stove. She was preparing his supper.

She was standing beside the stove and had a coal oil lamp in her hand. She was leaning over the stove and holding the lamp above her head. He put his gun to his shoulder.

What was in his mind he said he did not know. He declared that, except for the one evening when he was with her in the woods on the moonlight night and before her brother came, he had always hated her.

He hated being married to her. "She had such a scrawny neck," he said. He was a great fellow for details.

He said he stood looking at her and that he pointed the gun at her head. His hand trembled. It is certain his hands and his voice trembled when he was telling me the tale. If he was a liar he was a good one all right.

He could not bear shooting his wife so he raised the gun a trifle and shot the lamp out of her hand. The contents of the lamp ran down over the stove.

"Then," he said, "there was a blinding flash." It almost knocked him down. He recovered and stepping forward closed the door.

"I became foxy," he said. "What I did was the most natural thing in the world."

He had closed the kitchen door and had run back up the hill through the darkness to where he had been husking corn. He hid the gun in a corn shock.

As it turned out, no one had heard the shot and now his house was afire. In a short time some one saw the fire from the road, or they saw the reflection against the sky and came running.

He waited, he said, until they got there before he ran down the hill. Both his house and his barn burned to the ground.

No one ever suspected him, he said. I remember that when he said it he got up off the chair and stood before me.

He declared again that no one had ever suspected him of killing his wife and said that, in fact, he did not kill her. "I shot the lamp out of her hand," he said, and smiled. Then he went out of the room.

It might not have been true. At that time in my life I associated with a lot of mighty queer men. Some of them would have been entirely capable of inventing the tale Jake had told.

They would tell you tales like that and then, if you believed, they laughed.

Whether or not this one was a liar I never found out. As I have said, we were all itinerant workers. He did not come to my room for the next three or four evenings and when I inquired about him of the woman who kept the house she said he was gone.

Most of the men in that house were such abominable liars. He may just have been a liar or he may have been an itinerant workman, drifting about with that on his mind.

June

Warm still days. The spring has been late. Now the corn is well up out of the ground.

Went up, east of Wytheville, to see an apple orchard in full bloom. There was a roar of bees. There seemed millions in the orchard.

The nights are cool in the hills but during the days a gray warm haze lies over them.

The hills here have sensual lines. It should be a painter's country. Sometimes there is the impression of giant women lying asleep. Their great breasts rise and fall as they breathe.

Over by the old abandoned octagonal brick house, beyond Adwolfe, the hills have just the quality of old Italian masterpieces.

It would not at all surprise me to see a mailed knight riding down out of these hills.

Two Town Eyesores to Go

NEWS

After all, that now famous committee meeting at which Andy Funk and Jack Sheffey talked so feelingly of the weather and Dr. Zeb Sherrill got lost somewhere in the mazes of the court house yard came to something. Cut to the heart by our ribald account of the meeting Mr. Funk appeared at the meeting of the town council on Friday evening. On that evening the editor had gone off to the Riverside High School over in Rich Valley and coming home had got lost somewhere in the hills over near Nebo.

The town council was sitting and Mr. Funk was talking—with all of his well known and justly celebrated force. If there were any doubters on the council all doubt was quickly brushed aside. Mr. Funk was there to voice the good wishes of the Kiwanis Club and did most eloquently, they say, voice them.

With a whoop the town council passed unanimously the proposal to buy the lot belonging to Mr. Emmett Sprinkle, down by the handle works. There is a huge old building on the lot that will be at once reconstructed to house all of the town machinery, tar pots, pipes, etc., that have in the past littered our editorial front yard. The old eyesore building, now standing back of the court house, will be torn down.

The editor of this becomingly modest newspaper will then set out some young trees, put in some benches, have a bit of lawn there and places to play a few passingly innocent and interesting games, in the gloaming of summer evenings. A place too for the people of the county to gather on court days.

You see we have caught it from George Cook and Mr. Funk. We grow eloquent.

And we suspect the town will put in the retaining wall back of the Lutheran Church and some steps for church-goers to climb.

If the old lot needs any filling there is Charles Wassum. Is he not going to erect a new building on Main Street? What ho. Is not the town on the go?

And as far as the editor is concerned he has asked nothing from the town. If, after a few years, the town wants to put up a nifty town building on the lot we will gracefully move off.

The council was in the mood—as one might say—little birds were singing in their hearts. As every one knows the colored people of Marion have long been wanting a new school building. The one they have now is disreputable beyond words. Sometime ago they got together and told the town council that, if they would furnish the building materials, the colored mechanics of the town would build the new building free of labor cost.

A committee was appointed to see if they meant it. They did.

The town council did too. They did their share. Every one did.

It was a good night in Marion and the editor lost in the hills somewhere over about Nebo.

A Veteran

A VISITOR

A fine old man of eighty-eight, Mr. W. W. Roberts of Robert's Cove.

Age has bent his back a trifle but he is much alive and you never saw brighter old eyes or talked with a man who had a clearer mind.

He came into the print-shop and sat down on the bench by the door. For forty years he had taken our paper. He had a right to respect here.

And so we talked of the Civil War and the part he took in it.

"Were there many Union sympathizers in here?"

"Not so many of us.

"All of us from Robert's Cove went in on that side. There were four of us.

"And two killed."

"From where did you enlist?"

"From Cincinnati. I went out there."

"I was in the fighting right in this town, in Marion."

"Were you now?"

"I was. We were in Knoxville and were hemmed in there. We thought we were gone that time.

"Then, you know, Grant came in there with Sherman and they licked the Confederates that time. They came and got us out too.

"We came up here in the winter of sixty-four. We had a skirmish outside Marion and then we came on through. There was some fighting in the streets here. Our captain rode up to a man. He had a saber in his hand. 'Surrender,' he said. The man shot our captain and then one of our boys shot him.

"We went on up to Wytheville and destroyed the lead mines up there.

"When we were coming back the Confederate general, Breckenridge, got after us.

"We met, just outside of Marion, to the east and had a skirmish there but we were too strong for Breckenridge's crowd. There was a lot of shooting but not many hurt.

"Then we went on over to Saltville and broke that up. We broke up all the salt kettles.

"General Breckenridge and his men went off up Staley's Creek. They went on back out east to join Lee, I guess. We broke a lot of railroads up east of here.

"Some of the Union troops went back over the mountains toward Ohio. It got bitter cold and a lot of them froze their feet so that they had to be cut off.

"We went back west again and then south. We were down there when Lee surrendered."

Mr. Roberts of Robert's Cove, Grayson County, near the Smyth County line, was among the troops that pursued and captured Jefferson Davis but was not in at the capture. He came back in here.

He says that when he came back a Marion woman stopped him on the streets once. "You look like one of the Union men who took my saddle," she said. "I didn't take it," Mr. Roberts said and laughed. "I always managed to have a good horse and a good saddle. I was a cavalryman in the war."

"I never took her saddle," he said again.

"But was there much unfriendliness when you came back in here to live. Was Grayson County strong on the Union side?"

"No," he said. "They sent out five companies to fight for the Confederacy.

"I came back and went to the old farm, have been there ever since, the Roberts farm in Robert's Cove.

"I believed what I believed and so did those on the Confederate side. We never had any slaves on our farm, in Robert's Cove.

"Some of the worst ones to be bitter were people who had nothing to do with the war. They didn't fight. They stayed at home and talked.

"Those that fought weren't bitter when it was over. I was neighbors, same as I always was."

"Were you wounded in the war?"

"Some. Not much. I like to talk of it.

"We used to talk during the war, boys from both sides when they had a chance.

"Once, on picket line, when a messenger from the Confederates had come in they blindfolded him and left his escort on the picket line with us. One of them was from down this way. I asked him about a girl I knew. She was all right, he said. I said I was going to sneak down in here and have a look at her. 'I wish you would,' he said. 'That's a good warm overcoat you got on. I'd like to have it myself,' he said.

"He never got it though," Mr. Roberts said and laughed.

Mr. Roberts, of Robert's Cove, Grayson, went out. He is eighty-eight now. A fine old man. There is a merry twinkle in his old eyes. His eye is clear and so is his brain.

SECOND WEEK OF

JUNE

Buck Fever Says

Mrs. Malaria Fever, Coon Hollow, Va.

Dear Maw:

The morning after the town election was a clear fine morning and I was up early to see the joy of the elected candidates Maw.

And sure enough, there they were. All those elected had got up early and were running two and fro. They met in front of the court house and ran skipping hand in hand through the streets, singing, "Goodie, Goodie, Goodie."

They were all having a fine time dancing and carrying on like this and singing when Gord Snavely happened to think of those who ran for town office and wasn't elected.

So large tears of sympathy began to gather in Gord's eyes but Hash Rouse and Frank Peery hurries to him and wiped his tears away. "Think of all the good we can do," they cried and thinking of it made Gord feel better.

Then they had the ceremony of coronation. Dr. Buchanan and John Buchanan and Bob Anderson and Port Snider had been appointed a committee to get up early and weave garlands of roses to hang around the necks of those elected and they did it. They had been hid in the shrubbery over in Henry Mencken Park until the right moment but now they ran skipping forward and hung the garlands on them. John P. Buchanan wanted to hang something else on one of them but they wouldn't let him—but you know John.

Then they sang some more songs and the old town council, which is going out Maw was up and they sang, led by Dr. Thompson.

And then the old council and the new one, and Dr. Brown, Gord and Henry Gills all ran down to Henry Mencken Park and danced around the fountain down there, and it was a fine sight to see. So they bathed themselves in the fountain and all vowed the good they would do the town and went home and had breakfast, so they could get to their new offices early and do their duty and "put Marion on the map," as the saying is.

Your Loving Son,

BUCK

THIRD WEEK OF
JUNE

∽∽∾

The Request

Last December, when I asked you to tell my classes at Hunter College something about the way in which you write your short stories, you answered that owing to the pressure of your work you could not then find the time in which to take up my questions. At the risk of incurring your displeasure I am writing again with the same request. But I am willing to run that risk. I feel that the failure to have your views would mean that, in the symposium of statements given us by Manuel Komroff, Waldo Frank, Zona Gale, and others, there would be lacking the one writer whose stories have touched a truer emotional basis than has hitherto been known to exist in American writing.

To my questions, set down in that first letter, Komroff and the others answered with illustrative references to some one or more of their own stories. It is true, of course, that a writer's observations of his own creative processes are not always as clear-cut as his words would seem to indicate. Nevertheless, the bringing together of a writer's views of his work and examples from his own work serve at times to emphasize the organic relationship that binds the writer and his material. As you might suppose, this experience has proved tremendously invigorating to my pupils, many of whom have grown suspicious of the mechanical formulæ imparted in the textbooks of the short story. These students have shown themselves so receptive of the view that the story grows out of the life of the writer, that I have been encouraged to plan a book in which I want to include the writer's views of his craft together with an example of his work. The writers I have mentioned have already given me permission to print their views and to reprint their respective stories.

I should like to obtain your views. What you have to say on the subject, as I have found in The Story Teller's Story, is so heartening that every one honestly concerned with writing must be stimulated. Because of the interest you have always had in the many problems of the writer, I am bold enough to urge that you set down some of your experiences for the many young writers to whom your words are of rich significance. I need not tell you how deeply appreciative I should be if you were to enable me to include a statement from you in the book I am planning.

Cordially,
H. G. (a College Professor).

The Answer

Dear Sir:

After all—you must admit—it is a fairly large-sized order you have given here. I really cannot attempt to do it. I do not like such pawing over of my past emotions. Sometimes it is inevitable. There is the book of mine called, "A Story Teller's Story." That isn't autobiography. It is really a novel—of the mind of a man, let us say, of a man who happened to be a writer.

You are bound to find that most of your students will be thinking of writing as a way to make a living, to attain success, attract attention to themselves. The formulas are infinitely better for them. If they follow the formulas they will be much more likely to succeed.

Of course all kinds of emotions are stirring about in them. So are they in my colored cook, in the first man I meet when I go out into the street. And I understand your feelings too. You do not like the cheap little channels into which human emotions are poured in the ordinary conventional short story in the magazines.

You would like all of these young writers to be artists. Well, I would like all people to be lovers but do not know how to bring it about. I suppose there are only two sorts of really nice people in the world, the lover in love or the artist at work.

You wouldn't attempt to give a course in love-making would you, or get out a book of explanations by well known lovers?

How am I to attempt to lay down a formula for the channeling of the emotions of these people?

Let us say I am in love. God knows I have been many times. I see or meet some woman who is beautiful to me. I want her. How am I to get her? Well, I send her flowers and candy, I go to see her. Alas, this is a test for me. Am I up to it? Many doubts assail me. I walk with her under trees. It may be that I manage to get her off somewhere where we can be alone together. This would be difficult where I am now living, in a small town. In a city it might be managed better. But I am getting older now. It may be I am more discriminating. I do not fall in love so often or write so many stories.

But be that as it may, let us say I have pulled this matter off. I have got my lady to the seashore and am walking with her. On a certain afternoon, when I am with her, the matter between us is decided.

I come home from there, my dear man, and you take me aside. "I want you to tell my students just how it was done. What did you say to her? Repeat your words. Perhaps it was something in your eyes. Make your eyes look as they did at that moment. My students are worthy young men and women. They want to succeed in love. At the critical moment did you feel a certain emotion? Please feel it again now. My students want to see how you look when you feel it."

You see the probabilities are that Komroff, Frank and Miss Zona Gale were talking nonsense. When they really do it they cannot tell how they do it. Their explanations are as likely to be wrong as right.

You know that is one thing I like about painters. Most of them let some one else do the explaining. They paint. Ask one of them to tell you how he felt at a certain moment, how he held the brush in his hand, etc., etc., and he would tell you to go to Pittsburgh. And he would do it for just the reasons suggested above.

For each man and woman his own reactions to life, and lives are the writer's materials. If you are to have any individuality as a workman you have to go alone through the struggle to find expression for what you feel. You have of course to train your hand and your eye. Just because you ache to do something is no sign you can do it. Talent is given you. You have it or you haven't. A real writer shows himself a writer in every sentence he writes.

The training is another matter. It is a question of how keen is the desire, how much patience and perseverance there is. Sometimes I think it largely a matter of physical strength. How much disappointment can you stand before you throw up the sponge?

Right now, at this moment, I have a hundred stories in me I am not man enough to write as they should be written. How am I to tell another how to do what I cannot myself do?

FOURTH WEEK OF

JUNE

In New York
EDITORIAL

The editor in New York, to see the wheels of the big city go around again. Three days and two nights. One glorious night.

It was clear and cool. I could not sleep, did not want to. Rivers of motors in the street. Vast crowds of people. The great city has always been one of my first loves. There is no city like it. It has more individuality than Paris, or Berlin or London. Beside it, London is drab and uninteresting, Chicago like an ungrown boy.

I would like always to be a guest in the world, in Chicago, New York, London, Marion, in my own house. I do not want to say definitely that I will ever stay anywhere, be anything. I am an author now, a newspaper man. To-morrow I may be a soldier, a tramp. What does it matter?

A few people to love, not to see too much of them. The night in New York was like a song. There were a dozen parties going on to which I had been invited. I went to none of them.

I saw little enough of the literati. A charming German woman did my portrait for a book. She did not show it to me. I am afraid she made me look like Elbert Hubbard or William Jennings Bryan. They always do. But I am not like that. Unlike William Jennings Bryan, I have no passion for raw radishes.

I have other passions though. But we will not speak of them.

New York has as many moods as a temperamental man. It is brutal and casual, quick with sympathy sometimes, it is gay and sad.

Other authors have told me a great deal about the brutality of New York publishers to aspiring writers. This time a man told me that. "The editors are treating the writers brutally," he said.

I went to a man supposed to be the most casual and brutal of them all. I have found him always considerate and fair.

There are two sides to this matter. Oh, the egotism of writers. Every writer who has written a novel thinks he has produced a masterpiece. He does not say so but he thinks so. If it does not sell he accuses the publisher.

I dare say New York men expect you to look out for yourself. If you are a fool they will take advantage of you.

A typical New Yorker will not arrive at his office until eleven in the morning. In two hours he may do as much work as a Chicago man would do, with more fuss, in a day.

I have done what business I had to do in New York quite

casually, in a restaurant or speak-easy. "Will you do so and so?" "Yes," or "no." I have found few New York men who have not kept the word given me thus casually.

New York men know how to play. They are great diners out. They dance and drink. I like best to go away from every one I know—or perhaps with one person. That person not too close to my daily life. Then I like to go in and out of places, walk on the boulevards, see the rivers of motors—feel the power of the place. I like to spend money. If some one charges me ten or fifteen dollars for a dinner I do not care. I am willing to work to get the money back.

When I go to New York I do not sleep. My being there is a spree. I fill myself with the city and come home refreshed.

SIR OLIVER HOPKINS with SHERIFF SAM DILLARD

FIRST WEEK OF

JULY

The Fourth of July passed with a blare of bands and a big celebration at the fair grounds. There was a parade and great crowds from all over the county turned out. It rained a little just at noon but both the morning and afternoon were fair.

There were many kinds of races, for men, women, boys, girls, mules, ponies and horses.

There was a greased pig and a greased pole, a boxing match, horseshoe pitching, dancing and a ball game.

Greased Pig Has Bum Day
NEWS

The one unhappy witness of the big Marion Fourth of July was the greased pig. The poor pig was caught the day before the ceremony and given a shave. What pig would like that? Then he was greased. He was greased before a vast crowd of people. His privacy was invaded. Rough hands held him. Is it any wonder he squealed?

Then he was turned loose before all those people and a great

235

crowd of men and boys took after him. Four fell on him. They fought and struggled. Four men held him by the ears and shoulder. They marched around the race track and stood before the grand stand. Who did he belong to? The poor pig didn't want to belong to any of them or any one. Tex Anderson was appealed to. Sheriff Dillard came and quieted the clamor of the crowd. A Daniel among judges was needed. Some in the crowd yelled "hang on," others "turn him loose." How did they know it was a "him"?

The pig was turned loose on the ball field. Hugh Hutton was playing ball with the Marion team. Hugh has kind eyes. The pig rushed into his arms and was taken home to Hugh's house where we understand it is being given kind treatment. It must, after all, have been a lady pig.

SECOND WEEK OF

JULY

Summer

The whole country is lush with growth now. It is a joy to ride out and look about. All the land stretched away from the road on either side between Marion and Chilhowie is an especial delight to the eye.

And to the nose too. The elders are in bloom and the sweet clover and honeysuckle. There is one great field of sweet clover beside the road west of town. The air is heavy with the perfume of it. There is a delightful trick some good housewives have. They gather bunches of sweet clover and dry it. Then they put little bags of it in the linen closet. Try it. It will bring the fragrance of summer back on many a winter day.

Near Emmett Thomas' Texaco headquarters, where the highway crosses the river, east of town and on the river bank, the elders grow to huge size. The editor got down in there the other evening. There is no more exciting odor. Some of the elder flowers were as large as my hat. Thousands of bees had gathered. A basket of the blossoms brought home filled the house with perfume.

On the hillside, going up to the state hospital, they were cutting the hay that lined the road. That is a special fragrance too. The wind blew it down Main Street into the heart of town.

Out by the East End filling station the yard about the house of H. L. Wolfe is a sea of roses. In the mountains the rhododendrons are coming into full bloom.

The wheat fields are just turning color. Some are golden yellow and cutting has begun. Others are every shade from green to yellow. The fields are like wonderfully made quilts.

Park Plans
NEWS

Now our city fathers have definitely decided to move our beloved water wagon, our tar barrels, our piles of iron pipes, on which we often sit on moonlight nights to think of the errors and sins of our fellow men, we are to have our little park as we wish.

Well you see it is like this. Both Mr. Wassum and Mr. Lincoln are to do some building on Main Street and at once. There will have to be some filling done. These men both have the town's good at heart. We figured we could get some good dirt from them for the necessary fill.

But how are we to get it if we cannot get this stuff off the lot? That puzzles us. We lie awake at nights trying to figure it out. Now that the town fathers have gone this far we wonder if they would mind going the rest of the way. You know. Tell the boys to clear the stuff away. Then we will go and sing under Mr. Lincoln and Mr. Wassum's window. "Give us some dirt," we will sing.

Word comes to us that the women's club are all ready to help the park along with any number of bushes and shrubs. We are thinking of getting some landscape gardener friend to lay it all out for us. We aren't in any special hurry ourselves but we do want to hold those two men for the dirt for the fill.

THIRD   WEEK   OF

JULY

Trouble in Stoney Battery

NEWS

In Stoney Battery on Rolling Creek, near Thomas' Bridge, there is a little wooden church given over to the Dunkard Faith. The Dunkards address each other as "Brethren," so it is called locally "the Brethren Church." The Dunkards are a quiet, God-fearing people. They do not have paid preachers. Any man "called," may preach. A collection is taken up. The preacher gets what is taken in.

If you belong to the Dunkard Church you may not take an oath but you "affirm" and some of the brethren "affirmed" some pretty strong stuff.

The Dunkards baptize three times, all over, face-forward. They also tell straight-sounding stories when they are doing their "affirming."

On Monday there was a trial at Justice Buchanan's house near Thomas' Bridge and Justice Shuler, from Sugar Grove and the venerable Justice McClure from St. Clair came over to sit with

Buchanan. They sat under a pine tree in the yard and the audience and witnesses sat on a bench. Andy Funk was there as well as Hi Whistman.

The people on trial under the trees on Monday were Will Tedder, John Tedder, Earl Steele, Jake Tedder, Rosco Steele, Carrie Steele, Mrs. H. E. Steele and Wiley Kirk.

As the story came out John and Jake Tedder seemed to have been the bad actors of the neighborhood. The Steeles, that is to say Earl, swore that the Tedders had been making liquor. Earl, it seems, was out one day taking a walk in the woods and saw John, Jake and Willey Tedder making the stuff. Afterwards the Tedders were caught, and they accused the Steeles, Earl and his father, H. E. Steele, of "turning them up" which means telling Sheriff Dillard.

The Steeles were indignant about that, so indignant that they called the Sheriff to the stand to prove it was not true.

Evidently the Tedders believed it, however. The Brethren were having meetings at their church a week ago last Wednesday and the Tedders went down there. They saw the Steeles and there were words. We won't attempt to print the words. In their testimony the Brethren wouldn't say the words so why should we? Some of the witnesses weren't so particular.

The quarrel passed that time but the next Sunday evening broke out again. It is claimed one of the Tedders went and stoned windows out of the church. No one seems to know why he did that. Then he went and found Earl Steele. Earl was in a car belonging to Bain Richardson. Tedder went up to him and began handing out blows. Nothing loath Earl got out of the car and pitched in.

More Tedders came running and also more Steeles. There was some strong language used by many. People were passing up and down the road to the church. A lot got scared and went home.

John Tedder hit Earl with his fist and Earl claims he landed some good ones himself. Earl's mother came running. The claim is that John Tedder was going to hit her with a club but changed his mind. We didn't blame him when we saw Mrs. Steele. She looks to us like a woman who can take care of herself.

All the aforesaid accused got into it, some in an effort to stop the fight, others in an effort apparently to stop it by knocking the other side cold. John and Jake Tedder are still at large. It is claimed John has a broken jaw. He must be a hardy man, lying out in the bushes with a broken jaw.

Among the many witnesses called were Phiney Richardson, Aman Thompson, Bain Richardson, J. R. DeBord, C. B. DeBord, Karl Parsons, George Tedder, Roby Richardson, Vance Richardson, Bob Tibbs, Will West, Goldy DeBord, Mrs. Steele and Sam Dillard.

The Justices did not have Jake and John Tedder there to do anything to. They fined Earl Steele $25 and cost making $42. Earl appealed the case but later may change his mind and pay up.

Hot Politics in the Third Ward

Suit Wolf, Bill Watterson, "Strap" Mitchell, John Hankla, Paul McCoy, Sam Ray, Marvin Seaver, Max Robinson, Will Seaver, Bolt Britton and Tom Pruner, sitting in the parlors of the Third Ward Dude Club.

THE CONVERSATION

"Say what you talking about? Al Smith will sweep the world. He will carry every state in the union."

"Ah, you're crazy. Say you won't never hear of Al Smith after the first of next November. He'll go into a monastery. That's where he'll go."

"What's a monastery? What's that?"

"I'll tell you what it is. No, I won't either. I didn't come down here to educate you guys."

"I'll tell you what I'll do. If Al Smith's elected I'll crawl from here to the court house and back again on my hands and knees. And say, I'll carry Will Seaver on my back. That's what I'll do."

"All right. Will you sign up on that? If you will I'll tell you what I'll do. If that Hoover's elected I'll eat four dozen duck eggs, shells and all. I'll eat 'em on the court house steps, the day after election."

"All right sign that up. Sign it up. Sign it up."

"All right. Give me a pen. Give me a pen."

Another voice—"Say, if that Hoover's elected I'll let you sandpaper the nose right off my face. I'll do that. You can do it in front of the post office. I don't want no nose if Hoover's elected. I smelled enough with Coolidge in there, I did."

Another voice—"Ah you fellows shut up. I'll tell you what I'll do. I'll make you a proposition. All you fellows in here listen to me. I'm for Herby, I am. If that Al Smith is elected I'll make you all a proposition.

"Well, you can begin up by the post office. First Tom there can kick me, then Will and Max and Suit. You can all kick me. You can kick me clear down Main Street and right on into Wytheville. You can kick me clear to Roanoke. I don't care. Kick away. I don't want ever to see any of you guys again if Herby isn't elected."

Gruff voice—"Say you, give me six or eight of my kicks now. That Hoover hasn't got any more chance than I have getting into the cabinet. That's how much chance he's got."

Chorus—"Ah, you're crazy. You are all crazy. You are a lot of nuts. Why don't you sign up? Get the pen there. Why don't some one get the pen?"

Soft voice—"Ah, say it's hot to-night, I'll say. Who do you think will be elected?"

Chorus—"Al will. Hoover. Smith. Hoover. Smith."

Another voice—"I'll tell you what I'll do. If Hoover is elected I'll eat some preacher's pants. I sure will. I'll eat 'em raw."

Last voice—"Ah go on. If they ever elect that Hoover I'll tell you what I'll do. I'll plant oysters in Staley's Creek. That's what I'll do. If Hoover's elected I'll spend my money making Marion a seaport. I'll do that. I'll have ships going up and down Main Street. I will. That's how much chance I think he's got."

FOURTH WEEK OF

JULY

Sic\) *Again*

EDITORIAL

You will find them in every hospital. All doctors are familiar with the type. They adore operations. Illness is their greatest comfort. It is a method of gaining distinction, of getting attention.

It happens, I fancy, with women when they have not got something they want. What we all want of course is love. It is essential to a woman. Without love she cannot function and develop as a woman. Well, suppose she does not get it. There are a thousand handicaps in life for women.

To get what they want depends so much on physical attractiveness. A misshapen body, bad legs or ankles, an unattractive face. Between women there is always a war going on. It is the survival of the fittest.

All normal women want affection, a home, motherhood. The whole modern idea of women as functioning on the same plane with men is somewhat false. There is a physiological difference between men and women that cannot be ignored. Women want children. In the modern world they cannot get children, in the way they want them, safely, with the approval of society, without marriage.

The war between women goes on. Men often stand appalled

before the cold-blooded determination of the woman, after something she wants. The notion of "honor" as between man and man, when some woman is concerned, is a man's invention. Women commonly use it when it helps them to get or keep what they want. They ignore it when it gets in their way.

There is a reason for all this. If men cannot have children, if they are of comparatively secondary importance in the reproductive functions of life they have their own field. The arts are essentially masculine. Since the beginning most of the great figures in the arts and in all the fields of science and invention have been men.

To be sure this whole matter is somewhat confusing. Every male is partly female and every female partly male. Sometimes the line is hard to draw. We are all familiar with the masculine woman and the feminine man.

But let us go back to our subject, illness. At least half the illness in the world must be self-imposed. Men become ill when they can no longer face the facts of their own lives.

Man dreams—he pushes forward in life. He has hopes of happiness, achievement, success. In his own nature may be the qualities that defeat him. One day he wakes up. He is no longer young. Life is slipping away from him. "I am going to be a failure in life," he says to himself.

It is the nature of man always to defend himself. There must be a reason for his failure. Illness is a way out. "I am not physically strong enough. I am a sick man." What a comfort that thought is.

And there is the woman who has lost out, or thinks she has lost out, in the battle of the women. What a comfort illness is to her.

Even the cutting of her body by a surgeon is somewhat an approach, as by a lover. All surgeons who face the truth and have intelligence know that.

If you are a man surely you have had the experience of sudden and unexpected success, in love or in some other field. You were blue and discouraged, half ill, ready to become completely ill.

Then success came. But after all it does not need to be success. A bit of recognition of some finer quality in yourself may be all you need.

I remember an experience of my own. I had been writing for five or ten years. There was a certain quality I wanted to get into my work. Sometimes I thought I had approached it a little. At least I had become a little clear-headed about the matter. I had put aside trick writing, getting cheap flashy effects.

Oh, I tell you, if you are a man it means something to have done even a slight bit of work of which you need not be ashamed. If you are a woman, and even though you may afterwards have lost out, it means something to have inspired love, to have really inspired it. I remember that I myself once wrote a piece about the woman "strong to be loved." It was one of the best pieces I ever wrote. Few enough men knew what I was talking about. I think that all women who read it knew well enough.

But I am thinking of a moment when I got something I wanted. At that time I had written my Winesburg Tales. I had also written two or three novels. Some of my things had been published.

The critics had jumped on me hard. For my Winesburg Tales I was called "filthy minded." That is an odd thing to think about today. Surely we modern writers have done something in America. We have at least forced upon the public consciousness some public realization of the more obvious facts of existence.

The critics had jumped on me hard and those who had praised me praised me for the very qualities in my work I myself knew to be most false. It was pretty discouraging.

At that time I had a job I didn't like much. I was traveling through the Middle West for an advertising company. I was pretty discouraged, grew pale and thin.

The ugliness of life, that is always present, reared itself up at me. One day I was in Fort Wayne, Indiana. I had gone there to see a certain man, a manufacturer, had been sent there to see him and had lost my nerve. I remember going down to his factory. I got to the door and turned away. I was supposed to go to him and urge him to advertise his product. I remember walking about the streets of that town. "What do I care whether or not he ever advertises?" I asked myself. The truth was I did not care. "But what about your job?" "To hell with the job."

I was in an ugly mood. Instead of going to a decent hotel I went to a little hotel on a side street. I began to drink, was well on my way to getting drunk. The point is that I was walking on a little side street in that town when, on the news-stand, I saw my name on the cover of a magazine.

I do not suppose the magazine had a circulation of three thousand copies. It was a high-brow magazine. But what did I care about that. A man had written an article about my attempts as a writer. It was Mr. Waldo Frank. He was an intelligent man. He knew what I was trying for, knew of course where I had failed.

He did, however, know what I was after. He thought what I was after was worth going after.

I remember going into a railroad station nearby and sitting on a bench. Tears of gratitude came into my eyes. I was glad with an inner gladness hard to describe.

My point now is that I was ill, a sick man, and suddenly all my illness went away. My desire to get drunk, to wallow, went away too. If the thing had not happened, at just that moment, I might have stayed drunk for several days, wallowed about with cheap women. I had done that sort of thing before.

As it was I went out of the railroad station walking gayly. I went to the cheap little hotel and got my bag. No doubt that afternoon I went to see my manufacturer. Whether he decided to advertise or not I cannot remember. It is of no importance. I could sit in talk with him, did not hate him. Except in weak moments. I have never been a reformer. I have no notion that anything I can do will change any of the laws of life or governments or economics. Men and women in all walks of life, rich, poor and middle-class, have interested me about alike when I have been healthy and alive.

The point is that a bit of intelligent recognition of what worth-while I had done had on me an actual physical effect. It gave me new courage, restored in me my waning manhood.

It is the sort of thing every one needs. Let the sick woman find herself a lover who really loves and see how quickly she will get well.

Surely we all feel in us some hidden quality that makes us, at least at moments, worth while to ourselves. If it were not true we could not live at all.

And the love of God will not answer either. In spite of all the preachers say it will not quite see us through. We remain human and want human understanding and love. Without it we die—or we become ill.

And illness becomes such a comfort to us. It takes strength to live a life. When young artists come to me asking my advice I always look at them with curious eyes. How much physical strength has the man, how much reserve nerve force? It is a vital question. Illness begets illness, ugliness begets ugliness. No matter what you tackle in life and unless you are a cheap self-satisfied man you are in for a pounding. How much pounding can you stand? If you decide definitely that you will not practice trickery to get what you want in life very likely you will go right out and do some cheap tricky thing. You will have to go to your bed a thousand nights utterly discouraged with yourself and if you are to live at all you will have to have within yourself enough reserve strength and nerve force to start again the next morning.

And when you haven't got it you will become ill. To become ill is to throw the burden off on some one else. It is a way out.

Sometimes I wish there would be set up a new form of prayer. Instead of crying out always to God I would like to see men on their knees praying, "help me, my fellow men." If men did more of that perhaps they would realize more fully how very much every one else needs their help.

O Thou Happy Land

Takings of the town editor—some purple plums from Gil Stephenson, yellow plums from Mrs. Henniger of Chilhowie, beans from Mrs. Tom Greer, apples from Mrs. Greer (made into apple pies and consumed), dahlias from Mrs. Henniger, a jack knife off Jailer Hopkins, cucumbers off Jack Minnerick—and this only Tuesday. O yes, a glass of delicious peach marmalade from Mrs. Stephenson.

This is a grand year for berries. The blackberries are coming ripe fast in the hills now. There are acres of them along roads— free to any one who cares to go and pick.

We see hazel nut bushes heavy with nuts. Everywhere we go we kick up coveys of young quails.

On the top of Slemp Mountain a big pheasant hen walked as calmly as a barnyard fowl out from under the wheels of our car.

Zinnias in the yard of Mr. Francis at Chilhowie. Mrs. Henniger's phlox is fine. It is in great bunches and in many delicate shades.

People come in and say to us, "come and see my flowers." We wish we had time to cover the entire county and every blossom.

We have made some little study of mushrooms and have a book showing in pictures a thousand varieties. There are but three or four poisonous varieties. Others may make you ill temporarily or act as an emetic. There are also varieties that while they are very beautiful are tough and woody.

The average man thinks of mushrooms and toadstools. Some of

the most delicious ones are passed a thousand times and ignored. I have gathered great baskets in Chicago, in the grass along the busy streets. A friend and I went for an early morning ride in Boston and brought home enough for a grand breakfast.

Well, it is a bit of trouble. You have to learn the varieties. They are as varied as the trees of the forest and as easily distinguishable. All the puffballs, when gathered fresh, are delicious. And then there are the Rasulas, the Boletus, a huge family with many fine varieties. We get the toothsome Parasol Mushroom in quantities in the woods about our farm in Grayson.

In the fall the Brick Tops. When I lived near Chicago I loved to walk in the woods as I do now. I saw Italians with great bags on their shoulders. They were gathering Brick Tops in the fall, bushels of them. They dry and pickle them. Dried they are a delicious flavoring for soups.

And then the mushrooms that grow on trees. Often on the trunk of a dead tree enough Oyster Mushrooms for a meal.

The Beefsteak Mushroom grows chiefly on old Chestnut trees. It is red and tender, with a slightly acid taste—a connoisseur's favorite.

Some of the most gorgeous looking ones are not edible. There is the Bitter Boletus, as fine a looking mushroom as grows but as bitter as gall. There is a mushroom grows on old stumps. It is a handsome great yellow thing. At night it gives off a strange light.

The thing to do is to learn definitely the poisonous kinds. Go into the woods with some one who knows. Know the dangerous ones and then you may make some discoveries of your own.

Europeans do not let this fine food go to waste. There all mushrooms are gathered. Varieties that are passed daily in our woods, as toadstools, are to be seen for sale every day of the season in the markets of Paris.

P. S. The Coral mushrooms are a great species here. They are handsome things to be seen in the woods, like unto the coral growth at the bottom of the southern seas. We use them as we would spaghetti. They need a long cooking but are fine. Often we cook nuts with them.

The Fishing

It has been a fishing and a fishing story week. Cars, loaded with men, have been climbing daily over Walker's Mountain. Burt Dickson's brother came to see him and they went, accompanied by Dr. Dave Buchanan. It is said they got fifteen.

Then Mr. George Collins and Charley Rider lit out and came in with seventeen. Charles Rider is the son of Tom Rider and Tom is one of the famous fishermen of this section. Mr. Collins and Mr. Rider got seventeen—some of them beauties.

Marvin Anderson lit out alone. He was dressed in a gray tweed suit, the same sort the Prince of Wales wears when he goes after them. In his right hand he carried a pole, in his left a minnow bucket. These decorations added immensely to his appearance. The next morning Mr. Anderson walked so proudly through Main Street that strangers stopped their cars and asked where the parade was.

All week a procession of lucky fishermen coming home. Mr. Preston Collins, accompanied also by Mr. Charley Rider and with the editor along as spectator and to count the fish, went on Friday. Mr. Collins had a fine day but Mr. Rider was off form. The editor had a good day, acting as referee between Mr. Rider and the larger bass and also stringing and counting Mr. Collins' fish. The scenery was grand.

The Park

The little park, in the heart of Marion, is gradually taking form. The city government is tearing out the old eyesore building and moving the rubbish away. A prominent citizen said on the street the other day that the taking out of the old eyesore building had done more for the general appearance of the town than anything that has happened here for years.

Through the generosity of Mr. Charles Lincoln, Sr., and Mr. Charles Wassum we shall have good rich dirt to fill up the unsightly hole left by the taking away of the old building.

This fall we should be able to set out plants, young trees and grass.

Perhaps we shall have a sidewalk and steps up the hill to the church. We have no doubt that, when we get some flower beds laid out, the women of the town will give us flowers and flowering plants to fill them.

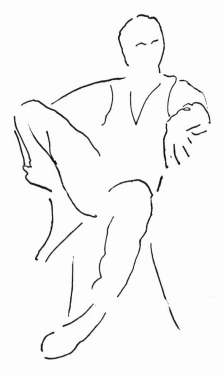

BUCK FEVER

FIRST WEEK OF

AUGUST

Marauder

Just before dawn I heard a faint, low rush
  Among the horse-weeds near my stable door;
I listened, fearing a sharp-toothed robber's raid;
  I listened—then I dozed away once more.

I scarce had sunk within sleep's yawning pit
  When a raucous squawk that ended in a gasp
Brought me to consciousness and sent me forth
  With a smoking lantern swinging from my grasp.

Garbed like a prowling specter, I emerged.
  And hurried down the path with slippered tread
To the low coop where dusk had sent my flock
  Before the moon had crawled above the shed.

Armed with a sturdy cudgel I appeared
  And the hens, crouching in terror near the door,
Seemed to implore my aid with shrill, high cries
  While their sickled chief lay bloodless on the floor.

But the sly thief had left with bulging flanks
  To join his mate along the bayou's rim

251

And he will seek for other wattled throats,
Scorning the rusting trap which yawns for him.

                                    JAY G. SIGMUND

Why Indeed

EDITORIAL

Why do intellectual men, writers, painters, etc., have such a passion for prize-fighters? A great fuss is made about Mr. Prize-
fighter Tunney's intellect. He probably hasn't much. A working
mind leaves its marks on the face. There is nothing particularly
sensitive about this face. It is not the face of a bruiser nor yet the
face of a thinker. On the whole it is a stupid face. Mr. Dempsey
is more popular. He is more a creature of impulse. I saw him once
and liked him. We were in the studio of a New York photographer. He took me into a corner of the room. "You are a writer,
eh?" "Yes," I said.

He told me that he had been acting in the movies. "I hate it,"
he said. He made no pretense of having a mind but I felt he had
one. "I enjoy fighting," he said. Well he meant he enjoyed the
rush of it, the plunge, the excitement. He was no cold calculating
man.

Before a fight the man was all nerves. He walked restlessly up
and down the room that day I saw him. It was just before the
fight when he lost his championship. Tunney had been in the
same place the day before. The photographer, after Dempsey had
left, showed me several photographs he had taken of the man
Tunney. He seemed to me a dilettante, with his fists, with his
mind, his feelings.

"He would be self-conscious," I thought. "That is no plunger."
He would be a man always thinking—"now, as I am a prize-
fighter I must look fierce." He would be a gentleman. "I must
develop my mind."

I could imagine Dempsey going off on almost any sort of angle.

He might get drunk, get into a saloon brawl—if there were any
saloons. He might take a sudden and violent fancy for some
woman. He might do any generous thing.

Mr. Tunney is going off to Europe to walk, it is said, with a
writer. I can fancy them going along the road together. They are
thinking. One is thinking, "Here am I, a man of the mind, the
fancy. I have a close friend who is a prize-fighter. How wonderful."

The other is thinking—"I am a prize-fighter but I am no brute.
I consort with men of the mind. I am really a remarkable man."

There will be a good deal of publicity about all this too. Already there has been a lot.

It is true that the man of the mind has always a liking for the
man of action. Primitive simple people appeal to him. He is trying
to understand human nature. These self-conscious calculating men
do not appeal. They are too much like himself.

And he is himself a man of action—in the true sense. The
painter, at his easel, when he is really painting is an excited man.
All of his nerves are on edge. I have watched painters at work who
were like Dempsey about to enter the prize-ring. One man I knew
swore violently sometimes when he was at work. If you had interrupted him at such a time he might well have hit you with his
fist. He might have beaten you brutally. "Get out of here."

He was trying to catch some delicate things. Thoughts and feeling elude like a fast opponent in the ring. You rush at your opponent—the idea. Oh, if I could only hit it squarely, send it sprawl-
ing.

I remember going once into an apartment in New York. A man
lived there, a writer friend. He had invited me to come and dine
with him.

I went in the late afternoon. The place was all quiet. I went
through his workroom. He was in his bedroom, lying on his bed.

A disheveled man. He told me later that he had been working

for two years to try and get just the feeling he wanted in a certain
piece of work. That morning he had got up feeling ill. However,
as he sat at breakfast what he wanted came clear to him. He had
written some twelve thousand words that day. The twelve thousand words were the very heart of a long book. After he wrote
them that day he never changed a word. It was marvelous writing.

And what a physical task. All day he had been hitting and hitting. There was perfect timing of the sentences. They rang like
bells. I have read over what the man wrote that day a hundred
times. I can see no flaw in it.

He told me that on the particular day of which I am now speaking he was so exhausted by noon that he could hardly sit in his
chair. He sent out and got a quart of whisky. During the afternoon he drank it all. "I was drunk later—when I had finished the
thing," he told me. "While I worked I was not drunk."

Well it was a physical task. When I saw the man he was so
exhausted he could scarcely raise his head from the bed. He was
as a prize-fighter might have been after a marvelous fight.

As for this Tunney, he is a bit too patronizing for me. He profits
by the prize-fighting thing and yet speaks of it with contempt. The
being intellectual is a bit too obvious. On my life, Mr. Jack Dempsey, or before him the negro Jack Johnson, had each of them the
better mind.

There is too much of this bunk about a man having a mind because he reads the classics. It is not Mr. Will Shakespeare's fault
that Mr. Tunney delivers lectures about him.

Strange Love

That office cat we had—I do not mean Nellie but the one that
came next after Nellie. That was the one, you will remember, that
never did get a name. He, or she, took up the roving life. Occasionally it comes to visit the print-shop. It watches Joe work on
the lino-type, rubs against Jack's legs, climbs up on Gil's make-up

table, leaps on Zeb's shoulder. Then it goes away as calmly and quietly as it came.

Recently it has taken a strange fancy. It has fallen deeply in love with a hen. The hen belongs to Mr. Hopkins, our well known jailer. The cat and the hen are inseparable. They go out together for evening strolls. Ofter they may be seen walking about the fountain in the park. The hen clucks and the cat mews.

It may well be that they are having intellectual conversations. Formerly, when we lived in New York and Chicago, when we knew more or less intimately the city intellectuals, we saw often strange male and female attachments. Among men and women also there are those who could not rightfully be called "he" or "she." There people often go in strong for the intellectual life. The coarser things of life, as one might well say, are thrown aside.

And so, we imagine, it is between this strange couple in Marion. They do not think or speak often of food. The more carnal lusts do not touch their pure and undefiled souls.

They stroll of an afternoon in the park and speak of higher things. It is beautiful to see them. We have recommended that our young Buck Fever form some such an attachment, say with a steer from one of our fragrant pastures.

There are so many problems in life that could be escaped if more of these attachments were made.

SECOND WEEK OF

AUGUST

Fire Department Runs Wild

NEWS

The Fire Department whistle let loose in good shape about 4 P.M. last Friday. We have seldom seen, or heard, a fire department

whistle blow with more intensity. It was a hot still summer afternoon. One of the most prominent of the Rialto merchants had
just been telling us that, with him, trade was not what it should be.

And then the whistle let loose and the merchant ran and so did
we. Accompanied by the whole fire department and about half of
the citizens we ran first to the house of Mrs. W. J. Matson. Mrs.
Matson was away but had left her house unlocked. There was no
evidence of fire. There we were, all set to put out a fire and there
was none.

So we ran around in Mrs. Matson's yard. A lot of the citizens
went on into Mrs. Matson's house, but as we had not been invited
we stayed out.

Some one had a bright idea. "Well, there must have been a fire,"
they said to themselves, "otherwise why did the fire whistle blow?"

It was a really bright idea. The man who had it is to be con-
gratulated. Some one called up central. "Quite right," said central,
"Mrs. Morgan's house is afire."

We went over there. Quite right again. Mrs. Morgan's house
was afire. In the same house lives Mrs. Mary Morgan, Mrs. M. M.
Miles and Mrs. M. M. Painter. They were all away. We put out
that fire. The editor did little about the fire but he did give a lot of
good advice. He gave advice to Mayor Dickinson, Dent Staley,
Billy Vines and several others. Mr. Earn Frances was going
about with a sign that said, "keep off this building." He hung it on
the editor by mistake.

So we came on home. We understand that the fire was started
by an electric iron, inadvertently left turned on. The damage must
have been considerable. It would have been less had Mr. Frances
hung that sign on the building instead of on us.

Contented Tar Barrels
NEWS

The boss is always giving me fool assignments. The other day
he wanted me to go on down to the new home of the town ma-

chinery and tar barrels and see how they were getting along in
their new home. Doc Brown and Bill Todd went down with me.

It is sure fine down there. I never saw tar barrels looking better
in my life. Their new home is a nice big old southern antique
house, the grounds of which are washed by Staley's Creek. We all
had a nice time down there. Mr. Wheeler, assisted by Bill Grundy,
poured tea.

Then we stood around awhile. "I expect your boss will want you
to write this up in some fool way, eh," said Doc Brown. "Don't
you like to be in the paper, Doc?" I said. "No," said Doc. "Then
for why did you run for mayor?" I said. I had him there.

We asked Bill Todd how he liked the tar barrels in the new
place. "Fine," Bill said. Bill has an affectionate nature. He went
over and patted one of the tar barrels on the shoulder. It was the
first time that particular tar barrel had ever had that kind of
individual attention from a town official.

Well we looked around at the road scrapers and the nice pile
of sand and the road rollers and all. It was as nice a walk as we
ever took. Everything down there is dry, roomy and out of the
way. Mr. Wheeler and his boys have done a good job. They have
got a swell blacksmith shop and everything they need.

BUCK FEVER

It May Be

A LETTER

To the Editor. My dear Sir:—I am afraid you are a hard-hearted
man. How much fuss you have made, for example, about giving
young Buck Fever, who works for you, a little raise. What is back
of this? The young fellow has as much to do with the success of
your papers here, if they are successful, as you have yourself. I do
not believe you are such a stingy man. I have seen you in both of
the two drug stores of the town. Men were drinking coco cola in

these places. You did not always smooch on the others. Once or
twice I have seen you set 'em up.

What I am thinking is this. I wonder if you really have any
comprehension of what such a young fellow as this Buck is up
against.

Well, he has come down here to live in town. He is going about
with town girls. Unlike a lot of other young fellows here he has
no car.

He hasn't any white pants, no tennis racket, bathing suit, golf
clubs. You would be surprised, Mr. A., to see how many times the
young fellow is humiliated. It is like this. Suppose you were a
young fellow yourself. You know as well as I do that Buck is a
rather handsome young man. Now that he is in town here and is
associating with the more cultured of our young town men, and
with our girls home from college, he has lost a lot of his country
crudeness. Why, Mr. A., you must have noticed it yourself. As a
writer Buck has a certain flare. You know that. He has a quick
sense of humor. There is something downright about the fellow.

I did think he wrote one piece, a few weeks ago, that might
well have been left out. I mean that one about the corn hoers. And
the one about the woman in Troutdale, behind the door. The
other night I asked Buck about these pieces. He says you egged
him on to it. He says it is your fault.

But I am getting off the point. Now that I am at it, Mr. A., I
think I shall unload my mind on you a little. As I have already
suggested I am a young man myself. I think, as a matter of fact,
that now that he is down here, my friend young Buck, looks up to
you as he might to a father.

You are tight with him and I know how he feels because my
own Dad is tight with me.

Just the other day my Dad and I had a falling out. It came about
like this. I had got crazy about a certain girl. My own Dad has a
car. I wanted to take the car to take the girl out.

Well, it happened Dad wanted the car himself. There was a visitor at our house, I told Dad I was going to take the car and just run downtown. Instead I kept it all evening. To try and square myself at home I got up a cock and bull story about running the car accidentally into a ditch. I had bent a fender a little, I did it purposely. Then I told Dad that I stayed out because I was afraid to come home.

The next day Dad and I had a row of course. He was sore at me. This wasn't the first thing of the sort I had done. I am a young fellow and have been selfish and pig-headed a good many times.

Anyway Dad got me into a room up at the house and talked to me. He told me a lot of things about character, how I would be nothing in this world until I developed some sense of responsibility to others. "You come home here, when you want to do something," he said, "and act as though you owned the place." It was quite true too.

My point is that if we young fellows are to develop the kind of character that you want to see in us you have got to have patience with us. I couldn't tell my Dad that. It is hard to talk to him sometimes.

I do such darned things. Well I get all set to have a strong character, to be nice and considerate with every one and then- bang-off I go. I was talking to a girl I had out the very night I got in so bad with Dad and she said that with her it was the same way.

But now I will go back to Buck. He is a friend of mine. I think you ought to come across with him. It may be, Mr. A., that you think by keeping him hard up like this, you are developing a lot of character in him but I think a man can get too much character. You didn't want it to grow on him like a hump on a camel, do you?

The reason I tell you this is that I saw Buck up against it the other evening. We were out with some girls. Buck got into a tough hole not having any money. Of course he passed it off with a funny crack but it hurt his feelings just the same.

Afterwards we took the girls home and walked around a while. Buck is pretty loyal to you and when I began to roast you for not treating him better—"Oh," he said, "I think the boss is all O.K. He is teaching me a lot and giving me a chance." He said that but, to tell the truth, he was all broken up not having the money to do his share with the girls.

So, Mr. A., if you are holding out on Buck just to develop his character I think you have done it enough.

And if you are just a tight wad, of course that is another matter.

A FRIEND OF BUCK'S

Fools

EDITORIAL

It is one of the most curious things in the world. I mean this matter of what is known as popularity. Any man of sense should know there is nothing in it. All men of sense do know it—with their heads.

They do not act upon it, however.

It is an axiom of newspaper offices that all people love publicity. "Do not believe them," says the old newspaper man. "They will come in and protest. 'Do not put my name in the paper,' they will say. Pay no attention to that. Slap it in and they will love it."

As a matter of fact, as an axiom, it is quite true. The notion of popularity carries with it the notion also of a kind of universal affection. That is sweet to all of us. We all like to think of ourselves as walking in a friendly world. On all sides are warm friendly smiles. Every one is wishing us well.

A quite charming idea but in practice it will not work. What you are in the public mind, if you are at all a public figure, is a built up thing. Shrewd publicity men know well enough that what is called, "the public" has no mind. Or it has the mind of a child. You must give it something it can feed upon.

And it wants simple plain food too. If I wanted to create the impression of being wise, a brainy man, I would walk through the streets often with a pile of books in my arms. It would be well to carry among them a few foreign books. You do not need to be able to read them. I have seen this worked. Occasionally go into a store, or wherever men are congregated. Put the books down and walk out, as though absent-mindedly. Some one will pick them up. There is a Greek book among them. Now you have got the report started. "The man knows Greek."

The public mind does not like subtle things. It likes big broad symbols. Roosevelt, the man with the big stick. There is a picture they can take. Wilson was a man too subtle to be popular. He was never a good showman.

An idea started in the public mind becomes quickly a fixed idea. Let us say you are an author. Your public is not very large but it is a public. It is like any other public.

Some critic starts a notion going about you. It is picked up by the next critic. Variations are played on the same theme. It goes on and on indefinitely—having all the time nothing to do with your real self.

Well, you become hardened. It does not matter. The public is nothing. It is a peculiar institution. Separate it into individuals and it is gone. What you come to live for and by in the end is individuals. You let the rest slide. When people write about you, saying over and over the same things, you do not read what is written.

You live by individuals, by the few people who may know you as a person and whom you may know in the same way. The rest is nothing. It is smoke. It is a thing blown away by the first wind. Any man of sense having been at all a public figure is soon fed up.

But all the same, like a child himself, he still clings to the vague notion of a warm and friendly world in which he can walk, admired and loved by all. To the end we remain fools.

In Court

NEWS

The sheriff, deputy Lamie and others said they were over in Lickskillet before day one morning. They had got information about liquor making over there. Lickskillet is just off Poor Valley.

The officers laid up over there. The brush was thick on the mountain top. Pretty soon they heard a sound. They say they looked up and saw two men, scrutched down, making through the bushes. They claim Drew Collins was one of the men. He had, they say, a big brass kettle on his head.

So the officers lit out after him and he dropped the kettle and ran. When they got up to where they had seen him they found a poke of flour, some empty quart fruit jars and the kettle. Nearby they found some mash and a still furnace. The flour, it seems, is used to paste up the cracks in home-made stills.

But Drew Collins says he wasn't there. He said he never went through the brush with no kettle on his head. Prosecutor Funk tried to get the kettle brought into court.

It seems the commonwealth did not make out a case. The Judge told the jury to bring in a verdict of not guilty. "All right," they said, and so they did it.

BUCK

Death of Chew

NEWS

Old Chew is dead. He was a big black dog known to almost every man, woman and child in Marion. How many times have we seen him lying in the court house yard. He liked the cool cement floor in the print-shop and loved to come in here on warm days. He would stretch himself out by the folding machine and lie there for hours.

Old Chew always had a certain dignity. He came and went like a man who knows his way about. Bill Johnson, the butcher, gave him bones or John McGhee gave him a chunk of meat. He was the property of Doctor Thompson's children and went there every night.

Sometime ago he became ill and went blind. The Thompsons took care of him. They fed and nursed him and gave him medicine. One day they all went away and Old Chew, gone blind now, wandered over into Prater's Lane. There have been a good many reports of mad dogs lately. Some one got excited, seeing the blind dog wandering about, and went and got a shot gun. Old Chew was wiped out. A dignified friendly citizen of Marion is gone to his rewards.

The Fair

EDITORIAL

The fair is an institution as old as mankind. When Cæsar went up into the wilds of Germany he found towns and villages there in the forests. Annual fairs were held there, among the wild men in the German forests, as they are held in American towns today. Well there were the broad-shouldered wild men of the forests riding their wild horses. There were exhibits too. The horse traders were there.

The same thing going on in far China and Thibet. Marco Polo, the first great traveler, speaks of the fairs of the far east.

And on the Russian Steppes and in cold Siberia other fairs being held.

Normal men have always loved horses. The automobile has rather taken the horse out of everyday life. For a time it was thought the horse might disappear out of our civilization.

Indications are, however, that the horse is here to stay. Horse racing is regaining all of its old popularity. Vast crowds in the cities now go to see the runners, the trotters and pacers. Purses are higher than ever. The horse has become an aristocrat.

O, the horse, the horse. This writer remembers when he was a young boy. He went horse crazy once. He got a job with a string of trotters and pacers. It was a lowly job. He was a groom and went about in horsey, evil-smelling pants. Well does he remember when he came home and told his mother what he was going to do. There were tears in her eyes. She thought the association of the tracks would be bad for her son.

Still she was one who hated to cross a son of hers. "If it gives you satisfaction, go ahead." The son did go ahead.

I dare say the associations were bad too. What profanity the boy heard. There were men about the stables who were artists at it.

Tough women hanging about too—and con men, flash men of all sorts.

The boy made friendships there he will never forget. There was Bert, the big negro with the big fists, and laughing long John Bottsford, a fellow groom, and Billy Stark the driver. Once he found a man who was with a little fake show. You paid ten cents and got a picture of your future sweetheart. The show had trouble sometimes, something slipped. One country white girl got a picture of a gigantic negro and another country girl a picture of a bull dog. That one gave the showman a black eye.

The fellow who ran that show walking about in strange towns with the editors talking, I remember, of poetry. We talked of Shelley. Would you believe that? He could quote whole poems.

And there was a fellow who was the wild man in a pit show. He claimed to have been a Virginia gentleman and a land owner once. Drink, he said, had brought him down. After the crowds had gone in the evening he used to sit with us and lie and lie about his past.

It was good lying. We learned a lot from that one.

And the horses and the cattle and the bands and the shows and the crowds.

And the glorious day when the boss got sick and let us drive Solarian, that great pacer, in the last heat of the free-for-all pace. And we won it too, not through any merit of our own but because Solarian only needed a light boy up who could hold the reins and talk to him to win it himself.

And then our name in the paper, to be mailed home proudly to mother. And after the fairs were over in the fall going home, ourselves to brag and brag and tell some of our own lies.

Lives there a man with soul so dead—who never to himself has said—"What Ho!—for the fair."

A Sentimental Journey

A STORY

Joe is a thin mountain man of forty with the figure of a boy. He is straight and tall. I remember the first time I ever saw him. It was a day of the late Fall and I was on a gray horse riding in the hills of our Southwestern Virginia.

It was a lonely land and I was at that time a newcomer. I was a little nervous. Romantic tales of mountain men shooting strangers from behind trees or from wooded mountainsides floated through my mind. Suddenly, out of an old timber road, barely discernible, leading off up into the hills, Joe emerged.

He was mounted on a beautifully gaited but bony bay horse and while I admired the horse's gait I feared the rider.

What a fierce-looking man! Stories of men taken for federal agents and killed by such fellows on lonely roads became suddenly real. His face was long and lean and he had a huge nose. His thin cheeks had not been shaved since the last Saturday. He had on, I remember, an old wide-brimmed black hat, pulled well down over his eyes, and the eyes were cold and gray. The eyes stared at me. They were as cold as the gray sky overhead.

Out of the thick golden brown trees, well up the side of the mountain down which Joe had just come, I saw a thin column of smoke floating up into the sky. "He has a still up there," I thought. I felt myself in a dangerous position.

Joe rode past me without speaking. My horse stood motionless in the road. I did not dare take my eyes off the man. "He will shoot me in the back," I thought. What a silly notion. My hands were trembling. "Well," I thought. "Howdy," said the man Joe.

Stopping the bay horse he waited for me and we rode together down the mountainside. He was curious about me. As to whether he had a still concealed in the woods I do not now know and I have never asked. No doubt he had.

And so Joe the mountain man rode with me to my house. It was a small log house I had built on the bank of a creek. "E" was inside cooking dinner. When we got to the little bridge that crossed the creek I looked at the man who had ridden beside me for half an hour without speaking and he looked at me. "Light," I said, "and come in and eat." We walked across the bridge toward the house. The night was turning cold. Before we entered the house he touched my arm gently with his long bony hand. He made a motion for me to stop and took a bottle from his coat pocket. I took a sip but it was raw new stuff and burned my throat. It seemed to me that Joe took a half pint in one great gulp. "It's new," he said. "He will get drunk," I thought, "he will raise hell in the house." I was afraid for "E" too.

We were sitting in the house by a fireplace and could look through an open door. While we ate "E" was nervous and kept looking at Joe with frightened eyes. There was the open door at her right hand and Joe looked through it and into his hills. Darkness was coming on fast and in the hills above a strong wind blew but it did not come down into our valley. The air above was filled with floating yellow and red leaves. The room was heavy with late Fall smells and the smell of moon whisky. That was Joe's breath.

He was curious about my typewriter and the rows of books on

the shelves along the wall, but the fact that we were living in a log house put him at his ease. We were not too grand. Mountain men are, as a rule, uncommunicative but it turned out that Joe was a talker. He wanted to talk. He said that he had been wanting to come and see us for a long time. Some one had told him we were from distant parts, that we had seen the ocean and foreign lands. He had himself always wanted to go wandering in the big world but had been afraid. The idea of his being frightened of anything seemed absurd. I glanced at "E" and we both smiled. We were feeling easier.

And now Joe began to talk to us of his one attempt to go out of these mountains and into the outside world. It hadn't been successful. He was a hill man and could not escape the hills, had been raised in the hills and had never learned to read or write. He got up and fingered one of my books cautiously and then sat down again. "O Lord," I thought, "the man is lucky." I had just read the book he had touched and after the glowing blurb on the jacket it had been a bitter disappointment to me.

He told us that he had got married when he was sixteen and suggested vaguely that there was a reason. There often is among mountain people. Although he was yet a young man he was the father of fourteen children. Back in the hills somewhere he owned a little strip of land, some twenty acres, on which he raised corn. Most of the corn, I fancied, went into whisky. A man who has fourteen children and but twenty acres of land has to scratch hard to live. I imagined that the coming of prohibition and the rise in the price of moon had been a big help to him.

All of that, however, came later. On that first evening his being with us had started his mind reaching out into the world. He began talking of the journey he had once taken—that time he had tried to escape from the hills.

It was when he had been married but a short time and had but six children. Suddenly he decided to go out of the hills, and into the broad world. Leaving his wife and five of the children at home in his mountain cabin he set out—taking with him the oldest, a boy of seven.

He said he did it because his corn crop had failed and his two hogs had died. It was an excuse. He really wanted to travel. He had a bony horse and taking the boy on behind he set out over the hills. I gathered he had taken the boy because he was afraid he would be too lonely in the big world without some of his family. It was late Fall and the boy had no shoes.

They went through the hills and down into a plain and came to a coal-mining town where there were also factories. It was quite a large town. He got a job in the mines at once and he got good wages. It must have been a good year. Joe had never made so much money before. He told us, as though it were a breath-taking statement, that he made four dollars a day.

It did not cost him much to live. He and the boy slept on the floor in a miner's cabin. The house in which they slept must have belonged to an Italian. Joe spoke of the people as "Tallies."

And there was Joe, the mountain man, in the big world and he was afraid. There were the noises in the house at night. Joe and the boy were accustomed to the silence of the hills. In another room, during the evenings, men gathered and sat talking. They drank and began to sing. Sometimes they fought. They seemed as strange and terrible to Joe and his son as these mountain people had seemed to "E" and mvself. At night he came home from the mine, having bought some food at a store, and then he and the boy sat on a bench and ate. There were tears in the boy's eyes. Joe was ashamed. He was only staying in the mining country to make money. His curiosity about the outside world was quite gone. How sweet the distant hills seemed to him now.

On the streets of the mining town crowds of men going along. There was a huge factory with grim-looking walls. What a noise it made. It kept going night and day. The air was filled with black smoke. Freight trains were always switching up and down a siding near the house where Joe and the boy lay on the floor, under the patched quilts they had brought with them from the hills.

And then the winter came. It snowed and froze and then snowed again. In the hills now the snow would be in places ten feet deep. Joe was hungry for its white wonder. He was working in the mines but he said he did not know how to get his money at the week's end. He was shy about asking. You had to go to a certain office where they had your name on a book. Joe said he did not know where it was.

At last he found out. What a lot of money he had. Clutching it in his hand he went to the miner's house at night and got the boy. They had left the horse with a small farmer across the plain at the place where the hills began.

They went there that evening, wading through the deep snow. It was bitter cold. I asked Joe if he had got shoes for the boy and he said, no. He said that by the time he got ready to start back into the hills the stores were closed. He figured he had enough money to buy a hog and some corn. He could go back to making whisky, back to his hills. Both he and the boy were half insane with desire.

He cut up one of the quilts and made a covering for the boy's feet. Sitting in our house as the darkness came he described the journey.

It was an oddly dramatic recital. Joe had the gift. There was really no necessity for his starting off in such a rush. He might have waited until the roads were broken after the great snow.

The only explanation he could give was that he could not wait and the boy was sick with loneliness.

And so, since he had been a boy, Joe had wanted to see the outside world and now, having seen it, he wanted back his hills. He spoke of the happiness of himself and the boy trudging in the darkness in the deep snow.

There was his woman in his cabin some eighty miles away in the hills. What of her? No one in the family could read or write. She might be getting out of wood. It was absurd. Such mountain women can fell trees as well as a man.

It was all sentimentality on Joe's part. He knew that. At midnight he and the boy reached the cabin where they had left the horse and getting on the horse rode all of that night. When they were afraid they would freeze they got off the horse and struggled forward afoot. Joe said it warmed them up.

They kept it up like that all the way home. Occasionally they came to a mountain cabin where there was a fire.

Joe said the trip took three days and three nights and that he lost his way but that he had no desire to sleep. The boy and the horse had however to have rest. At one place, while the boy slept on the floor of a mountain house before a fire and the horse ate and rested in a stable, Joe sat up with another mountain man and played cards from after midnight until four in the morning. He said he won two dollars at that.

All the people in the mountain cabins on the way welcomed him and there was but one house where he had trouble. Looking at "E" and myself Joe smiled when he spoke of that night. It was when he had lost his way and had got down out of the hills and into a valley. The people of that house were outsiders. They were not hill people. I fancy they were afraid of Joe, as "E" and I had been afraid, and that being afraid they had wanted to close the door on him and the boy.

When he stopped at the house and called from the road a man put his head out at a window and told him to go away. The boy was almost frozen. Joe laughed. It was two in the morning.

What he did was to take the boy in his arms and walk to the front door. Then he put his shoulder to the door and pushed it in. There was a little fire in a fireplace in a large front room and he went through the house to the back door and got wood.

The man and his wife, dressed, Joe said, like city folks—that is to say, evidently in night clothes, pajamas perhaps—came to the door of a bedroom and looked at him. What he looked like, standing there in the firelight with the old hat pulled down over his face—the long lean face and the cold eyes—the reader may imagine.

He stayed in the house three hours, warming himself and the boy. He went into a stable and fed the horse. The people in the house never showed themselves again. They had taken the one look at Joe and then going quickly back into the bedroom had closed and locked the door.

Joe was curious. He said it was a grand house. I gathered it was much grander than ours, in which he sat talking. The whole inside of the house, he said, was like one big grand piece of furniture. Joe went into the kitchen but would not touch the food he found there. He said he guessed the people of the house were higher-toned than we were. They were, he said, so high and mighty that he would not touch their food. What they were doing with such a house in that country he did not know. In some places, in the valleys among the hills, he said such high-toned people were now coming in.

And, anyway, as Joe said, the people of the grand house evidently did not have any better food than he sometimes had at home. He had been curious and had gone into the kitchen and the pantry to look. I looked at "E." I was glad he had seemed to like our food.

And so Joe and the boy were warmed and the horse was fed and they left the house as they had found it, the two strange people, who might also have heard or read tales of the dangerous character of mountain people, trembling in the room in which they had locked themselves.

They got, Joe said, to their own house late on the next evening and they were almost starved. The snow had grown deeper. After the first heavy snow there had been a rain followed by sleet and then more snow. In some of the mountain passes he and the boy had to go ahead of the horse breaking the way.

They got home at last and Joe did nothing but sleep for two days. He said the boy was all right. He also slept. Joe tried to explain to us that he had taken the desperate trip out of the mining country and back into his own hills in such a hurry because he was afraid his wife, back in her cabin in the hills, would be out of fire-wood but when he said it he had to smile.

"Pshaw," he said, grinning sheepishly, "there was plenty of wood in the house."

It had, after all, been only the snow-covered hills that had called him back out of the world.

FOURTH WEEK OF

AUGUST

They Do

NEWS

"Why," says a well-known citizen of Marion, "if there is any drinking nowadays I do not see it." That same day the editor drove to his farm. At one spot there was a Ford parked across the road with three drunken men in it asleep. The editor finally woke them. They managed to push the car off the road, falling down several times in doing it. The editor went on to his farm and came back to Marion. Some one told him that Herbert Fry, of Saltville, had been caught, red-handed, at a still by officers Holmes and Thompson and was in town trying to get bail. Hy Whistman had just arrested Reves Rolland. Reves, it seems, was full of corn and thought he was a wild and woolly man. He drove around shout-ing and waving a gun. He got down to Luther Buchanan's store, on South Fork, and it is said rode around the store shooting in.

Sheriff Dillard had just been out in the South Fork neighbor-hood and had got one of the Dipes boys. He was accused both of being drunk and of selling.

Si Price, over at Chilhowie, gathered up Russ Hankley. Russ

had bought some alcorub to rub on. It smelled too good, he said, so he drank it. It seemed to get results.

Si was also chasing Charlie Hicks of Charlotts Creek, which is at the entrance of Cleghorn Valley. Charley got filled up and wanted to fight some one. There was no one else about so he fought his sister

It is said the sister whipped him.

From a Boy

A LETTER

We are in receipt of the enclosed letter from our friend David Greear. David is about twelve years old. He is with his father John Greear, an engineer in the Wildcat Lumber Camp at Helen, Georgia. David says:

"I am sending you a subscription for the paper. A man here wanted it.

"I am water boy for the grade crew, building a railroad back up in the mountains here. I asked one of the mountaineers, working on the road if he would be glad if Al Smith got elected. 'No,' he said. He said he was afraid the price of liquor would go down and he couldn't get nothing for what he made.

"Another who was working with us was due to go to jail for bootlegging but he got them to let him off so he could make some liquor and pay up his fine.

"The other day I was going through the woods and felt my foot give a little and heard the sound of a rattle snake. I was standing on his head. I thought that if I got off he would bite me so I looked for an opening in the brush and made a leap. I got away all right so I caught him alive. Then I killed and skinned him and made me a belt out of his hide. I could send you a rattle if you wanted it because I have got two.

Yours Truly,

DAVID GREEAR"

Mrs. Jimmy Dutton

One of the most unique figures at the fair this year is Mrs. Jimmy Dutton, of the Dutton acts. These are the acts to be put on before the grandstand every afternoon and evening. You would never pick Mrs. Jimmy for a show woman. Well why not? She is gentle, sensitive, intelligent.

With her husband Jimmy she has been in the show business for years. The Duttons have played in almost every big city in America and Europe. Before the war she, with her husband, appeared before the Czar of Russia, the Kaiser of Germany, and other European notables.

In all the Duttons put on eighteen acts here, changing the acts constantly. When the boss sent me up there to see Mrs. Dutton she was frightened and troubled. Only four months ago her husband, Jimmy Dutton, died. The shows got to Marion on Monday. Her right hand man, William Bausmann, was taken sick here. He was rushed to Southwestern State Hospital where it was found he had appendicitis. As I write this he may be dying or he may be saved.

But I am not writing about him but about Mrs. Jimmy. I went to see her. The boss told me to. She was upset. She is a nice woman. She is as nice as my own mother. And she took me over to her horses. They were as nice horses as I ever saw. There was one lovely white horse given her by Mr. John Ringling, the big circus man, who was a friend of her husband, Jimmy Dutton.

Anyway there was Mrs. Jimmy and her hands and her lips were trembling a little. She said to me, "You tell 'em," she said. "You tell 'em that I may be up against it but I am going to give Marion the best lot of shows before the grandstand this year ever seen in their lives."

I guess she will too. I would lay a bet on that. She is all right. I had to rush down to get this piece in the paper. But before I went Mrs. Jimmy took me back over by the grandstand and showed me

the new lights intended to light her acts. "It's good, eh," she said.
I guess, whatever happens to Mrs. Jimmy she will always be a first
class show-woman. I admit I fell for her. I like her. I think the fair
is lucky to get her and her shows. She is O.K. with me and I bet if
you miss a show she puts on here you are out just that much.

BUCK FEVER

Fair Notes

The sky has been spotted with great white spongy clouds. No
one could have painted in a better background for the fireworks,
the parachute drop, or for Miss Vivian Devere's whirling figure
high up on the trapeze.

A bit later we hope to print the names of all prize winners at the
fair.

There have been corking finishes in many of the races. Nothing
pleases us more than to see two good horses fighting it out down
the stretch at the trot or pace, preferably the trot, a nicer gait.

There are people who see no difference between this rather fine
art, and a horse merely running. They like the run because it is
faster. The hoofs rattle. It is true the run can be a pretty gait but
it is not the trot. Ah, there is something. The horse has to learn
to hold that. There is better timing, a rhythm that has to be held.
There is a finer art in the driving.

There is something very charming about the technique of the
show people. They all do it, the tumblers, the strong girls, the girl
on the trapeze, the contortionists. The little artificial half run to the
front of the stage, the entirely artificial bow, the artificial but graceful movements of the arms and legs. This editor loves it all.

And there is a knack of picture making too. Some one connected
with the Dutton shows has it—we suspect Mrs. Jimmy. How very
well everything is handled to make the picture. That is not acci-
dental. It works best at night, against the night sky. Mrs. Jimmy
knows her business all right.

We like also the men at the cattle barn, the fat hogs lying there
on show, the baby beefs, all curried and washed, the chickens in
the poultry house, the bunches of corn and other grains, the hand-
work of the women on show.

You see how it is with us. The fair just suits us. How we hate
to see it pass. How we long for it to come back again. There is one
thing sure—we would not think of living in a county without
imagination enough to hold a fair and we think it rather significant
that Smyth County has the best fair we have ever seen in a county
seat town. And we have seen a lot of them.

Si Copenhaver, the starter of the races, has just the knack. He
knows how to handle horsemen. He is severe without being too
severe. He is a human, likeable man.

There was one very clever little race horse named Irish Luck. A
one-armed negro owns him. The negro's name is Reggy Smith.
He has got a sweet little horse.

H. S. Stout has his training headquarters at West Palm Beach,
Florida. He was here with five horses. Tuesday he started Checkers
and won·with him. He brought him back on Wednesday afternoon and driving a smart brainy race won again. He was ready
to start the same horse on Thursday when the rain washed the
race out. Mr. Stout looks to us like a smart driver.

One of the veterans of the harness horse world, here for the races
is W. F. Jenkins of Hawkinsville, Georgia. Mr. Jenkins is in the
late sixties and has been racing horses for forty years. He had
Mystery, 2.04; Dexter Lee, 2.06, and Lady T., 2.09. Any one who
saw him drive Irish Luck home to win in the last heat of the race
on Tuesday will not forget it soon.

The Bee Tree

Did they survive the cold? . . . when autumn locked
The creeks with glassy floors I saw them hide

In this dead burr-oak . . . scolding blackbirds flocked
And then the white snows wrapped the countryside;
Their last feast came from bloom of blighted clover;
I fear they hungered long before the sun
Grew friendly to the world it hovered over
And told them that the reign of ice was done.
I hope this linden's bloom will lure them here,
Now that the chopper's ax has spared their hold;
I think the thrasher's martial notes will bring
Their buzzing army out a million fold
And may they find each summer blossom filled
With mellow draughts some lavish god has spilled.

JAY G. SIGMUND

Soliloquy

I am constantly wondering about other men, how they manage
to live. Well, there they are and there am I. Sometimes the whole
idea of everyday life seems to me distorted, a little crazy.

I am thinking constantly of what I myself should be. Well, what
would I like to be?

I would like to be a man of more dignity. I would like not to
hurt any one.

There are so few nights when I can go to bed with any satisfaction to myself. At night I go into my own room and sit down. I
read perhaps a newspaper. The newspaper is an odd thing too.
There is the world spread out before me. Pride, crime, ambition.
How many pitiful things happen.

To-day I got a letter from an old friend. He was a man of forty-
two and fell in love with a young girl. How beautiful she seemed
to him. He let his whole life be wrapped up in her. Once, a year

or two ago, when I saw him last, he talked to me about it.

"It is dangerous," he said, "to be so absorbed in another but what am I to do? I cannot bear the idea of trying to think of myself, live for myself," he said.

He thought I was a luckier man than he was. He spoke of that. "You are not as dependent on people as I am," he said. He had the notion that my writing answered all the needs of my own nature. "It is something into which you can throw yourself," he said.

Well, sometimes, rarely, I can. Mostly I cannot.

Now my friend's wife has left him. She has fallen in love with a man nearer her own age. She came and told him about it. He made no fuss. "All right," he said to her, "I will do what I can." He has gone away from the city in which he has been living with her. In the meantime he provides her with money with which to live. Presently she will get a divorce. She will, I fancy, marry the other man.

And there is my friend sitting bitterly in his room writing to me. That is one of the sort of things that happen in this world. He is trying to be philosophic about it, to laugh.

His letter is a long one. He is trying to take it all as a part of life. "You bet and sometimes you lose," he says.

My mail is filled with all sorts of things. I am a man to whom people write letters. It is because of my books. I have written some story that has touched closely some man or woman. They feel close to me. A long letter sometimes results.

There is a woman in the east somewhere. She has centered her whole life about a little dog. The dog and the woman were on a beach. The moonlight was streaming down.

The little dog began to play. He ran madly in the moonlight. There may have been a kind of madness in the woman too. She had been ill for a long time. For some reason, when she went home, she sat down and wrote me a long letter. She described the moonlight, the sea, the dark look of the land behind her.

Her writing to me to describe all this of course meant nothing.

In a certain story of mine I once described some dogs, gone mad with moonlight. She remembered that and so, after she had come in from her walk, she wrote to me.

She took my name out of the front of the book and wrote me in care of my publishers.

She told me a story too that in an odd way capped the story told in the letter of my man friend.

She had been loved, in early life, by a man of whom she grew tired. She left him for another man. This happens pretty often in modern life.

Later she regretted what she had done. The second man grew tired of her, she said. He left her and she was alone. She lives alone. She has enough money to live comfortably.

I am in my room late at night and I sit here thinking. Sometimes I lay awake for hours after I go to bed. My room faces the town jail. I think of the men and women in jail. I think of friends kept and friends lost. I have lost a good many friends through my own foolishness.

This writing is a dangerous trade, too. Every writer has a desire to be clever. But cleverness is very dangerous. In being clever you sacrifice some one. You rob him of his dignity.

That ought never be done. Every man or woman should be left his self-respect.

For example, in New York recently I came face to face with a man who was my friend for a long time. He is a rather famous man, a writer. One day he sat writing. He thought up a very clever, and rather nasty phrase about me. It was one of those phrases close to the truth and yet not true. Once I was broke and was lecturing before a large audience in Brooklyn. I was doing it to get some money with which to live. Some man in the audience suddenly got up and repeated that clever and rather nasty phrase. I was humiliated before a crowd of people.

I see people trying to humiliate each other all the time. It happens almost every time I hear men talking together on the streets here in my town. It happens everywhere.

I do it sometimes in my papers too. I try not to do it but I do. The trouble with writing for a newspaper is that your stuff goes to press too soon. More than once I have awakened in the middle of the night. A day or two before I had written something I thought was funny. Perhaps it was funny too, but at some one else's expense. Sometimes I get up early and run downstairs into the print-shop to throw something of that sort out of the paper.

I am trying to give you here a picture of a man's thoughts, as he sits in his room at night, or after he has gone to bed and is lying quietly there.

Sharp pangs of regret, a feeling of cheapness. Often I lie in bed thus for hours thinking these thoughts. I wonder how many others are doing the same thing. "I am a muddler in life," I say to myself. I wonder how many others are saying to themselves the same thing.

I think I must have become a writer because of this trick in myself. I could not bear thinking of myself when I was alone and so I tried valiantly to think of others.

I began with people I knew. I tried to be some one else.

I imagined myself being a horseman, racing horses on the race tracks, I tried to imagine myself rich, or poor, a youth, an old man, a United States Senator, a sport, a woman, a young girl. I remembered little things I had heard people say.

There was a man walked in a certain way. Another man was always saying disagreeable things to people. There are all kinds of people everywhere. They are doing and saying all sorts of things. They are actuated by all sorts of desires and ambitions.

You cannot think far into other lives without becoming intensely humble. How do people manage as well as they do?

The habit of trying to be some one other than myself has grown on me. I do it constantly. I remember once being a murderer—in fancy of course. I began having all of the thoughts of that man. There was a tense moment, while the desire to kill was growing in my mind. It became a definite thing. He did kill. While he was killing his man I sat writing. This was on the deck of a steamer at sea. I remember how vivid everything was. I was thinking every thought the man thought, having his emotions. He got his man killed. I got through describing it all.

Just then a man came along and spoke to me. "Hello," he said. His voice startled me so that I came near leaping into the sea. The world I had been in, in which I had killed a man, was ten times more real than the real world. The man's voice had jerked me back too suddenly into the real world. I turned and walked rapidly away from him and went into my stateroom. I stood inside the room shivering, although it was a warm, fair day.

If I had not been a writer or a painter, some kind of an artist, I would have had to live too much with myself. I could not have stood it. Long ago I would have gone mad.

FIRST WEEK OF

SEPTEMBER

∞∞∞

County Housekeeping

That is what Mrs. Homing-Pigeon says it is. She was in yesterday. "Such things as the colored school and the county jail are a matter of county housekeeping," she says.

If the county thinks it is good housekeeping and good sense to let things go, they will.

"What is the use talking of money? Such things depend on whether people want them or not.

"If they want twenty-five or -six men penned up in an unsanitary place, if they want the colored people not to have a decent school, then they won't have a new colored school or a larger and more sanitary jail.

"If disease breaks out in these places and infects the town or the county, well then something will be done.

"It takes a real disaster to stir the feelings of most people," Mrs. Homing-Pigeon says.

Squeak

NEWS

Another print-shop cat has come and gone. This one was named "Squeak." When he was a little thing Dent Staley brought him down here in a paper poke.

Gil

He was a handsome cat, Squeak was. But all of our cats that do not die seem to have the wanderlust. Squeak was an automobile cat. He couldn't resist them. Let a car stop in front of the shop and he would get in.

He went away on two or three automobile pilgrimages and came back. Doc McCarty brought him back once.

We fancy he finally got on a through car. He had extended his field of operation to the Rialto. Heavens knows where Squeak is now. He hasn't been seen for a week.

Buck Fever Says

We have a book in the library called, "My First Two Thousand Years." The author writes:

"The book will offend no one but the Catholics, the Protestants, the Mohammedans, and the Free Thinkers."

The boss gave me this book to read. I was afraid.

He wants to have it read first by a special town committee. "Did you buy the book?" I asked the boss. "No," he said. I knew he didn't. He never buys anything.

I think some safe person ought to read this book and report on it. It may not prove to be half as bad as the authors hope.

Land Locked Sailor

No other man along the ridge
Could splice a hay-rope's strands,
And he had queer, blue anchor things
Tattooed upon his hands.

He swore the sort of heavy oaths
Which only seamen swear;

His clumsy footgear was the kind
Which old salt sailors wear.

Rough days he'd ask: "How would ye like
To climb a mast to-day?
For she'll be choppier than Hell
And soak the deck with spray!"

While other times he'd sit and dream
While rainbows curved their stripes;
Some brighter days he'd whistle tunes
Filled with the lilt of pipes.

I've seen him let his hay be wet
While whittling out the prows
Of tiny, masted, sailing boats,
Or larger fishing scows.

But one day when a windstorm broke
I saw him almost cry,
Because two lost, bewildered gulls
Went veering through the sky.

                                   JAY G. SIGMUND

On the Witness Stand

EDITORIAL

This writer finds life a lot more interesting, trying to think what
others are thinking than spending too much time over his own
thoughts. Too many of his own thoughts are not very cheerful.

I never see a criminal go on the stand to be tried without a
feeling of relief that it is not me.

As every one knows there is the continual accident of life. There

are so many laws that every one breaks them. Well, I personally
do not break in houses, I have not struck any one or been struck
for years, I never shot any one, I pilfered a bit when I was a boy,
as most boys do, but the fact that I do not do it now does not let
me out.

In spite of all the bodies of lawmakers the real crimes of life
are not reached by the law.

How many times have I been cruel and ruthless, pushing my
own purposes against the purposes and interests of others.

It is possible to make some other human being, who cares for
you, suffer hell by neglect. A housebreaker, who breaks in some
one's house and steals goods, probably does not do one-half the
harm done by a scandal-monger.

The real crimes of life are done of course by those of us who
do not get on the stand to be tried for them.

To be a criminal is stupid. As a young man I went sometimes,
as most young men do, into houses that were not very respectable.
Writers sometimes write of such places trying to throw a glamour
over them.

There is no glamour. Women who lead loose lives professionally
are not intellectually interesting.

It is a question if all people who lead lives of crime are not men-
tally defective—or near it.

How stupid they are. When caught how stupidly they lie. Go
into the court room and watch. How obviously the witnesses lie.
It is difficult sometimes to prove they are lying, but every one
knows they are.

Well, here is a case in court. The witnesses are sworn. It is a
form. The witnesses go and put their hands on the Bible.

"Will you tell the truth, the whole truth and nothing but the
truth?"

It would be a hard oath if any one thought about it. Truth, eh.
Most of the better brains of the world have been seeking truth
for ages. They have not got very far with it.

Now the witness is on the stand. Let us say there are five witnesses. They have all agreed on a certain story.

"We will swear to this—John, who was seen leaving the vicinity of a robbed house at night was not John. We will all swear John was somewhere else.

"We will swear he was at Will's house and we were all there. We were playing cards."

But how are we to fix the time?

"You Bert, will say that you looked at your watch. You asked John what time it was. Your watch was eleven minutes slow. You set it."

And now an odd thing happens. One by one the witnesses who are to swear to a lie get on the stand. They become confused. Their stories get mixed.

However, they are all clear about one thing. Bert's watch was eleven minutes slow. They all have a childish belief that, if they agree on the eleven minutes, if they all remember that, their whole story will be believed.

The man who has committed a crime is in the docket. He is watching the witnesses. Sometimes it happens that, to save their own scalp, his own people are compelled to testify against him.

He is watching the faces of the jurors, the judge's face. Let us say he is facing a prison term. He looks out at a window. Others out there are walking about, are free, free.

A sickening hunger for freedom. What chance has he in a dash? Officers are sitting about. They have guns. He has to give that thought up.

He becomes indignant. The criminal on trial, like all people, has to save as much as he can of his self-respect. That is the great thing. Even to feel himself a dangerous man is something. The Kinney Wagners are trying to make people respect them. That is what they are up to. It is a great egotist who dares kill another man.

There is a twist in the brain.

Most criminals have convinced themselves that all society is armed against them. "I never had a fair chance," they all say.

That is another way to save their self-respect. If I can convince myself that society is in a conspiracy against me I can say to myself—"what chance have I?"

It is a fascinating, terrible spectacle, this watching people being tried for crimes. There is so much stupidity. Crime is stupidity of course. There is often great cunning in the criminal but never intelligence.

Who Shot the Horse?

NEWS

This is a question that has torn the social life of the Rich Valley since early summer. A horse, belonging to Mr. C. F. Chapman, got out one night in early June and wandered, with two other horses, loose on the road, into the field of Mr. W. F. Keezee. Mr. Keezee is foreman on the large cattle farm belonging to Richardson and Clark.

Something happened there in the early morning and there are many conflicting stories about it. A young man, then employed about the place, says that Mr. Keezee got out early and saw the horses in the field. He had been annoyed before by the same horses and lost his temper.

There was a twenty-two rifle at the house and he went and got it and shot one of the horses twice.

Mr. Keezee denies the story. There is an intimation that the young man who told the tale was sore, having been discharged, and that he himself shot the horse and then "threw off," as we say in Grayson, on Mr. Keezee.

There was much conflicting evidence about what happened in the early June morning. At least two dozen witnesses testified. People saw and heard things. Others saw and heard something else. The jury were also puzzled. They were out a long time.

To shoot another man's horse maliciously is a felony and is punishable by a long term in the penitentiary. The jury finally brought in a verdict against Mr. Keezee but said the horse, while shot intentionally, was not shot maliciously. They fined Mr. Keezee $125.

Jack Pruitt's Story

NEWS

Jack says that on an Easter Sunday, two years ago, he went to the house of old Jimmy Lamie, in Rich Valley. He was on his way down there, he says, when he met Jim Bowling and young Henry Lamie. "Would you like to stick your head into a barrel of mash?" he says Jim Bowling asked him.

This sticking your head into a barrel of mash, it seems, is an exquisite pleasure. Mash is the stuff out of which moon is made. It is the grain in the process of fermentation. Sometimes it is called, "the beer."

"Yes," says Jack. And so, he says the boys took him down to the site of an old sawmill. "Scrape the sawdust away," they said. Jack says he did. We gather he kneeled down, it being Easter Sunday, and drank long and perhaps loud.

"Ah," says Jack. So he says he and Jim and Henry went up and sat down under a tree. They rested up. Then another sticking of heads into the barrel and another and another.

Then Jack went on down to the Lamie house and had dinner there. He wanted to rent some land. Old Jimmy didn't much want to let him have it, but did.

He says he stayed about then and during the Easter afternoon went several times, with Jimmy and Henry, to again stick heads in there, that is to say into the barrels of mash.

And so evening came on, Easter evening. Jack says Henry spent the afternoon cleaning a gun.

They had all of them decided to make a run. And so, in the

evening, they went up and made it. They got, from what was left of the mash, some five gallons.

So he got a gallon for himself, agreed to pay $2.50 for it.

"Did you ever pay?" "No."

"Did you ever pay the rent on the land you rented from Uncle Jimmy?" "No."

So Jack went away with his gallon and got drunk with it. He was arrested. There is a provision of the law that, in such cases, if you tell on the others involved, you get free yourself.

Jack told on Jim Bowling, Henry Lamie and Johnnie Phipps. Jim Bowling and Johnnie were convicted on Jack's tale. Henry Lamie wasn't. The jury didn't believe him. You see, Jim and Henry and Johnnie say it is all a pack of lies. They say Jack only told it to get out of some scrape of his own.

And so Henry Lamie went free, but on the same story Johnnie Phipps and Jim Bowling are doing time.

Being Their Own Lawyer

NEWS

Clyde Moore and Estill Grogg were up on the charge of having liquor in their possession. They live near Broadford. They decided they would do their own pleading.

The two young men were caught at the back of a church over there. The sheriff, accompanied by another, had come along about eleven one night. He may have been told the young men were drinking. Seeing them loitering about the church he got out to investigate. The young men ran. They were both caught.

They had been sitting on the front steps of the church and beside the steps he found a bottle of moon.

It was the purpose of the young men, acting as their own attorney, to convince the jury that the bottle of moon was not theirs.

"But how did you get that way?"

They had got that way, they said, walking down the road. It

was in that uncertain hour between light and dark, a quiet evening it was. As the poet would say, "all was at peace."

One of them saw something shining in the grass. It was a half gallon jar of home brew. They climbed over the fence, got that and drank it.

Then they went walking again. Pretty soon a car stopped in the road. Some total strangers were in the car. They asked the boys to drink with them.

They would and did. Then they went on down to the church and sat on the steps. They say that there, beside them, within reach of their hands, was another quart of moon but they didn't know it. It was what you might call a remarkable evening. All nature about Broadford had become a kind of booze Christmas tree. The jury swallowed hard but just couldn't believe the story, even though they told it themselves and didn't have any lawyer to help tell it.

The jury said 90 days and $50.

Sir Oliver Sows

It was a noble thing to see—Sir Oliver Hopkins, the jailer, sowing grass seed in the park. Mr. Frank Copenhaver started to sow it but Sir Oliver stopped him. To every occupation in life there is a sort of rhythm, expressive, as one might say, of the inner nobility of the thing. We hope we are not getting too poetic.

Anyway Sir Oliver stepped off with a certain indefinable grace. He was bare-headed, his noble brow exposed to a strong September sun.

It is a shortcoming of our own that we did not have the band down. The sowing of grass should be a ceremony. What nobler occupation in this life?

We wish that all Smyth County could have seen Sir Oliver step.

Ex-Mayor Dickinson, Mrs. Colonel Homing-Pigeon and Mr.
Preston Collins were in attendance.

Suddenly, carried away by the grace of Sir Oliver, Mrs. Homing-Pigeon began to sing. She has a surprisingly sweet soprano
voice. It was grand to hear the lovely lady sing and Sir Oliver step,
his arm swinging in gentle rhythm to the song as the blue grass
seed went down into the ground.

SECOND WEEK OF
SEPTEMBER

A Note on Story Telling

They happen everywhere. The best story tellers are often un-
educated men. The stories of a man like Lincoln, when retold or
put into print, are often pretty bad. The man's great reputation
must have been founded on something more substantial than the
occasional flashes of wit that remain in the tales repeated.

Men in the country who lead simple lives, who do not see newspaper funny strips or read humorous books, often tell me tales
that are infinitely better than anything I see in print.

There is an old country builder, all his life a mountain man,
who has, during the last year, told me four stories I have been
trying ever since to get into words.

I want words that will convey just the flavor of his telling. I
haven't found them yet.

One of the stories I watched grow. He and I stood in the road
and there were two neighbor men on horseback. It was, I fancy,
just the Abraham Lincoln sort of story telling.

It went well but he wasn't satisfied. I could see that.

Several days later I gave him another chance. Again four or five people were standing about. I laid the groundwork for the story—led up to it, that is to say, and made a faltering attempt to begin telling it myself. That was for bait.

I stopped. I could see his eyes shining, his lips moving. "You tell it. It's your story," I said.

Well, he did tell it, that time. He had been at work on it. All real story tellers are alike. The old man had been thinking of the attempt in the road. Nights, after he had gone to bed or when walking in country roads alone, he had been practicing. He had left a bit out here, added something there. His vocabulary was meager. It is amazing how little vocabulary has to do with story telling. One word can be made to serve many purposes. It must be fitted just so into the whole. The whole thing must have a design, form.

The old man told his story the second time magnificently.

All writers, I am sure, have an experience I am constantly having. There are certain people that feed me.

They appear at the most unexpected times and places.

There was a man, an Irishman, used to work at a desk near my own when I was a copy writer in an advertising agency. God only knows how many stories I got from that man. He had the trick. What he did was to put his finger on the essential spot. I grew so ashamed after a time, having fed upon him so much, that I told him about it. "You should write the stories yourself," I told him. He tried. How he came out I don't know.

Not so well, I fancy.

He had read too much, had too much respect for stories in books.

Many good story tellers, when they take their pen in hand, become quite impossible.

What a writer has to learn, first of all, is not to have too much respect for the printed word just because it is the printed word. Such contempt is a very difficult thing to learn. Some people never learn it. You are a writer or you aren't.

A novel—a story.

Who cares for a novel because it is a novel?

Form is something to talk about. It isn't at all what critics, who write so much of "form," think it is. People who write about writing are very fond of playing with the word.

It is as intangible a thing as love. Did any one ever succeed in telling you what love was?

There is a certain advantage to be gained by what is called amateurishness. God knows, I, a story teller, do not care much about associations with writers. When a writer has begun to succeed a little he becomes a professional. The fun is out of the game. Such a man is too niggardly. He is always thinking of using all the material he can get his hands on. I have had professionals tell me a story quite openly and well. Such a man has, for the moment, forgotten himself. He has let go.

Then he remembers. I am another professional—or he thinks I am. I may be. God knows I hope not. Most of the praying I do is an appeal to God to help me escape professionalism. I have had such a man, after telling a story well, say to me, "Look here. That's mine. You can't have it."

The idea back of the remark made me a little ill.

If, just now, American writing is on the whole better than English writing, and I think it is, it is because it is more amateurish, more free, less professional.

What a writer wants is an escape from talk of writing. Thinking of it is all right.

Well, a man should think of writing. He should think of his story. He should hunt it day and night until he gets it, the soul, the very meat of his story.

Talking with other writers very likely only throws a man off. He gets on the subject of style. If you want to create a new method of writing prose, that's all right too, but it has nothing to do with the story itself.

What is the matter with James Joyce? None of the critics put their fingers on the spot when his *Ulysses* appeared. The man is scientific, an experimenter. When he tries to tell a story he is a poor story teller, God knows.

On the whole, I find myself better off associating with farmers, working men, business men, painters—any one except other writers. I can get what they have to say in their books.

And what stories I occasionally get from people, how beautifully told. People who lead rather isolated lives, like farmers, do it best. Perhaps they have more time to brood.

I remember a story I got last summer. It was told me by a man met on the road.

We were both on horseback and had stopped to gossip.

How he came to tell the story I can't remember. I wish I could tell it as he did. The story, his telling of it, lit up my whole day.

He was a man of about thirty, a farm hand. His name was Felix.

He had been in the war. He went in as a private and after he had joined was transferred, as he said, out of the National Army into the Regular Army. What that means I don't know.

Anyway there he was, a countryman, a rather heavy slow-speaking man thrown into a regiment where practically all the others were city men.

When they had got overseas they were stationed somewhere in the south of France. It was near the Italian border.

There was in the regiment an Italian-American from New York. He had been in America for nineteen years, had come here as a boy with an older brother and then he found himself with the American army near the Italian border, within some thirty-five miles of where his father lived.

He asked for a furlough, to pay a visit home, and they wouldn't give it to him.

There had been some kind of a general order. Felix, the farm hand who told me this story, said that in his opinion the head men of the army must have spent most of their time issuing general orders. There were so many of them.

The Italian-American, when they told him he couldn't go for a visit home, simply ran amuck.

"I'll go anyway," he said. "I warn you. If you want to keep me here you'd better lock me up."

What they decided to do was to let the man go for the visit home, but to have an American-born soldier go with him.

They chose Felix.

There was where Felix's best story telling came in. He described the walk over the Italian hills with the Italian-American. After they got outside the American lines the man spoke hardly a word of English and Felix had no Italian.

It did not matter. The American farm hand—he was from the hills of Virginia—got it all.

He felt the growing joy of the man, the feeling for his own hills. He said the man kept jumping and shouting in the road. He would walk for a mile singing at the top of his lungs.

They came to the house where the father lived. It was a little stone house in a valley. There was a hillside road leading down and in the road the man kept meeting people. They did not know him but he rushed at them shouting. He hugged and kissed men women and children. You are to bear in mind he was dressed in the uniform of the American army. Felix said the people did not know the man but felt his joy. Felix felt it too.

It was enough for every one.

At the door of the little stone house in the valley, when they came to it, the father and the son stood facing each other. The older man, the father, was almost deaf, he was almost blind.

However he felt something. He just stood staring at the two men in the American uniforms. Minutes passed. Felix said he could hear nothing but the ticking of a clock in the house. A young woman came into the room where the old man was and stood with her arms crossed.

There was a gun hanging on pegs on the wall.

Suddenly the old Italian man grabbed the gun and, pushing the two young men out of the doorway, ran into the yard.

He began loading and shooting.

He shot a rooster, a goose, a pig, a goat, and then another pig.

All the time he laughed and shouted and screamed. Felix, the man from the mountains of Virginia, as I have said, knew no Italian and yet he knew just what was going on. He even knew the old man's words. As the old man loaded and shot off his gun, making a regular slaughter house out of the barnyard, he kept yelling.

"My son! My son! My son!

"A feast! A feast! A feast!"

That, I thought, when Felix told me the incident, was story telling. Giving me, as he did, just the sense of that home-coming, the joy and wonder of it.

He did it with less words than any story teller I have ever heard. It was like Old Testament story telling.

And there was something else added. It concerned the woman who was the Italian-American soldier's sister. She had been a babe in arms when her brother left for America and did not, of course, remember him at all. His coming home couldn't have meant much to her, but her father's joy meant a lot.

Well, now she was a grown woman and married. Her husband, a poor laborer, was in the Italian army. They hadn't any possessions but she was living for the time in her father's house and he had given her a goose. He wanted it back to make a part of the feast for his son. He, the son and Felix had eaten up everything else on the place and had drunk all the wine.

She hung onto the goose because she wanted to give it to Felix as a present when he and her brother had to go back to the army. It was her way of expressing her thanks to him for bringing her brother home and making the old father so happy.

Felix said he carried the goose under his arm the whole thirty-five miles back to camp. It wobbled its long neck and hissed at every one along the road but he hung onto it. When he got back to camp he made a pet of it and for a month or two it went waddling and hissing up and down the company street. Then, he said, the regiment had to move to another place and he put the goose into the company mess. He said the piece he got—a wing it was—didn't taste very good. He said he kept thinking of the Italian-American's sister. "I was kind of stuck on her," he said. "When I was carrying the goose home," he said, "over the Italian hills, I kept shutting my eyes and trying to imagine I had her instead of the goose held tight like that in my arms."

THIRD WEEK OF
SEPTEMBER

It Rains

Rain, rain and more rain. The corn is down. Fall work is held up. The fair in Tazewell was spoiled. It happened again in Marion, the last two days, and no doubt will happen at Galax.

People on the street are restless and depressed. We all respond to weather more than we know. It is a time to be patient with each other, as gentle as we can be.

A dozen men have told me that they wanted to go away. They are restless under the gray clouds. It is at such times that men sometimes do dark evil things or think dark evil thoughts.

Life should be gay. It cannot be sometimes. I have had people speak sometimes of my own gayety when inside I was so depressed I spoke with difficulty.

And I knew they were speaking of my own apparent gayety because they were depressed. It is so difficult to help each other out. Almost every one does foolish things for which he has to pay.

I wish it were possible for me to be the friend of all men but I cannot be. I am like every one else, too much absorbed in myself.

Every one walking about—isolated figures. The gray days following each other—rain, rain and then more rain.

In the Mayor's Office During the Fair
NEWS

Mr. N. D. Wiles, a stranger visiting this fair, was brought in. He was passing through Chilhowie and Justice Charles Francis was also coming to the fair. Mr. Wiles was accused of reckless driving. He was said to have torn a hub cap off the Francis car. He was fined $5.00 and costs.

Mr. Levi Blankenbeckler of Adwolfe was arrested at the fair and accused of driving a car while intoxicated. He was bailed out and will have to appear before the next grand jury.

Three colored boys tried persistently to crawl under, or over, the fair ground fence. They were warned off several times and then arrested and brought before the Mayor. All three were from Chilhowie. They were fined $2.50 each with costs of $2.00, or $4.50. One of the boys paid up and the other two were put into jail.

Cal Brooks, from Cleghorn Valley, was on a bad one. It took three officers to bring him down from the fair ground and O what a head he had next morning. The Mayor fined him $20 and costs.

Will Harrison, who is in jail on a bootlegging charge, had a hot evening. He was in the upper tier with the two men from the state asylum, brought in intoxicated. They were bad ones, that pair. Will spent the evening hidden away on top of the cage. He crawled up there and just lay still until the state hospital men came and got their treasures.

Horse and Rooster Day in Court

NEWS

Mr. R. L. Cole bought a horse of Arthur Bowman. He didn't like the horse he got and from all accounts no one can blame him. That case wasn't called when we went to press. We will pass that one.

But the rooster case was fought out to a finish. Mr. George Cook and John P. Buchanan were on that one. It was fought so hard that at one time Mr. Cook's client broke down and cried. It seems M. R. Jones of Atkins had some steel traps set about his place, H. B. Atkins had some chickens. Hens and roosters they were. One of them went over to Jones' place and got into one of the traps. Then Atkins went over and got both the chickens—that is to say "Rooster," and the trap, too. Jones had him arrested for stealing the trap. There was a justice court trial of the case.

Then Atkins sued Jones for twenty-five hundred dollars for malicious prosecution.

"But why do you feel you should have that much money?" he was asked. He said it was on account of his reputation. Suppose his children should hear that he stole a steel trap. "But have you any children?" "Not yet." The man isn't even married yet.

But we are not trying this case. We are just pointing out what kind of cases sometimes get into our courts. It took an entire morning for a judge, several jurors and two of our best lawyers. But apparently there is no way to throw out such cases, if the men engaged are willing to pay for them.

Old Factory

EDITORIAL

With me ill health, physical weakness, weariness comes often from having too much going on inside. I am like a factory whose walls are not heavy enough for the machinery housed in it. Within an hour I have emotions that shake me to pieces. Sometimes I want to paint, write, dance, play—all at once. People speak of a writer's seeking materials. I never did it in my life. If any one here thinks I am here to get materials for stories they are foolish. There is too much material everywhere. Using the materials, handling them, is another matter. It takes a man to do that and sometimes, too often, I am but half a man, a tenth of a man.

There are days when every face in the streets shouts at me. Every one has a story to be told. On such days every scene resolves itself into a painting. I grow so weary at such times that it is with difficulty I raise my eyelids. I want the body of a giant, the nerves of a draft horse. I am a factory with too thin walls. The machinery inside shakes me to pieces.

FOURTH WEEK OF

SEPTEMBER

Fall

The change from summer to fall comes as suddenly and as subtly as the change in a child, that becomes suddenly no longer a child.

Fall is here. The summer is gone. There is a new feeling in the sky, in trees, in the grass under foot.

The summer went away like a bird that flies into a bush. There may be hot sunshiny days yet, but they will be fall days. With this writer it came after the rain that wiped out the last two days of our fair. They had but one horse race on Thursday. The trotters came out but the mud was too deep for them.

Some runners came out and ran, slashing through the mud. It was as though they were throwing summer out from their flying heels.

Then three days of solid rain. A cold clear day, a gray day and then more rain. Summer was having a hard time getting away. The gray clouds were a cloak, concealing her departure.

She is gone now. It is fall. It can be a glorious time in this country but it is not summer.

Alas, this editor was born poor. Winter is ahead. As a child the coming of winter always brought fear of cold and hunger. The old dread holds. In contemplation of winter I am always afraid.

Mamie Palmer, Bootleg Queen, in Dying Condition

NEWS

Mamie Palmer, the young woman who was picked up with a load of booze by the sheriff some time ago, is in a bad condition. She went before the grand jury and pleaded guilty.

In the meantime it had been found that she was in an advanced state of tuberculosis.

Her condition has now become so bad that today Judge Stewart telegraphed Governor Byrd asking that she be pardoned. Lying in the jail in this condition she is, of course, a menace to all the other prisoners. Even though we may feel that the guilty deserves to be compelled to take such chances—a very doubtful human point of view—how about the other prisoners, either not guilty or not proven guilty?

Our jail conditions here are terrible. Because the conditions in most county jails everywhere are bad is but little excuse. In Marion we have also a state hospital. Often men from the hospital, mental defectives, get out and get drunk. They are thrown into jail. Syphilitics and tuberculars are thrown in there. In these days of automobile accidents, bootleggers, etc., any man might be put in the same jail. A disease might be contracted that would result in slow horrible death.

The county jail and the negro school building are the two Marion sore spots, both unsanitary, either one likely at any time to spread disease through the entire community.

The Modern Age

EDITORIAL

The editor and his wife to see some pictures thrown on the screen at the office of Sprinkle Motors. It was night. The room was darkened. There was a young man there from the factory. The pictures were all concerned with tests made in a modern great automobile factory.

The exhibition made me determined to get some magazine to send me out to Detroit. I want to spend a day or two in one of these factories looking about. I would like to talk to the workmen there.

From these pictures—taken largely from the testing side of modern manufacture—most of the men employed are young men. The colleges must be turning out an endless number of these young scientists.

I was curious to see the faces of the workmen in the factories. The pictures were not large enough.

With me, always, the man is the most interesting side of any such industry. Who can doubt the efficiency of the cars made with such elaborate precaution against mistakes. Of course they are all right. Everything used is tested to an extent almost unbelievable. It must be so in all the later great manufacturing organizations and the larger the organization the more careful the tests of parts and materials can be. It is so because cost can be distributed over a greater number of cars.

Who can doubt that we could make each copy of this paper infinitely cheaper if we had a circulation of millions.

But there is always something lost. The something lost is of interest to me too.

O, it is not in manufacture. The amount given for the money cannot be criticized. It makes no difference to me that a few men, controlling these great industries, get enormously rich.

I do not think it matters so much who gets very rich. Who wants to be very rich? To want it is childish and foolish.

When you pass a certain point in the accumulation of money, money also loses its significance. How many men in New York to whom it makes no difference whether the house in which they live costs them, per month to maintain, a thousand or fifty thousand?

There is a sense in which these men are truly royal. They are royal about things that concern you and me closely enough.

As the young salesman from the factory talked I watched him closely too. He was a nice young man. He was saying certain words. In how many places had he been saying the same words.

Significant words too. He had in some way lost the significance of the words he said. Perhaps he had said them too often.

They were true words too. That was the interesting thing about it.

What puzzles me is an old question. To tell the truth how many men here in Marion are interested in automobiles? I mean really interested. Here is a machine closely interwoven into all of our modern life.

There is however no such relation between the men and the machine there was formerly between the man and his horse. Many men seldom lift the hood of the machine they drive. There are delicate, strange things down in there. The motor is itself a strange thing, the differential, the apparatus for lighting the machine and the road.

It is all wonderful, strange. We take it all for granted. What is wrong is the very thing that makes it right too. I mean that in perfecting modern industry the individual man has simply got lost. We all feel lost.

Formerly, at one time in my life, I had something to do with making motion pictures. No, I did not write for the movies, I had a job doing publicity for an actor. I never did much. I was put on the payroll and pretty much forgotten. At home I was at work on a novel.

I did however spend certain hours and days about the studios. It was a strange life. There were men and women there, acting in pictures, the story of which they had never heard. They did individual scenes that were afterwards patched together in the office to make the story.

It is so in modern industry now. Formerly at least the whole machine was made in one factory. Now there is a system of factories often in different towns. A great factory makes one part and another great factory another part.

Great assembly plants put the machines together. There is always this strange feeling of the separation of the man from the thing his hands make. It affects all life in a way few people realize. Much of the boredom of modern life is concerned in it. If there is any way out, any way to give back to the workman the feeling that here is a thing his own hands have made—a peculiarly healthy satisfying feeling—I do not know what it is.

ZEB

Decided He Did

NEWS

Two young men went into the Whitworth Store in Marion on Saturday and, after standing about for a time, went out. After they had left two lumbermen's jackets were missing. Mr. Whitworth immediately called up the Sheriff's office and Mr. Hopkins responded.

He went at once to Mr. Whitworth's store and after getting a description of the two men went out looking for them.

One of the young men had got out of town but the other, Buddy Austin, was at a nearby restaurant.

Mr. Hopkins went in. "Where did you get that jacket?" "At Whitworth's," he said. He had too. Mr. Hopkins took him over there.

"You stole it." "No, I didn't."

"I got it at Alexander's," he said. They went up there. "No, that isn't the place. I got it at Weilers."

They started up there. "Look here," the young man said, "I did help myself to it. Take me back there."

Mr. Hopkins took him back. He decided to pay for both jackets and Mr. Whitworth decided to let him off.

Bear Hunter Gates Gets One
NEWS

It was away up the northest corner of Smyth, where both Taze-well and Bland counties come into Smyth. Beartown is up there. There is also a great gorge and tall peaks reaching up to the sky.

C. F. Gates, John R. Petts and Albert Baker (colored) were up there looking for stray cattle when they came upon a huge black bear.

It was an unlucky meeting for that bear. Mr. Gates is the champion bear-killer of Southwest Virginia and has held the title for many years.

He pulled down on that bear and got him. He was brought to Chatham Hill. T. B. Ward, who told us about it, was one of the people who had a meal of bear steak.

Plays for the Boys
NEWS

Welden Reedy, a famous mountain banjo picker, who used to live in Smyth, was in town the other day with two other mountain men, also experts on the banjo and the guitar.

The boys went around to the jail and spent the afternoon play-ing for the prisoners. It was as good mountain music as we ever heard.

No, your editor was not in jail. He was with Park Commis-sioner Frank Copenhaver in Sherwood Forest.

We were wandering among the tall trees of the forest and feed-ing the little birds when the dulcet strains of music fell on our ears.

It was the boys inside the jail getting a real treat from three thoughtful men. Whatever the boys in that jail can get that helps while away the hours is surely coming to them.

Election
EDITORIAL

To the editor every election is a miniature war. In any hard-fought election some of the same influences that are so apparent in times of war come to the front.

Men and women lose their dignity and judgment. Each side is intent on winning. Often it doesn't matter how they win. The end justifies the means, etc.

What was intended by man to be a process of selection of their governors, on merit, becomes a game, often merely a tricky game.

I often wonder how any man can bear to be in a high political position when it is so generally known what price has to be paid to get there.

I have lived through two wars. During the great war I went about praying always for the end of it. I look forward with pleasure to the end of this political campaign. Misrepresentations on all sides, lack of human dignity.

But I have no illusions that in what is called "the good old times," it was any better. In the early days of our republic there was the same thing going on. I have not read my history in vain. Bitterness always—always ugliness when one party was trying to defeat another.

Long rows of men who have been president and who, after being president, have left no mark, nothing they can be remembered by. The school teachers tell the children their names. Nothing remains but a name on a long list of names.

No great achievement, nothing left of all the hard, bitter struggle that once went on but a name on a list of names. It is hard work for a sane man to see much sense in most of the election furor.

The Education of an Artist

To watch people, listen, be aware. Who has solved the riddle of human life? The man is angry. Why? Is a man ever angry at another. Perhaps he is dissatisfied with himself. He is taking it out on another man or on a woman.

What can you learn in the school? Almost everything they teach you is wrong.

Most writers never know enough poverty. They do not suffer enough disappointments. Success of any sort is a terrible handicap.

The world is ruled by the paradox. Who loves luxury as does the artist? If he is a good artist he is a sensualist. He is as unmoral as a dog. A fine dog has the sense of smell highly developed. The artist would have all of his senses developed like that.

There the man is, trying to train himself all the time. Color, the feel of fabrics, the seductive lines of the human form.

The lines formed by hills falling away into valleys. Horses pulling loads up hills.

Voices heard in silent streets at night.

Every impulse of the artist is toward luxury. Nothing destroys like luxury.

There is a type of mind that will never in this world understand the artist or his impulses. I call it the scientific mind. I may be wrong. What do I know of the sciences?

I am thinking of the type of mind that accepts surfaces. For every cause an effect. What are you to do with God? Where is your cause and effect there?

Absolute knowledge is vulgarity. How do you know you are right?

Cleverness is also vulgarity. The clever men are the popular ones. Why not? They are always saying things that sound smart. If you let any clever thing soak in it becomes as nothing. Cleverness is pure froth.

Most critics go around with little patent formulas in their heads. That is the easiest way. A formula is like a foot rule. You may measure things with it. However, do not blame the critic too much. We are all caught and held fast in traps. The critic has to pass upon works of art, one after another, rapidly. What about a man like Mr. Broun or Mr. Mencken? They have too much to do. I cannot blame them if they overlook some delicate things I have just caught in my prose. Pretty often I am coarse and hurried. If they do not catch me at it I am thankful.

I parade myself before the public. What contempt I have for publicity. However, let some editor of a magazine write asking for my photograph. He always gets it at once.

I am a proud man, arrogant, a fool. If I write something that does not attract attention I am angry. If it attracts too much attention I am angry.

There was a story of mine called "I'm a Fool" that every one praised. I liked the story when I wrote it. After every one had praised it I hated it.

When I contemplate my own childishness I am so sick of myself that I feel like suicide. What prevents is that I know others are as childish.

All of this sounds very serious. People reading my stuff think of me as a serious-minded man. I am not that at all.

Personally, in my relations with others, I am rather jolly, almost what is called a "good fellow."

I am always up in the air or down in the pit.

I knew a doctor once who had good sense. I went to him for an examination. "You have a disease for which I can do nothing. You are getting older."

I am presumed to be talking of education, the education of an artist. I am a profoundly ignorant man. It may be the only road to knowledge is through having diseases. I call myself a profoundly ignorant man but if some one else were to say it I would be offended.

The situation of the author in America is unique. I write stories, novels, what I call poems—sometimes. Recently I built a house. The house is in Grayson County, Virginia. It is a stone house and a stone house was never before built in that part of the country.

The house was built almost entirely by what is called "unskilled labor." What an educational summer that was for me. We gathered the stones along the road. As the house is far from the railroads what ingenious devices we have had to resort to.

O, the ingenuity of those workmen. Formerly I was also a workman. Many of the men were better workmen than I ever was. All summer, as I watched them, I grew more and more ashamed of myself.

Surely it is more important to build a house well than to do some of the things I do and for which I get well paid. For talking a lot of nonsense on paper I often get as much, for two or three hours' work as some of these men got for working all summer.

It is sheer brutal folly. If I took it too seriously I would go mad.

Everything in life seems to me like that. It is a mess, sometimes a strikingly glorious mess. "What the hell," I say to myself. I grin and chuckle over life as much as any one.

Great God, see what happens. I get better paid for much less important work than those men. The house they have built is mine. I can order any one of them off the place. Suppose a good workman got drunk and came by the place late at night. He is swearing furiously. In town he got into a quarrel with another workman. He is thinking of him, going home, swearing at him. "I'll cut his damn heart out." There he is, shouting under my window, disturbing my sleep. For doing that I can have him arrested. "Never set your foot on my place again." He may have been the best builder I had. But for him I might have had an ugly house. I have a beautiful house. It is solid and has lovely lines. I did not do it.

I have myself been drunk, shouting in roads at night.

I have known writers who have got serious about such matters— John Dos Passos, Upton Sinclair. Such men, always mourning about workmen, pretending they are workmen, that they feel like workmen.

What rot. An artist is an artist. He isn't anything else. Anyway, whether I am a good or a bad artist, I have accepted myself more than that.

Well, I hate money. I love it. I hate people. I love people. I hate work of any kind. Work is the only thing in life that interests me.

All of these contradictions wrapped up in me. I sound very serious as I write this. I am writing with my tongue in my cheek.

How am I going to educate myself. It may be that acceptance of self is the only education a man needs or can get. If you were like me you would find acceptance of self pretty hard. I assure you of that.

Well, here I am. Formerly, that is to say perhaps ten or twelve years ago, I wrote a lot of stories. I gathered them into a book and got them published. There I was, an absolutely unknown man sitting in a garret. I made my living every day by going to an advertising agency and writing advertisements. No doubt there was a certain purity in my stories at that time. There must have been a certain purity in me.

When my book was published I got nothing but abuse. People sat down and wrote me letters. My book of stories sold only two or three thousand. Sometimes it seemed to me that all my readers were writing me letters.

Most of the letters came from women. "You have a filthy mind. You have a filthy mind." That sentence ground into me day after day.

The book, that was so filthy, that came from a man with so filthy a mind, became suddenly pure. It began to be praised. Suddenly it blossomed out, was in all of the public libraries. It was reprinted in one of the low-priced libraries. How many have been sold I do not know, perhaps fifty, perhaps a hundred thousand.

Nowadays the book is almost universally praised. How pure and sweet it is. What has become of the man who wrote it? I do not know. This hand, that now pounds this typewriter, wrote the book, but the hand is now attached to the body of a far different man. People nowadays sometimes write me letters, saying, "Why are you not pure and sweet as you were once?"

What I am trying to get at is the simple fact that here I am. I am a man trying to educate myself. Education for me means an understanding of people. How am I going to understand?

I dare say that if I were a scientist I would be all right. I could get a fact under my belt and keep it there. As it is I have never in my whole life been able to lay hold of a fact. When I get ahold of one it melts away to nothing before my eyes.

You see how fond I am of swearing at scientists. I know nothing of science or scientists. A man has to have some one to swear at. I grow so tired of always swearing at myself.

There is another thing. I will mention that briefly and then I will quit. It is about this matter of uncertainty, groping in the dark, all that sort of thing.

You see, to write of this matter at all, I have to presume that the readers of this tirade have also read some of my books, that they have listened to what has been said of me and my books. That may be the greatest nonsense of all.

It may be that this whole article is an attempt on my own part to interest people in me, to send them to buy my books. I assure you I would be entirely capable of that sort of sly whipping-up of interest. If there ever was a sly man in this world I am one.

However, to resume this matter of groping, of "uncertainty." If a man calls me an uncertain man, a groping individual, it means surely that he, having so pronounced on me, must be quite sure of himself.

Really, the country is full of that kind of educated men. There are any number of men who know positively that—well, they know that if the proletariat were to come into power the world would be a better place.

They know where they are going when they die. They know about women.

They know what is good and what is bad, what is beautiful and what is ugly.

Why I do not myself become better educated through knowing these men I cannot say. I have gone toward them so hopefully so often. They apparently know but they are unable to teach me. They give me certain facts which I devour greedily. They give me no sustenance. It seems I am doomed to starve in the midst of plenty.

SECOND WEEK OF

OCTOBER

On the Rialto—Rain

Politics on the wing. A good deal of sharpshooting. Some shooting from ambush, too. Not many dead yet.

The big rain sent a mighty stream of water down the Rialto hill on Friday night. The council had just killed the boss' sidewalk bill. When the boss got home the mud was banked an inch deep against his front door. The boss says some one is groundhogging on him.

Weiler department store sprung a roof leak. A lot of valuable goods injured.

In the Curtis Beauty Parlors the water was six inches deep on the floor of the shop. The Deep Sea Club sent boats out to carry off the customers.

The back of Doc Thompson's drug store, where the Senators sit on winter nights, was all flooded.

All the Third Ward suffered. There were a good many cars parked along the curb. As the water rushed down the hill the wheels of the cars threw the water across the sidewalks and into the stores.

Saw both Doctor Dave and Bob Anderson, but neither man was willing to attach any political significance to all the water. I didn't think they would. It was the boss' idea.

                                                              BUCK

Painting in the Print Shop

More and more these days our print shop walls are flaming with pictures. We were able to buy, just after the war, some marvelous reproductions by German printers. We have a water color by Marins, paintings by Bonner and Matisse and a young Russian named Zawado, photographs by Stieglitz and Man Ray, woodcuts by Lankes, a fine charcoal by Jerry Blum, some delicate etchings by Roy Partridge.

These men are all fine workmen. It will pay you to study the walls of the print shop these days. Others are to be added. Some of our painter friends have offered us paintings that will come later.

We have also a fine Lincoln and a Lee, and the Jefferson given us by Governor Byrd. Also a fine early print of Maud S. at full speed.

Modern painting is just fitted for such a shop as this. It is infinitely better to have these fine things here than in a picture gallery. Men work here, farmers come in, the town merchants and lawyers.

The modern painter tries for color that means something in itself. These paintings, in the print shop may not mean much to you at first but after you have seen them for a time they make the old stupid paintings, so common in most places, look pretty tame.

Ester Woods Not So Gentle

NEWS

She is described by neighbors as a "roadside-sitter." Her name is Ester Woods. Some time ago, that is to say in early August, she came along the road in a Ford car. She was out of gas and oil. So she just sat there. A man would hardly describe Ester as "a lady in distress."

She is a stout courageous soul, Ester is. After she had been sitting in the car for a time Jim Osbourne came down out of the hills and got her and her Ford. He brought a mule down and hauled them home.

Ester said, in her trial before Justice Farris, that Jim was all right but wasn't the fighter she is. They seem to have struck up a partnership. They began living together.

Carl Kimberling had rented some land of Jim to put out to corn, on shares.

Ester says Carl turned his mule into the corn to eat up Jim's share and that Carl had Jim bluffed out. Ester says Jim was afraid to say anything but she wasn't.

She took up for Jim, fought for him.

She was brought to trial for going down to where Carl was

cutting corn in the field and cutting loose some real language. She cut a little loose in court. Squire Farris fined her ten and costs for being a disturber. "That's all right," Ester said; "now how much extra will it cost me to beat up Carl right now?" Ester looked as though she could do it too. I wouldn't want any of that kind of road-sitters or mule-stoners on my road. Ester is the real thing.

BUCK

THIRD WEEK OF

OCTOBER

On Trial

NEWS

The editor's horse got out of his pasture, over at the farm one day last week and was taken up by a neighbor. We offered $5.00 to pay the damage, but the neighbor wanted $20.00. I guess he thought we were rich. Well, we are but not in money. Our riches are in friends, good health, work that we like to do.

So the neighbor and I fought it out before Squires Johnson and Lum Sebastian over in Grayson at Grant and the squires soaked us three dollars.

The neighbor had to pay his share of the cost and so he was out of money. Had he been more neighborly he would have been $5.00 ahead. Had he been a good neighbor he probably wouldn't have charged us a cent.

Poor Male

There are some flax plants glowing under the window of Tom Greer's office. A year or two ago he threw a handful of seeds out the window and the tall plants have been growing there ever since.

Reporter—"But why are some of them dead and dried while the others are still green?"

Mr. Greer—"The dry dead ones are the males. As soon as they serve their purpose they die. They are however the only ones that bear any flowers."

Reporter—"Thanks for that."

Mr. Greer—"Well, after a time the females die."

Reporter—"Can the females survive or get anywhere without the males?"

Mr. Greer—"They can't do a thing in this world."

Reporter—"Many, many thanks for that word of comfort, Mr. Greer."

To the Band

The Marion Band has been playing at more places. When our band goes some place people listen to it. "Oh," they say, "is that the Marion band?" The band boys practice faithfully. They sit up in a hall and play. The music floats out over the town.

The band ought to come out of the hall oftener. They ought to make the town band-conscious.

Boys, on the nights when you go to practice, and when the weather is clear, get out and parade once or twice up and down the Rialto. Play as you march. No use waiting for some special occasion. You make it a special occasion just by getting out on the street.

People will say, "What's going on?"

Well, the band is going on.

We do not wait until some one asks us, "Why don't you get out another copy of the paper?" We go ahead and get it out. The band should appear more often on the street. They should make the town know they are there and improving all the time.

Mamie Palmer Dies

NEWS

Our readers will remember Mamie Palmer, the bootleg queen. She was picked up on the highway near Saltville by sheriffs of the county with a load of liquor in her car.

When brought to Marion and sent before the grand jury, Mamie plead guilty and was put into our well-known jail. At once County Health Officer Ward, Judge Stewart, and others about the court, interested themselves in Mamie. She was already far gone in consumption but was a cheerful soul. Every one in jail liked the poor thin woman with the sharp voice, the sharp tongue and eyes.

Whatever else she was, Mamie was a true stoic and a sport. She took it all, even her approaching death, as a part of life.

At once Judge Stewart wrote to Governor Byrd, telling of the dying woman's condition and the governor pardoned her. Mamie was so evidently a woman who had been through a rough life but many a woman in a good comfortable home might have learned something from her. There is many a woman needs her spirit and her gameness.

We had written about Mamie in the papers and two men of Marion—names withheld on request—came in and asked us to see her and see if she needed money.

She didn't. There were West Virginia friends ready to take care of her.

They did try. But Mamie was too far gone. She went to her friends in West Virginia and was there for a week or two when she was taken with a hemorrhage and died.

The Moderns

EDITORIALS

"Great things are about to happen," says my friend Alice. She had come down here from New York to talk to me. Alice and I are old friends. I connect her in my mind with the idea of the Moderns because Alice has always been so modern.

She was in step with the young people of thirty-five years ago. That crowd went on. She caught step with a younger crowd and a younger and a younger. There are people like that. They are not so young in their bodies but stay young in their minds. Because they are so young in their minds the bodies do also stay surprisingly young.

Alice had come down here to Marion to talk with me about the kids of today. She is quick with sympathy for them. "Anyway, they are brushing aside a lot of bunk," she said.

While she was with me Alice talked of many things. "Suppose the young people of to-day do succeed in breaking down old moral standards. They have pretty much done that."

"Do they solve anything by that?"

It is as difficult to live now as it has ever been. Young people may neck and they may kiss each other. They may go even further. There is excitement in it.

But life is not based on that. Love between man and woman is a strange thing. You cannot fool with it. Do you or don't you?

To love you have to think constantly of the other person. "I care for another not myself," you say to yourself. There are obligations on all sides. The physical forms of love without the reality become at once vulgar. Every sensitive person knows that.

Perhaps the old expression of morality centered too much on the form, the word, and not enough on the reality. It is like Christianity itself. Who can doubt the pure worth of Christianity as a force in the world?

But the forms of Christianity without the inner reality—of what worth is that? It is vulgar to pretend to Christianity when you do not have it.

My friend Alice has an idea that the young people of to-day

are finding these things out. They are finding out, she thinks, through experience. It may be true.

And what things are to be found out. There might be established a real sense of morality and decency in the world.

For example, there is a great deal of wealth in America. People still cling to the idea that there is distinction in wealth itself. How foolish. You have but to know a few wealthy people to see the falseness of that idea.

They do not get fineness with their wealth. Are you poor? You walk past the house of some wealthy man. You go along the street past some wealthy club. There are clubs in America that cost as much as fifty thousand dollars to belong to.

Do you think anything interesting is going on in the clubs? You ought to go in there—sit around in there. I have done it. Nowhere in this world will you find such dull bored people.

They can talk of nothing but money and the cost of things. Hardly any of them know how to spend money. There is rarely any development of the mind or the imagination. Such places are horribly dull.

Alice thinks that young people will gradually get disillusioned about these things, about wealth, pretense, all kinds of bunk.

But in finding out will they vulgarize themselves beyond repair? That is evidently the question faced by the moderns. If the old morality is to break down there must be a new morality. Any sort of decency is beset with difficulties on all sides.

If the moderns, the kids, are really brushing aside bunk are they building up another kind of bunk to take its place?

I think myself that is the difficulty. It is always easier to destroy than to build up. Decency starts deep down. Anything in the worth of a thing has got to be got at by patience, by work. It is all right and fine to throw the bunk aside, God knows there is enough of it, but if in throwing aside the bunk the reality is also destroyed then surely nothing has been gained.

The Writer's Trade

Writing is both a trade and an art. Ordinary writing, such as the writing of articles, newspaper stories, etc., has little to do with art. I can see no reason why it should not be an honorable trade.

I see no reason why it should not be a fair trade to write clever plot stories for magazines. I am always wishing I could do it. Well, I haven't the knack. There is a section of my brain that will not work that way. It may be a defect. Should I be proud of my own defects?

But what about truth? What is truth? Truth, where are you? Come here. You see—Truth does not come.

A great fuss is sometimes made about this matter of Truth. I suspect there is no such thing. People ask, "Why does not such and such a one, who is very clever, produce art?"

It is because he is not an artist.

The men who write popular stories and plays should respect their own trade. Most of them I have known spend too much time apologizing. Or they brag too much, which is but another form of apology. They should be more self-respecting. It is perhaps as important for people to be amused and excited by the popular methods as it is that they be moved more deeply.

I think most men write as well as they can. You cannot really make a success, say of a patent medicine, unless you believe in it. You cannot make money writing popular short stories unless you have that kind of mind.

A few of us who write are sometimes given credit for making what is called "contributions" to the art of writing. That is as it turns out. The man who sets out to do such a thing would be an ass.

In my time I have written letters for men in love, advertisements of soap and patent medicines, pleas for forgiveness for men who had got in bad with their wives, newspaper articles,

applications for jobs, funeral orations, speeches for politicians—
what kind of writing have I not done?

And for that matter what kind of writing will I be doing an
hour from now?

An hour ago a man came in here to the office of my country
newspaper. He is a sewing machine agent and wanted an advertisement written. I did it for him, of course.

Yesterday I wrote an advertisement for a stallion. His name is
Hamrick. There was pleasure in that, surely. Hamrick was
"standing" up at the Groseclose barns, on the great Virginia
highway, east and west. As I wrote about him I could smell in
fancy what old George Borrow—what a writer that fellow was—
what he called "stable hartshorn." Henry Fielding called it that
too.

"O, thou Hamrick," I said to myself as I wrote that advertisement. In fancy I saw the noble fellow, a gigantic dapple gray with
a broad back.

"Would that I had such a back myself, such strength, such
spirit," I was thinking as I wrote. I could be more delicate about
life and about my work if I were stronger. I would not then be a
nervous irritable scribbler. I could be delicate with prose then.
O, how delicate I would be, being strong enough to be delicate.

Well, at times, I know how to write. It is my trade. At moments, when I have been fired by some strong feeling, I have
written poetry. There are a few stories that have crept out from
under my pen of which I can say, after a long time, that I am not
ashamed.

There have been many times in my life when I have wished I
had a lot of money. If I could make thirty, forty, fifty thousand
dollars a year writing thrilling detective stories, or cowboy stories
—fair women being rescued in the sage brush—or movies, would I
not do it? O dear yes. See what I could do!

On certain days I have a strong desire to travel. I am restless.
Life grows stale to me. I want to see new places and new faces.

If I had more money I would pack my bag and go. I would not write about them. I would myself be an adventurer, a cowboy—if I could find some cows—a sailor, an explorer. I would become as skillful and as practiced in love as George Moore used to be—in fancy.

I have always been a man who made, in one way or another, a good deal of money. But money means nothing to me when I have it. I spend it too rapidly. To be sure, as compared with real money-makers, I make nothing.

And how much I could spend. Every day I think of marvelous ways to spend money.

But why should I compare myself with those who do make it? Perhaps I have sometimes a certain pleasure in the process of doing my work that they do not have. On certain days I walk about the streets. I see men at work on buildings. Other men are doing other kinds of heavy work. When I go into the country I see farmers in the fields.

As compared with the labor these men do my own efforts are as nothing. I wear better clothes than they do, I drive a car, I live in a better house. Often when I talk to some farmer I am ashamed of the bellyaching about conditions under which they must labor, of all the men and women of my sort. I mean the actors, painters, writers, musicians I know. The farmer may work all year to raise a crop. One frost or a windstorm will wipe it out. I remember a sight I saw when I was a small boy. There had been a heavy hail-storm and a large wheat field, almost ready for the harvest, was destroyed. I happened to be fishing in a nearby stream on that day and had got under a tree. The farmer who owned the field came down after the storm and knelt in a fence corner. I heard his prayer. He was praying for strength not to give up. "Give me courage to plant again next year," he prayed.

And I have lived in the houses of city and town laborers too. I know too well how they live. I know the dreadful terror of too much and too heavy labor. It takes your strength, your spirit. The fancy cannot play. You feel yourself caught and held, as in a vise.

Very likely your wife is a slattern and you have underfed crying children about.

But I see no reason why the underdog should be given the upper hold of things. Surely he would be cruel too. Because a man has led a life that has brutalized him is no reason for putting him into a position where he has power over other lives. And I see no reason why a man should feel himself raised up because he has got his name up a little in the world.

When I am writing, out of some deep feeling from within, I do feel raised up of course. I am exalted, like a man or a horse, running a race. Often when I am writing well the figure of a white running boy comes into my mind. I seem to myself to be that boy. It must be some dream of my own youth that has carried on in me.

But why did I not remain a white slender boy? Where was I running?

There was something desired. Was it a goal?

Why should I set myself up above any one—any thief, any prostitute, any man who has got rich by lying, cheating, stealing—if he has got rich that way? How do I know how men get rich? What is it to be rich?

I am as confused about money as I am about other things. Critics are always abusing me because of my confusion. If they have themselves a solution for the difficulties of life why do they not tell the rest of us about it?

I admit my own confusion about money, government, sex, all kinds of relationships. Does this seem naive? It does not seem to me a sign of sophistication to accept the easy worn-out solutions always being handed out.

If I am exalted sometimes so is any farm boy in love. I would like to be in love all the time. When you are in love you see some one else as beautiful. There is nothing on earth more dreadful than falling out of love.

There is this matter of women.

There is a woman you have loved. The lines of her figure were beautiful to you. There may have been some blemishes.

The woman's eyes were a little too close together. There was a line, from her ear to her shoulder, that was not so good.

Why did these bad lines suddenly become all important? There must be some virtue in being steadfast. Yesterday, or last month, or last year, what was fine in her figure, in her person, overshadowed all the rest.

Then suddenly what was bad began to overshadow what was good.

This is what is confusing to me about love and marriage.

Certainly I want an eye. I want to be able to see, hear, taste, feel. My senses are everything to me. When they begin to atrophy I die. I find that even the finest paintings, sculpture, music, prose, song, do not always remain lovely to me. How can women be different?

Everything dies and sometimes comes to life again. With me love and friendship does the same thing.

I presume that, as a writer, I should be able to stand apart from all this. I should be able to analyze it, understand it.

I should be an impersonal thing, standing apart. I might come closer to understanding it if I could do that.

I can't do it. When people about me are in a muddle I get into a muddle too.

That is why something in me protests against any sort of special honors paid me.

And then sometimes I am quite sure I would be glad to be marked down as a kind of special thing among my fellow-men—loved, honored and all that—if I were not afraid people would find me out. I would like to be acclaimed—"here he comes, the marvelous one—hurrah."

As for writing—I do try constantly for a kind of simplification. There must be a great deal in style. I am working for it all the time. I am pretty sure it is not what most of the critics declare it to be when they speak of style.

By "style" I mean a kind of dance, an overtone. I mean color and life in prose.

I mean something different from the subject matter of what I am writing but at the same time a part of it. The gown worn by a woman is not the woman and yet if it is not the woman after she has put it on it is nothing.

Only today I have got a letter from a foreign radical magazine, asking me certain questions about a working class art. How confusing that is. Laborers working are often beautiful to me. The banker, who sits in his banking house making money, is not likely to be beautiful.

But the banker has money with which to buy rich beautiful things. Money—that is a beautiful idea. It excites me. I rarely look at a banker without wishing to thump him on the head, grab and run but I have never done it yet. I trust this declaration will frighten no one. I lack nerve perhaps. My own class, the artist class, is supported by the rich. If money were not accumulated by the few how would anything beautiful ever be present in this world?

Certainly we would never get it through democracy. Democracy has nothing whatever to do with the arts, justice equality morality has nothing to do with them. There may possibly be a higher morality, the artist sometimes knows, and I suspect there is.

Often enough I am deeply moved by the wrongs done to labor but as I am feeling that way I look up.

Over my desk there is a small Chinese figure. It is the figure of an artisocrat.

Another aristocrat made the figure. Surely artists are aristocrats. Any laborer I have ever known would have thrown such a figure aside. What value would it have for him?

Now you see I am ready to brush all down-trodden people aside. Well, let them go, let them suffer. If they become slaves, let them be slaves.

I am as aristocratic as any man in the world can be.

I am as cruel and heartless too. I am, as Mr. Bernard Shaw once said of a character in one of his plays, "a very simple man, perfectly satisfied with the best of everything." I do not want equality. Look what would happen to me if we got that.

Sometimes I return to my craft of writing as a trade. "Let me take it that way," I say to myself. "Whenever any one wants something written let me write it as best I can."

I have even thought sometimes of setting up a little shop somewhere. What do you want written? Are you a woman in love? You have certain fine feelings about a certain man but you have difficulty in expressing them. Very well, come to me. Tell me about it. Pay my fee.

I will make a study of the man and see if I cannot devise a way to get him interested in you.

Or you are an old man, about to die. You want a funeral oration written, to be delivered over your grave.

Why should I not do that for you? Why should I not write speeches for a candidate for office, advertisements for a bawdy house or a patent medicine?

Why should I ever in any way superimpose my own opinions on any one?

After all, there must be something amateurish about this notion that any one can ever do anything about life.

Why do I not fully, wholeheartedly, accept my position as writer? Why do I not say to myself, "I am a worker. Why not accept my trade?" Well, I do sometimes and when I do I have the most fun.

If I set myself up—if I have opinions of my own, if I make myself stand for certain principles in life, as sure as I am alive I will do something tomorrow that will do to the cause, for which I am trying to stand, a thousand times more harm than it will ever do good. And besides, what have I to do with causes? How am I to know a good cause from a bad one? Who am I, a scribbler, a teller of tales, to be fooling with causes? I should have the dignity of my own trade.

I should be afraid of nothing but power—a thing that has ruined every man I have known who has got it—and I should be un-ashamed. I should be unashamed of my own trade I mean, the trade of the scribbler.

So here we are, the scribblers. Bring on your ink, your pencils, your typewriters. We write plays, stories, advertisements, news-papers, what not. We are of an old brotherhood. Every kind of man or woman, good or bad, strong or weak should be unafraid of us if we are really working at our trade and not trying to put something over for ourselves.

FOURTH WEEK OF

OCTOBER

THE YEAR'S END

Books and More Books

The fall books are rolling in. There is no lack of authors. Some years it does not rain much. There are no apples some years. There are such things as wheat or corn failures.

But there are no author failures. New ones and old ones they are on the job. Often I go out for a walk. I see people I do not know. "They will probably become authors," I say to myself with a heavy sigh.

In the print shop in Marion we run a lending library. It is a non-profit making plan. The money that comes in goes to buy new books. Any one may join. The more members the more books. Let us all sink together.

On the Rialto

Bill Wright, the banker, and Joe Wright, the mail carrier, both from Troutdale, in town for the day. They are not brothers but friends. Joe is a rep and Bill a dem. Joe says his route is to be extended to take in Coon Hollow. He says he saw my sister Spring at Oak Hill Academy the other day. Jim Blood, he says, spends all his time shining his gun and getting ready for the fall bird shooting. If Jim doesn't shoot anything but birds he will be lucky.

The town full of bankers on Saturday. The boss wanted me to go to all their meetings. "You see if you can't find out some new ways to borrow money," the boss says. I says, "I can find out more about that right on the Rialto than I can from a banker," I says.

At the skating rink saw Chip Ewalt, Raymond Morris, Olden Dillard, Frank Debord, Billy Baxter, Williard Lincoln, and a lot of others cutting the high wide and fancy. Senator Glass didn't have time to get down there.

Preston Collins to Baltimore, where he went with Mr. and Mrs. Henry Staley for a visit. He has been missing some of the best mushroom hunting of the season.

A lot of people knew that Col. Pendleton could make a crackerjack political speech but didn't know he was a singer of verve and feeling.

Charles Lincoln, Jr., off for a long trip. There are big things brewing, they say, in the Lincoln organization. Mr. Charles, Sr., John P. Buchanan and Charles, Jr., always going off to New York. Some say they are fixing it up for the Marion band to play in the Metropolitan Opera during the winter.

The new Wassum and Lincoln buildings going up fast now. They were waiting for structural iron but it has come at last.

The boss's New York correspondent in town over night but he lit right out again. Heard on the street that he just come home to hide a hundred thousand dollars. Don't believe it. Followed him around all evening and never saw him hide a thing.

BUCK FEVER

Catch the Bank Robber
NEWS

Rumors run through a town sometimes as they do through an army. On Monday the whole town of Marion was rocked by a story that there had been a big bank robbery in Chilhowie. As the story flew about details multiplied. The story had no foundation in fact.

Here is what happened. A man named Walter Baldwin is said to have stolen some cattle from the farm of Dr. McKee, near Chilhowie. He took them to Rich Valley and sold them. Afterward he tried to cash the check at a Chilhowie bank. The bank did not let him have the money but held it for him. Later the fact that the cattle had been stolen was found out. Baldwin came into the bank and tried to get the money.

The officials of the bank tried to hold the man until Sheriff Dillard could get there. Sheriff Dillard made a record run from Marion. People saw him whirl out of town. Some one knew the bank had called him. That is how the story started.

Baldwin, however, growing suspicious, had lit out. The Sheriff and Si Price spent the whole afternoon trying to locate him without success.

Deep Sea Club on Cruise
NEWS

Leaving the harbor at Main and Staley's Creek the Deep Sea Club made a hard and daring run right to the top of Whitetop at the end of last week. Commodore Ellis was on the quarter deck and boatswain Kent at the wheel.

"Well, Commodore," says we, "did you hit any hard winds?"

"Hit 'em," says he. "We ran right over 'em.

"Hell and harsh weather," says he, "we cruised right over White-top and slid down the other side." "Then," says he, "back we came to Marion and got some ladies aboard. They was sick ladies," he said, "they needed some sea air. We ran 'em into Saltville."

"Were any of them seasick?"

"Oh, I wouldn't call it that," says the hardy Commodore.

BUCK

Virginia Falls

Saturday, the 20th—a peculiarly exciting day. It was a painter's day. The light had a peculiar quality. Colors stood out with amazing vividness.

I lunched with a photographer from New York. The light must mean everything to a photographer also. We lunched at the Hotel Lincoln. A big crowd there.

Afterwards to a convention of bankers. Their talk seemed far, far away. They were talking about the cost of running a bank. I left there and drove over the mountains to the farm.

All the way over the same amazing effect of light. Individual trees stood forth. A young maple, far up the side of the hill, was touched by a stray wind. It seemed to dance. It was like a young girl running down the hill.

I imagined Christ walking with his disciples. Did God often let such a light fall on him? Did he think of trees, fields of grass, cattle on hills, flowering weeds, as well as men? I myself get well fed-up on men and women and their everlasting souls, their problems, not so important after all.

Some of the pagan people see God in trees, cattle, weeds, fields of grain. I am more than a little a pagan myself.

In the evening the moon shining. There was a winding road

with the river below it. How silent the woods. Day had passed im-
perceptibly into night. The moonlight had much of the quality of
the day just passed.

The noises in the woods. Little things running on dry leaves.
The water in the river made many noises. I stood a long time
listening. How many tones could I catch? Oh, that I had an ear.

There was something special and sacred about the day and the
night. I could not sleep afterwards but then I did not want to sleep
so it was all right.

The Singing Print Shop

Warren Johnson, well known Marion colored man and team-
ster, was hauling us some manure for the grass in Sherwood
Forest. This was on Wednesday morning. It was a cold morning
but the sky was clear and the sun bright. When Warren had got
the manure all unloaded he came into the shop. We get out the
Democrat on Tuesdays but were late this week. Too much news,
etc.

Anyway the presses were running and Warren came in and
sang us all a song to the tune of the presses. When he had got
through singing Warren looked up at the picture of old Maud S.,
over the editor's desk. "That was a good hoss," Warren said as he
went out. Here is the song he sang for us.

YOU MUST HAVE JESUS ROUND YOUR HOME

Now, you must have Jesus round your home,
My brother, you must have Jesus round your home.
You can say what you want to,
You can do what you choose,
But you must have Jesus round your home.

Your body lies molded in the clay.
My brother, your body lies molded in the clay.
Get your heart right with God,
Cause you can't stay here always,
You must have Jesus round your home.

My Sister, you must have Jesus round your home,
My Sister, you must have Jesus round your home.
You can say what you want to,
You can do what you choose,
But you must have Jesus round your home.

My Sister, your body lies molded in the clay,
My Sister, your body lies molded in the clay,
Get your heart right with God,
Cause you won't stay here always.
You must have Jesus round your home.

Little Children, you must have Jesus round your home,
Little Children, you must have Jesus round your home.
You can say what you want to,
You can do what you please,
But you must have Jesus round your home.

Little Children, your body lies molded in the clay,
Little Children, your body lies molded in the clay.
Get your heart right with God,
Cause you won't stay here always,
You must have Jesus round your home.

Will You Sell Your Newspapers?

It was a good deal like asking—"will you sell your wife?"
Well, newspapers are sold. Mr. Harding, when he was elected

president, sold his paper. There are men who deal in country
weeklies, buy and sell them.

But there isn't any one going to elect me president. I don't even
know of any one who wants to give me another steady job.

And it may be that running a country weekly is more important
than being president. Think what Harding might have escaped.

I have been running two country newspapers, in Smyth County,
Virginia, for a year now. One is the *Smyth County News* (rep.)
and the other *The Marion Democrat* (dem.). Only last week a
man came in and offered to buy the papers. For some reason the
idea struck me as absurd. I can imagine giving them to some one.
"Here, you can do this job better than I can." As a man might
walk out on his wife—when he no longer loved her, or when she
loved another man.

Another man came in and wanted me to make my papers a part
of a "chain," like the drug and grocery stores.

"But, my dear sir," I said, "a country weekly is such a highly
personal thing. It is about the only kind of personal journalism
left. If you put it into a chain it becomes as impersonal as a city
daily."

"Of course now—if this town suddenly became industrialized
and grew big. If we had to run a daily here. I could sell a daily
perhaps as I would any other property."

"Or if a war broke out. I would sell then in a hurry. Imagine
having to run a country weekly during a war like the last one. Suppose you were at heart a pacifist. I am a man of peace of course. I
couldn't run any kind of a newspaper during a war. It is difficult
enough to run one during a presidential election. I almost went
crazy during this last election."

Suppose you had to turn in and begin calling all the Germans or
the Japanese "devils"—singing the song of hate—or hating dems
or reps.

But a war. . . .

Days passing in a town—in any town, anywhere.

Before I came here I had been a city man a long time. I had almost forgotten about the towns. But American cities are no more than small towns grouped together. There is a negro section, a Greek, Italian, German, Irish section—the quarters of the intelligentsia. I lived among the intellectuals for a time. I still go to the city to visit them. There is a section where the rich live and another for the very poor.

Long streets of middle-class houses and apartments. Tough streets.

Sections of the city where you can go and get yourself a woman for hire.

In a small town the band plays on summer nights. People are driving around in cars. There are drug stores, hardware stores, print shops like ours, clothing stores, dry goods stores, shoe stores. There are hotels to which traveling men come.

Boys go swimming in a creek or in a river in the summer.

Wait now, we have but touched the rim of the towns. Young men walking along with feverish burning eyes. Are they young poets?

They are young men filled with lust.

Lust in girls too, in school teachers, preachers, husbands, wives.

Do you think women lust after one man or men after one woman?

"I am as full of lusts as a tree is full of blossoms," says the poet.

All men and women are poets sometimes for swift passing moments in life.

Let me catch it as I can. Clutch it.

Do you think the rich man who has got power is satisfied with his riches and his power? You are a fool.

Yesterday I drove my car down a street of our town I had never been on before. I did not know the street was there. Men hailed me.

Women and children were sitting on doorsteps. "It is our editor."

"Well, you have been a long time getting down here."

When I drive on a country road in this county farmers or their wives call to me. "Come in and get some cider, a basket of grapes, some sweet corn for dinner." The women of the town and county keep the print shop fragrant with flowers.

I have a place in this community. How difficult to feel that in the city.

I am bored sometimes. Who isn't? Suppose you have to report an amateur theatrical performance—that happens—the actors all wanting praise of course—just as do the professionals in cities.

I have been just as deeply bored in a playhouse on Broadway as I could be in Marion.

The town spreads itself out, it performs for me as I do for it. Now look you.

A man in the town has done a tricky thing. Do you think he is satisfied with himself? Now he is going about explaining himself, explaining and explaining.

Do you think he would do that if he were satisfied with himself?

There are forests near the town.

See the majesty of the river in the sun. See birds flying over the river.

River talk. Creek talk. Town talk. Woods talk.

Women's missionary societies meeting and talking. A Kiwanis Club. A Rotary Club.

Men sitting at table with their wives, their minds straying far. Women's minds straying.

Improvement, culture, lectures heard, books read, music listened to.

A man has flown across the Atlantic. There is an announcer shouting over the radio. Did you hear the Dempsey-Tunney fight? That was a good announcer.

Birds building nests in trees in the woods above and below town. Corn growing in fields.

In the winter gusty days. Snows come. Engines creak on the rails of railroad tracks.

A man in a house on a certain street gets suddenly angry and strikes his wife. Her nose bleeds. Her blood falls down on the bosom of her dress. The man goes out of the house and slams the door.

Will the woman leave her husband? Will she divorce him? No, she will keep right on living with him.

There was a drowned man pulled out of the river. He was drunk and fell in and drowned.

There are rainy winter and fall nights when the editor walks about in the streets or in country roads, sick with disgust of his own life, that he is so ineffectual in life. Tears come to his eyes sometimes. It happened when he lived in cities just as it happens here, in this small town.

Even as I sit writing a man, a merchant here, comes in. He tells me of another man, a friend. "He was at my house last night. He is in deep trouble. He is in love with another man's wife and cannot get over it. Is there any cure for such a man? Can he get over it?"

"Alas, yes. He will. That is the pity of it. A man really in love, no matter what the difficulties, is a poet. Men and women in love are about the only poets we have. Save your pity for the man or woman no longer capable of falling in love. There are that kind here too."

"But perhaps he is only lusting. Love does not come to many people. You have to be capable of holding it."

But to come back to the town—do you know about the man who suddenly after a long life of sin got God? He had been a wicked man, he said. After he got God he used to stand on the street corners and preach. What was he up to? He had a daughter who was ashamed of him. "Don't do it, Father, please don't," she begged. She explained that it humiliated her too much. He kept saying that he had to do it, that he had to testify to his God.

There are a thousand tales in this town as in all towns. Where shall any one begin? There was a young man, a farm hand, came to town and saw the military company drilling in the street on a summer evening.

He stood at the curb, his brown hands clutching the door of a Ford car. He thought the men marching were beautiful. He thought their uniforms beautiful. He thought, "if I could only belong to that military company I would be the proudest and happiest man in the world."

Do you know about the rich young man? He was born rich. He was taught that he was something special and believed it. It spoiled his whole life. It spoiled his body, the way he walked, his voice, everything.

He could not love. No one had taught him how to love. Even as a small boy he had no fun. He put on airs and the other boys laughed at him.

There was a farmer, a renting farmer, who lived on a farm near town. He got in a quarrel with another man who owned a beauti-ful dog. He was afraid of the man so one night he crept out and shot the dog.

"Will you sell the newspapers?" What an idea. I have been the editor of an American small town paper for a year now. Mr. Sin-clair Lewis has not described the life of our towns, Mr. Dreiser has not done it. Nor have I.

I have got an occupation here, something to do. I like the smell of the shop, the business, the uncertainty, the position it has given me in the community. For a long time I have been a writer. Much of the writing here, on my papers, must be quick and passing. Even on a weekly the time for going to press comes all too quickly.

Too often I do not have time to think of what I write. For convenience sake I live directly over the shop. Sometimes the presses run in the night. They shake the building. I lie in bed and tremble sometimes.

I am afraid the people here will not like my papers, but they are amazingly kind. When an old farmer, or a laborer from one of our factories, comes in to pay up for another year I am childishly pleased. If he says, "it is a good paper. It is good reading," I am delighted. I run about telling the men in the shop. I walk up and down in the shop and brag. The men, Jack, Joe and Gil smile at me. They laugh a little. Even Zeb, the printer's devil, smiles. They have been doing this thing for a long time.

One of the men in my shop has worked on an American country weekly in Virginia for forty years.

The men are indulgent with me, as is the town and the county. They know I am a green hand. Why I have been running an American country weekly for only a year. Do I want to sell it? Of course not.

I must have a job and I never have had another job that gave me so much pleasure.

A man has to work. He cannot be just a teller of old tales. He has to find somewhere a place into which he fits.

The presses in the print shop are persistent things. They eat up thousands and thousands of sheets of paper. They keep demanding and demanding. They will not stay quiet.

It is good to have something like that, crying and crying. New weeks come as the seasons come on the farm. The fields have to be prepared and the crops planted. The paper has to be got ready. It certainly serves to take your mind off yourself.

END OF THE YEAR